The Civil War in Pembrokeshire

The Civil War in Pembrokeshire

by
Terry John

Logaston Press

LOGASTON PRESS
Little Logaston Woonton Almeley
Herefordshire HR3 6QH
logastonpress.co.uk

First published by Logaston Press 2008
Copyright © Terry John 2008

ISBN 978 1904396 90 1

Typeset by Logaston Press
and printed in Great Britain by
Bell & Bain ltd., Glasgow

Contents

Acknowledgements

I would like to thank the staff of the Pembrokeshire Record Office, the National Library of Wales, the Carmarthenshire Record Office, Tenby Museum, Haverfordwest Library and Carmarthen Library for their help in tracking down documents, books and other sources of information.

For their interest and encouragement I would also like to thank Steve Ash, David and Glenys Bennet, Janet Bray, Doris Edwards, Sybil Edwards, Trevor and Mary Goodman, Thelma Golden, Huw and Karen Jenkins, Steve and Eva Laugharne, Nesta Kirk, Frieda Rowe, Jean and Gordon Wheatley and Deborah Williams; and last but not least Andy Johnson of Logaston Press for making possible the publication of this book.

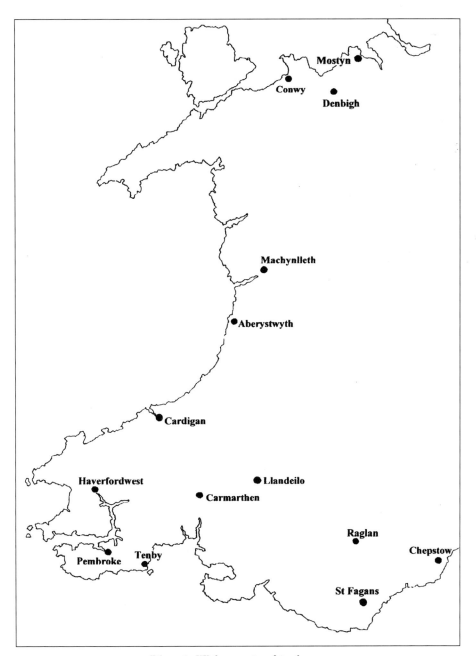

Places in Wales mentioned in the text

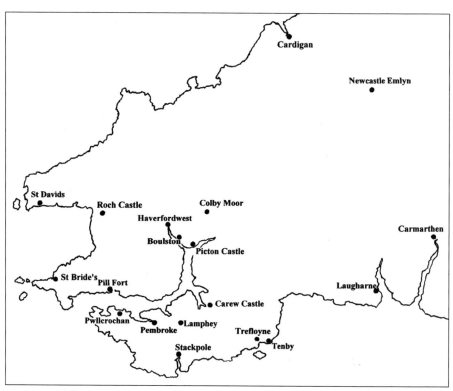

Main sites of conflict in West Wales (1642-48) mentioned in the text

1 Retribution

On the morning of 4 April 1649, a military court was convened at Whitehall in London to try three men on charges of treason.[1] The accused, all from Pembrokeshire, were John Poyer, a former mayor of Pembroke, Colonel Rice Powell of Jeffreston and Major-General Rowland Laugharne, whose ancestral home lay on the shores of St Bride's Bay. During the first Civil War, they had upheld the Parliamentary cause in west Wales, often against considerable odds.

Poyer, by his prompt actions in the autumn of 1642, had ensured that the town and castle of Pembroke was held against the Royalists, whilst Rice Powell had been a constant presence in south Wales throughout the conflict, commanding garrisons at Tenby and Cardigan and capturing Aberystwyth Castle. Laugharne, through his skills as a military commander, had won the respect even of his enemies, ensuring that by 1645 the Parliamentary cause was supreme in west Wales.

In the spring of 1648, to widespread consternation, the three men had declared for King Charles, an action that many believed precipitated a new round of fighting. After a six-week siege Pembroke was finally taken by Parliamentary forces and the ringleaders brought to London for punishment.

The trial of the three men lasted until 12 April. When the final witness had been heard and all evidence had been presented, the members of the tribunal considered their verdict. It was not long in coming. Laugharne, Powell and Poyer were condemned to death.

Their relatives wasted no time in petitioning Parliament to be merciful towards them. Ann Laugharne begged that her husband's recent actions 'might not cause all his former services to be forgotten'.[2] The three sisters of Rice Powell also sought a pardon for their brother, whilst Elizabeth Poyer was active on behalf of her husband. It was even rumoured that the two town maces of Pembroke, made originally for the community in 1632, were taken secretly to London to be used as a ransom to free the men.[3]

These appeals, backed by a personal plea from Poyer himself, were partially successful. The Council of State announced that only one man should forfeit his life. The decision as to who this should be was left to the guilty parties to decide. Not surprisingly, they refused to make such a choice. Eventually, lots were drawn and a victim selected. On 25 April, John Poyer was taken from Whitehall in a closed and guarded coach to Covent Garden, where he was executed by firing squad.

News of his execution was widely reported in the broadsheets of the day, which carried a full account of his final words. In the shattered town of Pembroke, where people were slowly repairing their burnt and roofless houses, there must have been some who considered that he had received his just deserts. Others may have wondered how three such prominent men, once widely regarded as heroes, could have come to such a pass.

2   The Key Players

John Poyer

The image of John Poyer which has been handed down over the centuries is of a man of forceful character, impatient, stubborn and rapacious, who held passionate beliefs and acted resolutely upon them. One senses, however, from the statements made about him and from his actions, that there may also have been at the core of his personality seeds of self-doubt and insecurity, which were rooted in his background.

Poyer's place and date of birth are uncertain, but there is no doubt that in the years before the Civil War he was a figure of consequence in Pembrokeshire and west Wales. In a pamphlet published in 1648-49, whilst he was a prisoner at Whitehall, he describes himself as a merchant dealing in wool, coin, skins, butter and tallow. He claimed to have employed more poor people in cloth-making than anyone else in Pembrokeshire.[1]

There is also evidence that for several generations his family had occupied a respected position in Pembroke. A merchant named John Poyer, presumably the father or grandfather, was appointed in 1604 as one of the two bailiffs who were to assist the mayor in his duties. In 1616 and 1617, the same John Poyer again held the post of bailiff, describing himself as a gentleman.

This may have been a recently achieved social position. The county gentry of the day could look back upon generations of ancestors who had held the family lands for centuries and who had occupied influential offices within local government. There are no records of any earlier Poyers amongst their ranks and John the bailiff must have clawed his way upwards by his own efforts. Few of the hereditary gentlefolk would have applauded him; most were suspicious of, and often resented, those merchants who had become wealthy enough to buy land and claim a place amongst them. This hostility may be what lies behind many of the stories about John Poyer which were recounted in the news-sheets of the day and have been repeated ever since.

In 1648, the year when Poyer abandoned his allegiance to Parliament, a pamphlet appeared which stated that his parents had been servants to Owen

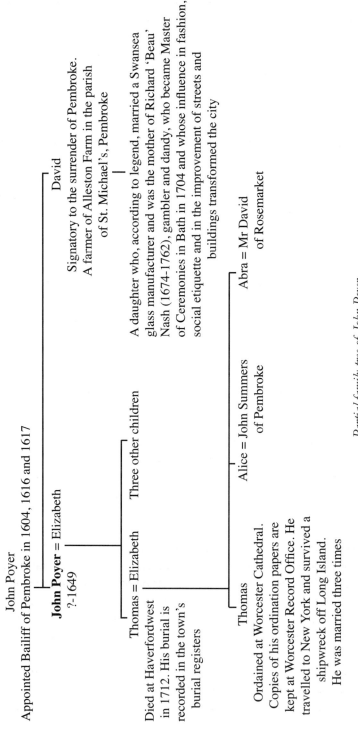

John Poyer
Appointed Bailiff of Pembroke in 1604, 1616 and 1617

John Poyer = Elizabeth
?-1649

Thomas = Elizabeth
Died at Haverfordwest in 1712. His burial is recorded in the town's burial registers

Three other children

David
Signatory to the surrender of Pembroke. A farmer of Alleston Farm in the parish of St. Michael's, Pembroke

Thomas
Ordained at Worcester Cathedral. Copies of his ordination papers are kept at Worcester Record Office. He travelled to New York and survived a shipwreck off Long Island. He was married three times

Alice = John Summers
of Pembroke

A daughter who, according to legend, married a Swansea glass manufacturer and was the mother of Richard 'Beau' Nash (1674-1762), gambler and dandy, who became Master of Ceremonies in Bath in 1704 and whose influence in fashion, social etiquette and in the improvement of streets and buildings transformed the city

Abra = Mr David
of Rosemarket

Partial family tree of John Poyer

After his execution his descendants adopted the motto 'Destiny is Against Me'

Eliot of Narberth.[2] Eliot was Sheriff for Pembroke in 1609 and his son John became Poyer's bitterest enemy and the source of many of the scurrilous tales about him. It was John Eliot who published the story that in his youth Poyer was employed as a scullion in the kitchens of the Powell family of Pembroke, where one of his jobs was to turn the spit to roast the meat, and that he was no more than 'a poor, ragged boy which was hired to run to and fro on errands'.

Eliot also had something to say about Poyer's mother. He does not name her, but implies that she was of loose morals and that she was 'generally famed in the town … and in that regard Poyer is by instinct of nature possest with more than ordinary impudence'.[3]

Poyer, in the pamphlet published during his imprisonment, naturally denies most of these assertions. He admits that his origins were humble, but explains that he quickly raised himself to a respectable position in society. He became an exporter of farm produce and Welsh flannel to Bristol and says that the best gentlemen in Pembroke bound their sons to him in apprenticeship.

Poyer also points out that in 1633, he was appointed as commander of the trained bands of Pembroke.[4] This was an indication of his trustworthiness, for the trained bands were a form of citizen militia created to defend communities in times of warfare and invasion. The commanders were usually well respected, even authoritarian, figures in their localities. It is known that Poyer held the post of bailiff of Pembroke in 1633, when he was recorded as a glover.[5] He also enjoyed sufficient respect to be elected as mayor of Pembroke in 1641.

In an unpublished manuscript, now in the National Library of Wales, Edward Laws suggests that, if Poyer's background was indeed a humble one, he would have needed considerable financial backing in order to succeed as well as he did. If the money did not come from Poyer senior, then who provided it? Laws also suggests that Poyer's mother may have had an admirer who provided the ready cash, but mentions no names. Was it perhaps Owen Eliot? Poyer's parents were supposedly Eliot's servants, so is it possible that Owen was John Poyer's natural father? It would explain John Eliot's hatred of him, though there is absolutely no evidence to back this theory.

The Poyers may, indeed, have been landowners themselves, in a small way. Local tradition states that they owned property, perhaps a few farms, in the Narberth area of Pembrokeshire. Some records mention a holding at Cold Blow, whilst at Templeton there is a building, probably of 17th-century origin, which is still known as Poyer's Farm.[6] These possessions may have been in the family for some years, or they could have been bought as a result of John's prosperity as a merchant.

Laws says about Poyer's later life: 'In 1643, the Governor of Pembroke fell in love: there are reasons for supposing that his sweetheart Elizabeth – her maiden name has been forgotten – was a Tenby girl. Well educated (she wrote a good

5

letter in an excellent hand) she was taken up by Madam Laugharne'.[7] Laws does not give his sources for this statement, but in making it he opens up yet another mystery in the life of John Poyer. Who exactly did he marry?

A story generally accepted today is that Elizabeth Poyer was in fact a sister of Ann, the wife of Rowland Laugharne. This theory seems to have been first put forward in G.T. Clark's *Genealogies of Glamorgan* where the two women are described as daughters of Sir Thomas Button of Cottrell in Glamorgan. The relationship has since become an accepted fact and is repeated in several histories of the Civil War.

Clark's entry for the Button family shows that Sir Thomas had several children. There were three sons – Miles, William and Rice – and at least one daughter, Ann, who is recorded as having married Rowland Laugharne. Elizabeth's name is also included, showing that she married Poyer, but Clark had no firm evidence for assuming that she was a member of the Button family. This becomes evident if one studies Clark's research notes, where a hand-drawn family tree shows Sir Thomas' children, to which Elizabeth's name and her marriage with Poyer are appended by a dotted line. Beneath it, Clark has written, 'This match seems to have existed from an entry in the State Papers Domestic, 1660, p.43'.[8]

The entry to which Clark refers begins: 'Miles and Florence Button and Eliz., widow of Colonel John Poyer Governor of Pembroke', and goes on to seek monetary recompense from the newly restored monarchy for services rendered by the petitioners during the Civil War. Some historians have assumed that because Elizabeth was thus linked with Miles, she must have been his sister and therefore Ann's. The wording of the petition contains no evidence of a family relationship and no contemporary source mentions it.[9]

Miles Button must have known the Poyers and was probably an acquaintance of long standing. The Button family owned land in Pembrokeshire and Miles was amongst those who supported Laugharne and Poyer during the Second Civil War. As a result, both he and Elizabeth Poyer were experiencing financial difficulties in the aftermath of the war and they may have decided that they stood a better chance of recompense if they presented a joint plea rather than separate ones. Miles may also have been encouraged to support Poyer's widow by Ann Laugharne, who probably sympathised with a woman she had known for years and who was struggling to bring up several children on her own. Other petitions exist from Elizabeth and from Ann, but none of these later ones are in their joint names, nor do they include Miles.

There is one further clue to the lack of a family relationship between Ann and Elizabeth. It comes in the form of a letter written by Elizabeth to Ann in 1647, when Poyer had arrived in London to answer a number of serious charges brought against him by, amongst others, John Eliot. Elizabeth had accompanied her husband and was clearly living in a state of near poverty. She wrote to Ann

Laugharne to beg the loan of five shillings, as she had no decent shoes to wear. She addresses Ann as 'most honoured' and as 'Madam Laugharne' and ends the letter with the words 'your pardon for my presumption and humblemost your servant, Elizabeth Poyer'.

Though the letter is short, there is no trace in it of sisterly affection and no mention of a family relationship. Elizabeth would surely not have couched the letter in such formal terms had Ann been her sibling. The final sentence seems to indicate that she regarded Mrs Laugharne as her social superior, not as an equal. It seems unlikely therefore that the two ladies were related.

With this letter, however, most of our knowledge of John Poyer's marriage and of his wife's possible relationship to the Button family comes to an end.

Rowland Laugharne

As with John Poyer, there are certain facts about Rowland Laugharne which are obscure. His date of birth is uncertain, but he was probably born in about 1612, although some authorities give the earlier date of 1607. Whatever the truth, he belonged to a family that could trace its history back through two centuries of Pembrokeshire's history.[10]

The Laugharnes first appear in the records of Haverfordwest at the beginning of the fourteenth century. Richard of Talacharn (the town of Laugharne in Carmarthenshire) was Reeve of Haverfordwest around the year 1300, when his name was added as a witness to a grant of burgage in the town.[11] In 1362 and again in 1372 another Richard Lagharne (*sic*), presumably the son or grandson of the earlier Richard, also held the post of Reeve and witnessed further burgage grants. His name appears on documents dated 1380 and 1382, though by then he was no longer Reeve.[12]

In the middle of the fifteenth century, Thomas Laugharne married the daughter of John de St Bride and acquired the manor

This arched gateway is one of the few remaining fragments of the manor of St Bride's, the ancient home of the Laugharne family

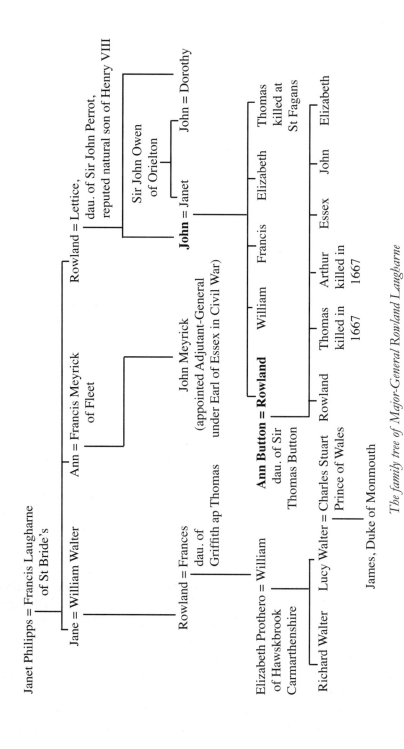

The family tree of Major-General Rowland Laugharne

of St Bride's, about ten miles west of Haverfordwest, which became the family's principal estate in Pembrokeshire. Here, perched on low red sandstone cliffs above a sandy cove and adjacent to a medieval church, stood a centuries old house recorded in 1298 as 'le Hille'.[13] Today, only shattered fragments of the building remain, but in Rowland's day it was a substantial house, forming the southern façade of a courtyard. The other three sides consisted of a battlemented wall topped by a wall walk. An arched gateway was the main entrance into the court, whilst in the west wall another archway gave access into the largest of several walled gardens; this garden still exits. Outside these enclosed areas stretched a wide lawn, divided up by pathways and dotted with oaks of 'large girth', but stunted and twisted by the sea winds.[14] There was also a bowling green.

To this house, successive generations of sons brought their brides. Inter-marriage with the daughters of other gentry families endowed the Laugharnes with further wealth and estates at Orlandon, Fenton, Walwyn's Castle, Llanrheithan, Llanunwas, Eweston, Farthingshook and at Pontfaen overlooking the narrow, wooded cleft of the Gwaun Valley.

In addition to gaining so many properties, these alliances enabled the Laugharnes to become part of a powerful, close-knit and influential circle of country families (see the family tree opposite). Perhaps the most notable of the marriages took place in 1584, between Rowland Laugharne, grandfather of the later Rowland, and Lettice, the daughter of Sir John Perrot, the reputed natural son of Henry VIII. Rowland senior's sisters also made advantageous marriages: Jane to William Walter of Roch, whose great-granddaughter was Lucy Walter, the mistress and perhaps the wife of Charles II and mother of the Duke of Monmouth; and Ann to Sir Francis Meyrick of Fleet near Pembroke. Another stitch in the tapestry of family relationships was the marriage of the Earl of Essex's sister Lady Dorothy Devereux to Tom Perrot, the son of Sir John Perrot, doubling the link between the Laugharnes, the Meyricks and the Perrots.

The unions of Rowland and Lettice and Ann and Francis Meyrick brought the Laugharnes into the orbit of the Devereux family, Earls of Essex. One of the great magnate clans of Tudor England and Wales, the Devereux family had seized the opportunity offered by the dissolution of the monasteries to gobble up some of the old monastic holdings. In addition to the ancient episcopal palace and manor of Lamphey in Pembrokeshire, they held sizable blocks of land scat-tered through Carmarthenshire and Cardiganshire. By the mid-sixteenth century they had become the leading family in south-west Wales.[15] At various times its members held the mayoralties of important boroughs or served as MPs for Carmarthenshire and as Chief Justices of South Wales. Claiming descent from the ancient Welsh princes, their prominence allowed them to build up a network of influence based upon patronage, privilege and clientship and they worked diligently to ensure the placement of their nominees into offices within local government. Robert Devereux, the second earl, wrote to the Justice of Assize in 1585, 'I am desirous to countenance my friends and servants in their county as far forth as I am able'.[16]

This placeman system allowed Devereux to build up such a reputation for leadership in Pembrokeshire that he could regard himself almost as the first man of the county.[17] He spent much of his youth at Lamphey Palace and was familiar with the area and its gentry. He recruited into his service a number of local gentlemen. Amongst them was Gwyllyam or Gelly Meyrick, the brother of Francis who had married Ann Laugharne. Gelly Meyrick, the son of the Bishop of Bangor, became steward of Essex's household and was knighted by him in 1596, during the Earl's attack on Cadiz, which had been intended to forestall the preparation of another Armada. Gelly was assiduous in building up further layers of support for Essex in the region, often encouraging into his camp gentlemen of a similar political and religious outlook.[18]

For much of his adult life Essex was regarded as one of the most powerful and militant supporters of the Reformation in Europe. Although, like Queen Elizabeth, he stated that he did not want to pry into people's private beliefs, he was prepared to make public displays of his own Protestant piety. He gave his support to clergymen who had been removed from their own churches for their puritan beliefs and invited them to preach in his own house, occasions which drew large congregations.[19] This endorsement of the more radical varieties of Protestantism was even more marked in his son, the third earl, who proved to be a staunch ant-papist and who, when the Civil War began, was regarded as a champion of the Church of England. It provided families like the Laugharnes and the Powells with a focus for their Parliamentary and puritan sympathies.

Essex's attempted coup in 1601, which aimed to restore his ascendancy at court after his failure to put down rebellion in Ireland, involved few of the gentry of south-west Wales. His execution was followed by that of Gelly Meyrick and a few other conspirators, but perhaps Rowland Laugharne the elder and his son John had stayed quietly at home. They may have distrusted Essex's impetuosity and hot temper, or perhaps their loyalty to the ageing Queen Elizabeth was too strong.

During the early years of the seventeenth century, John Laugharne married Janet, the daughter of Hugh Owen of Orielton near Pembroke. This was one facet of a double union between the families, for Laugharne's sister Dorothy married Janet's brother Hugh Owen the younger, heir to Orielton.

Rowland Laugharne the younger, as we have noted, was born between 1607 and 1612, the eldest of a brood of four sons – Rowland, William, Francis and Thomas – and a sister, Elizabeth. Little is known of his early childhood, but the link with the Devereux family survived. At some point, probably in the early

1620s, Rowland and his brother William entered the household of Robert, third Earl of Essex.

This Devereux was a man dogged by ill-fortune. The son of the executed second earl, his family estates had been alienated to the crown and were only restored after the accession of James I. Married shortly before his fifteenth birthday to the beautiful Lady Frances Howard, daughter of the Earl of Suffolk, Essex had suffered the ignominy of seeing the union annulled on the grounds of non-consummation. Free to marry her lover, James Carr, a favourite of the King, Frances and her new husband were shortly afterwards accused of the murder of Sir Thomas Overbury. An associate of Carr's, Overbury had opposed the marriage and Frances managed to have him confined to the Tower of London, where he died in mysterious and agonizing circumstances. Rumours of poison were rife and Frances and James Carr were charged with murder. Found guilty, the couple were sentenced to death, and it was rumoured that Essex was working behind the scenes to secure Frances' execution. However, the King intervened and exiled them from court, to spend a period of incarceration in houses outside the capital.

Laugharne probably joined the earl's household not long after his eighth birthday. This seems to have been the average age at which the sons of the gentry were sent away from home. A placement with a noble family was seen as advantageous in many ways. A young man could complete his education there and would learn how to behave in society. Most importantly, he would make contacts which could be useful in later life and might, if he were talented enough, catch the eye of the monarch or of one of his ministers.

For Rowland and his brother William, the time spent with Essex certainly widened their horizons. In 1620, the earl was one of a number of gentlemen volunteers who joined Sir Horace Vere's regiment to serve in the Palatinate in the opening phases of the Thirty Years War. He took with him Francis Meyrick, a cousin of the Laugharne brothers, and it is likely that at the same time, Rowland also accompanied Essex. If so, whilst abroad he would have encountered several personalities who were, two decades later, to become famous during the Civil War. Sir William Waller, the future Parliamentary Major-General of the Southern Association, was one, as was Ralph Hopton, who became the King's General in the West.[20]

Little is known about Rowland's career as a page in Essex's service, but by the 1630s he had become one of the earl's principal servants. According to Arthur Wilson, who was at that time Devereux's secretary, Rowland played a part in arranging the earl's second marriage.

At the Christmas celebrations given in 1630 by the Countess of Hertford, Devereux met Elizabeth Paulet, whose father, Sir William Paulet, was an illegitimate offspring of the Marquess of Winchester. Elizabeth was poor, but possessed 'a most sweet and bewitching countenance and affable and gentle conversation'.[21] Essex decided to marry her, using Rowland as a go-between to press his suit.[22]

The marriage resulted in an earthquake within the earl's household. Arthur Wilson did not approve of the union and openly voiced his dislike of Elizabeth. In return, Lady Essex did her best to turn her husband against his once-trusted secretary. In due course Wilson was dismissed and Rowland was appointed in his place, a position he was to occupy for several years.[23]

We have few glimpses of Rowland during his time with Essex. We know nothing about his appearance, or of his impact on other people, though we can infer that he was probably a young man of some tact and discretion to have been entrusted with the details of the earl's courtship. It is likely that during this period he rarely came home to Pembrokeshire.

The first record of his presence in Pembrokeshire, presumably on a short visit, comes on 22 June 1638, when he was named in a document concerning the grant of the manor of Angulus (Angle) made by John and William Ashburnham to Rowland, Miles Button and Phillipp (*sic*) Bowen for an annual rent of £300.[24] Another document drawn up three days later transfers the manor from Rowland and Phillipp Bowen to Miles.[25]

The Button family owned an estate at Sandy Haven on the Milford Haven waterway, as well as other properties within the county, though their main holding was at Cottrell in Glamorgan. Miles had inherited the family estates from his father, Sir Thomas Button, upon the latter's death in 1634.[26] A close connection appears to have existed between the families for some time, as a number of leasehold agreements were drawn up for Sir Thomas during the early 1630s, all witnessed by members of the Laugharne clan.

The linking of Rowland's name with the Button family probably indicates that he had by now married Ann, Miles' sister, or was shortly to do so. The exact date is uncertain. It may also have been around this time that Rowland left the Earl of Essex's household and took up an appointment as secretary to the Earl of Pembroke.

Essex and Pembroke, though they were both to support Parliament in the coming war, were not the best of friends and their antipathy became more marked as time went on. This move by Rowland into Pembroke's orbit raises some intriguing possibilities. Did it take place because of a rupture between Devereux and his once-trusted servant? If so, over what? Or did it come about because Rowland wished to better himself, especially if he was betrothed or recently married?

There is one piece of evidence which indicates that Rowland's departure was not amicable. On 8 April 1644, reporting on the successes achieved in Pembrokeshire by forces under Laugharne's command, Essex had Rowland's name erased from the record, so that the entry in the Commons journal read, 'It hath pleased God to give us good success in Pembrokeshire by the care and valour of Mr. XXX a servant of the Earl of Pembroke, to whom his Lordship gave a commission at the beginning of these troubles, whereby these places have been preserved for the Parliament'.[27]

The reason for the omission is unknown, but it may indicate a falling out between the two men, which Essex did not forget or forgive. What is certain is that Rowland appears to have spent much of his time outside Pembrokeshire, possibly in London, in the service of the Earl of Pembroke. It is not until 1643, when he arrives before the walls of Tenby, that he becomes a permanent presence in his home county.

Rice Powell

Of the three main protagonists of this story, Rice Powell is the one about whom we know the least. He came from a family well-established in the Pembroke area; they are often described in contemporary documents as 'of Greenhill', an estate at Pwllcrochan to the west of Pembroke, indicating that they held property there. They may also have owned land at Jeffreston, a parish about five miles north-east of the town.

Rice's grandfather was Morgan Powell, who had married Maud Wogan, the daughter of another influential Pembrokeshire family, themselves related to the Owens of Orielton. Morgan and Maud produced several children, of whom the most important to this story were Lewis, Jane and Frances. Jane married, as his second wife, Richard Cuny of Welston, a house about three miles north-east of Pembroke; Frances became the wife of John Marychurch of Manorbier.[28]

Lewis Powell married Mary, the daughter of John Prys of Rubarton and between them they produced a large brood of children. There were said to have been ten in all, of whom Rice (or Rhys) was probably the eighth.[29]

The Powells were thus part of a group of inter-related families based in and around Pembroke. Several had been supporters of Sir John Perrot during the reign of Elizabeth I, whilst others had followed the star of Robert Devereux, second Earl of Essex. During the opening decade of the seventeenth century, this tight-knit clique featured in two court cases which made plain their political, religious and familial loyalties.

The first of these occurred in 1602, shortly after the execution of the Earl of Essex. Richard Bathoe, a preacher resident in Ireland, complained to the Star Chamber that during a visit to Pembroke he had been assaulted by an armed gang. The instigator of the attack was John Meyrick of Fleet, a relative of Rowland Laugharne. Meyrick had taken offence at some slighting remarks made by Bathoe about the dead earl. Others involved in the attack included Thomas Adams, Hugh Powell, John Cheere, John Shakerlyne and John Lynch. They were

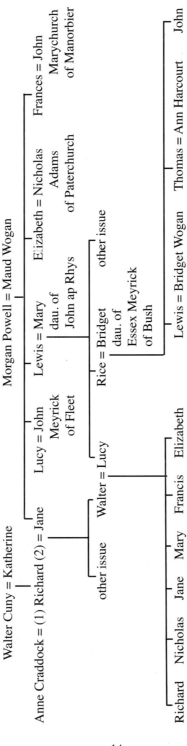

The relationship between the Cuny and Powell families

egged on by Morgan Powell's wife, Maud, and by Jane Powell and Meyrick's wife, Lucy. It is quite likely that the assault on Bathoe had as much to do with current suspicions of Irish refugees who had flooded into Pembrokeshire during the Irish wars of Elizabeth I's reign, as with resentment over the remarks concerning the Earl of Essex.[30]

The second case, however, seems to have been more firmly rooted in group loyalty to Essex's memory. After Devereux's execution in 1601, the manor and palace of Lamphey was left not to his 9-year-old son Robert, but to Walter, a second, illegitimate offspring. The estate was then leased to Rhys Philips Scarfe of Laugharne, who later refused to give up the tenancy. A plot to seize it back was devised by Nicholas Adams, John Meyrick, Richard Cuny and the under sheriff, Lewis Bishop. Adams, Meyrick and Cuny were married to daughters of Morgan and Maud Powell, whilst Bishop was said to be 'much practised and experienced in oppressing, wronging and deceiving of others'.[31] They accused Scarfe of breaking into Lamphey Palace at the head of a band of 'disordered and vagrant persons', seizing goods worth £400, corn to the value of £200, over 400 sheep and other livestock, which had then been sold, and remaining in occupation of the palace. It was also alleged that Scarfe still owed £240 in arrears of rent.[32] The case came before the Star Chamber and eventually the estate was restored to Robert, third Earl of Essex. He seems to have enjoyed good relations with the Powells. On 1 October 1620, Lewis Powell and his wife took over the lease of the manor, mansion house and lands of Lamphey from the previous lease-holder, Richard Cuny of Welston, who had obtained the lease in 1618.[33] The relationship between the Powell and Cuny families was a close and enduring one.

Though we know a great deal about the marriages and actions of Lewis Powell and of his relatives, the date of birth of his son, Rice, is uncertain. There are no clues to where or how he was brought up. He may have become a page in a noble household, as did Rowland Laugharne, but there is no evidence of this.

It is possible that Rice spent part of his youth on the Isle of Wight, or that the family had connections there, for in some documents he is described as 'Captain Rice Powell of the Isle of Wight'. Certainly his eldest sister, Martha, married a gentleman named Stephen March of the Isle of Wight. Rice himself took as his bride Bridget, a daughter of Essex Meyrick, though some authorities describe her as a member of the Cuny family.[34]

Rice seems to have decided upon a military career even before the Civil War began, possibly because as the younger child of a large family he could expect to inherit little in the way of money or lands. In 1642 he was in Ireland, fighting against the Irish rebels and he was obviously a soldier of considerable experience. A document he signed on 28 March 1644, assigned to Walter Cuny 'a large sum due to him for service in Ireland against the Irish rebels'.[35] Lord Clarendon regarded him as a soldier of fortune, and one of his acquaintances believed him to be 'a well experienced soldier that came from Ireland to endeavour the relief, and not like many other, the destruction of his bleeding country'.[36] Rowland Laugharne describes how, at the outbreak of war, the threat posed by Royalist forces to Pembrokeshire persuaded Powell to 'quit his command, forego his arrears and repair home'.[37]

3   Wales on the Eve of War

The Land

The Wales into which John Poyer, Rowland Laugharne and Rice Powell were born was regarded by some contemporaries as a land of poverty, economically backward and under-developed, its soil badly cultivated.

There were cogent reasons for this view. The majority of the population made their livelihood from agriculture or in the trades dependent upon it and some farmers struggled to provide a basic living for themselves and their families. William Vaughan of Llangyndeyrn in Carmarthenshire noted that fields were so bare of corn that a stranger 'would think that the earth produced such a grain naturally wild'.[1] An estate in Anglesey was described in the 1630s as consisting of 'coarse and wild grounds without hedges … not a stick of wood growing upon any of them nor any firing besides gorse and ferne …'. In addition most of the houses were 'not fitt for a civil man to rest himself in for an houre or two much less to lodge in it'. [2]

Almost two-thirds of Wales is a barren upland, where shallow soils and a wet climate hinder cultivation. Settlements in these areas in the 1600s were small, the farmsteads remote and scattered. Even in the more fertile coastal plains of the north and south, agricultural methods were often those that had been practised for generations. In a few areas, such as the hundreds of Dungleddy and Castlemartin in Pembrokeshire, the old medieval open-field system was still in evidence.[3]

In the two decades before the outbreak of the Civil War, a series of poor harvests caused widespread misery. Between 1620 and 1623 and again for much of the 1630s, conditions were particularly grim. Not only did the cost of corn rise sharply, but on many farms the profits from wool, sheep, butter and cheese showed a considerable loss. Sir John Wynn of Gwydir in Caernarfonshire, writing in 1623, lamented that he was £3,000 in debt. There was a shortfall of £1,000 in his income from rents and, what was worse, 'my tenants have not wherewith to pay, the bread corn is that exceeding rate that a number do die in the country for hunger … the rest have the impression of hunger in their faces exceeding the memory of any man living'.[4]

There were others who viewed Wales in an entirely different light. The poet Thomas Churchyard, writing his descriptive poem *The Worthiness of Wales* at the close of the sixteenth century, regarded the Welsh as both prosperous and honest. He took a far more positive, even rosy-tinted view of the nation's well-being:

> There markets good and victuals nothing deare
> Each place is filled with plenty all the yeare
> The ground manurde the grain doth so increase
> That thousands live in wealth and peace.

Despite the bad harvests and several visitations of the plague, the population of Wales steadily increased. In 1536, it numbered some 278,000 people. By 1630, this had risen to between 350,000 and 405,000, the majority of whom were concentrated in the lowland areas.[5] The three south-western counties of Pembrokeshire, Cardiganshire and Carmarthenshire accounted for roughly 25% of the total population; Glamorganshire housed the largest number, well over 40,000 people.

This steady increase may have led to, or been the result of, improvements in agricultural methods and improved yields. Some careful landlords ensured that their lands were regularly fertilized with lime, manure, seaweed or marl; marshes were drained and trees felled in order to put previously unproductive land under crops. As Thomas Churchyard put it:

> They have begun of late to lime their land
> And plough the ground where sturdy oaks did stand,
> Convert the meres and marish everywhere ...
> They tear up trees and take the roots away
> Make stony fields smooth fertile fallow ground,
> Bring pasture to bear good grass for hay.

In many of the Welsh shires, these improvements were accompanied by the enclosure of freehold lands and even old manorial demesne lands, which became intensively farmed. In many places, where land was parcelled out into a patchwork of small plots or strips, the impoverished tenants were ousted and the holdings were concentrated into units of much greater acreage. This led to some ill-feeling between landlords and tenants and to several protracted court cases which dragged on even after the Civil War had ended.[6]

Trade

Many of the most important exports of Wales were linked directly to agriculture. Because of the growing demand for meat in the expanding towns of England, there was a continual movement of cattle along the drovers' routes leading through the lush, cascading valleys of the border lands to markets in the Midlands and beyond. In the ports of South Wales, cattle were crowded aboard coastal trading vessels for shipment to Bristol and the West Country.

There was also a vociferous demand for dairy produce and where English towns could not meet the demand, Wales supplied the need. Glamorgan became one of the kingdom's biggest butter and cheese producing regions.[7]

The woollen industry still provided employment for many in the Welsh countryside. From the three counties of the south-west, unworked wool was exported to the cloth industry of the west of England, though there were still weavers guilds dominating the craft in towns such as Haverfordwest, Brecon and Carmarthen. In the rural areas, especially in the north, wool production was based on the hill farms and villages and was sent by packhorse to markets in Oswestry and Shrewsbury.[8]

Coal had been mined in Pembrokeshire since at least the 14th century and there were mines in Flintshire, Denbighshire and Glamorgan. In addition to coal, culm, a slow-burning mixture of coal and clay, had been exported to Ireland from Tenby and Milford Haven for many decades. Coal was a necessary fuel in several Welsh industries. Potteries and salt refineries needed regular supplies, as did brewing and lime burning. In 1615, Robert Mansel founded a glass factory at Milford Haven, using Pembrokeshire coal to create the molten glass.

Many of the major landowners exploited the underground natural resources of their estates, sinking shafts for coal, lead and copper, sometimes in partnership with other members of the gentry. Walter Vaughan of Golden Grove in Carmarthenshire owned mines at Llangennech, Llwynhendy and Cydweli.[9] When Roger Mostyn of Flintshire raised a Royalist foot regiment at the beginning of the Civil War, it included coal- and lead-miners from his Flintshire estates.

Society

Scattered across the coastal plains of Wales and nestling in the river valleys below the moors and the mountains stood the houses of the gentry and the mansions of the aristocracy. To modern perceptions, there may seem little difference between these two ranks of society, but at the beginning of the seventeenth century, the divide was clearly understood.

The great nobles of the day owned vast estates from which they derived considerable wealth. Their titles had been granted by earlier monarchs and in some cases had been handed down from father to son for generations. Commanding great respect and wielding immense influence, few of them lived on their Welsh properties, finding it more profitable to remain at the centre of government in London and rent out their Welsh manors. An example was Robert Devereux, third Earl of Essex, who held manors in several Welsh counties, of which the richest plum was Lamphey in Pembrokeshire. Originally an episcopal palace belonging to the bishops of St Davids, it passed into Devereux hands in 1546 and on the eve of the Civil War was tenanted by the Gunter family, who were said to have originated at Tregunter in Breconshire.

Next in importance were the gentry, a group which contained subtle distinctions of rank. First in precedence were the knights and, after the creation of the rank in 1611, the baronets. They were followed by esquires and then by gentlemen. All derived their position from privileges granted by the sovereign and by inherited land and wealth.

In general, the Welsh gentry were not accounted as wealthy as their English counterparts. Their riches came mostly from land and there could be considerable variation in the amounts received. Some families collected only £20 a year from their estates, whilst many owning a larger acreage enjoyed incomes of £300 or more. A few were even worth in excess of £1,000, placing them on an economic parity with the aristocracy.

Whatever their financial condition they could be sure of one thing: their ancestry, whether descended from the ancient Welsh royal houses or from the first Norman invaders – and many families could claim descent from both – gave them an undoubted standing in their communities. Their influence and patronage was widespread and pervasive, extending into all the crevices of Welsh life, and they could expect to hold office as justices of the peace, county sheriffs, even Members of Parliament.

A closely-knit group, inter-related and self-confident, the gentry were proud, often quarrelsome and were prepared to be litigious over land rights and property, but they were also aware of their duties and obligations. They were expected to be liberal in hospitality, with a measure of charity to the poor. It was commonly accepted that a gentleman should be a patron of scholars and poets, perhaps even a writer himself. Sir James Perrot of Carew published, in 1596, *The Discovery of Discontented Minds*, and followed it with several other books including, in 1630, *Meditations on the Lord's Prayer,* an influential and well-received religious text. George Owen of Orielton also produced several works, the most well-known of which was *The Description of Pembrokeshire*, regarded today as one of the prime sources on late sixteenth-century Pembrokeshire.

In 1626, William Vaughan published *The Golden Grove*, in which he set out 'the means to discern a gentleman'. These were, firstly, that 'he must be affable and courteous in speech and behaviour. Secondly, he must have an adventurous heart to fight, and that but for just quarrels. Thirdly, he must be endowed with mercy to forgive the trespasses of his friends and servants. Fourthly, he must stretch his purse to give liberally unto soldiers and unto them that have need; for a niggard is not worthy to be called a gentleman. These be the properties of a gentleman, which whosoever lacketh deserveth but the title of a clown or of a country boor'.[10]

George Owen, writing at the end of the sixteenth century, has left us an idyllic description of the gentry of Pembrokeshire in their hours of relaxation. 'Such is the quietness and love that is amongst the gentlemen of this country that hardly are they found asunder if they be in one town, but always together at meals and meetings in such sort that it is joyful to behold. So gentle in speeches, so courteous in behaviour to each other, striving to exceed in courtesy and kindness the one to the other, no one faction, side or quarrel among them, so that it is a rare and seldom thing to hear of an affray or quarrel among the gentlemen of the chiefest sort ... With this is God pleased, the Prince well and carefully served, her laws duly obeyed and justice duly ministered'.[11]

Within two generations this idyllic world was to be torn apart, its courtesies, its pleasant, carefully measured rhythms fractured by the realities of war.

The Peasantry

It has been estimated that the peasantry made up at least 90% of the population of seventeenth-century Britain. For the majority of them, hard, grinding work and economic uncertainty were facts of everyday existence.

The most prosperous members of this group were the yeomen, occupying freehold lands which they worked for themselves. They could receive an income of up to 40 shillings a year, but William Vaughan noted two further qualifications: yeomen tilled the soil and made their living by selling corn and other produce in the markets.[12]

Some yeomen were wealthy enough to live in comfortable, stone-built houses and possessed goods of value. They were willing to involve themselves in trade and kept alehouses and bakeries; many developed skills in a range of crafts, or were able to loan out money, crops or livestock to others less fortunate. Their lineage might be as ancient and distinguished as the gentry and marriages between the wealthier yeoman families and the lower ranks of the gentry were not unknown.

At the lower end of the yeoman scale were those who worked much smaller acreages and were economically more fragile. They in turn overlapped with the husbandmen, a group of tenant farmers who by dint of hard work and luck might become reasonably prosperous. Few were so lucky. They were at the mercy of circumstance; a series of bad harvests or a period of inflation would leave them with a reduced store of seed for the next year's sowing or without cash to buy an extra supply. These were the families most likely to lose their tenancies and to sink down into the ranks of the landless labourers.

The bulk of the labouring class found employment on the land. They occupied tenancies of a few acres or even less, paying cash rents to the gentry as lords of the manor. In addition they performed a range of services which dated back to the medieval period. In 1609, a survey of the manor of Beere (Manorbier) in Pembrokeshire listed the dues owed by the tenants to their lord. These included the gathering in of the hay crop, which was to be transported to the castle at the tenants' own cost; new millstones to be transported to the mill, the cart, horse and driver to be supplied by the tenants, who must also fetch timber for the repair of the mill; and 'likewise to give to the lord for every messuage a hen at the feast of the birth of Our Lord yearly'.[13] Other labour services might include a number of days of compulsory ploughing and reaping on the lord's land, the carrying of lime for the making of lime mortar or the collection of firewood.

It was from the ranks of their tenants, workers and other dependants that the gentry were able to recruit foot soldiers for the regiments they raised at the onset of war. Where the numbers were insufficient, recruiting drives were launched through the villages and market towns of Wales.

Lawyers and Merchants

Separate from the groups mentioned above, but often derived from them, or aspiring to rise beyond them, were those of professional status – clerics, lawyers, apothecaries and merchants. Many of the clergy were from yeomen stock and they were usually appointed to their livings by the lords of the manor.

The legal professions attracted the younger sons of the gentry families, though they did not always achieve the riches or social success they might have hoped for. There were exceptions; Thomas Canon was the son of a Haverfordwest attorney who was educated at Jesus College, Oxford, and at Clifford's Inn and Lincoln's Inn. In 1606 he was appointed County Feodary, which involved collecting the incomes of people who had been made wards of court, a post he held until 1636. He was knighted in 1623 for his services to the Crown and was mayor of Haverfordwest on five occasions, as well as serving thrice as the town's MP.

One of the most prosperous, energetic and influential groups amongst the professional classes were the merchants. In every town and seaport their business premises and storehouses dominated the harbours. Inside these buildings, clerks scurried to and fro, tallying casks of cheese, butter and salted fish, hogsheads of ale and vinegar, barrels of salt, ballets of canvas, dickers of animal hide and fardels of linen cloth, whilst wagon-loads of coal and culm rumbled down to the quaysides to be shovelled into waiting ships, which carried the produce of south Wales to ports in the West Country, Ireland and the Continent, returning with spices, silks, wines and fruit.[14] These merchants formed a tight-knit, closely related group, who supported one another and exercised considerable influence over the affairs of the towns from which they worked.[15] They jostled one another on the benches of the Town Councils and were regularly elected to the mayor-alties or other civic offices. Some became prosperous enough to live out in the countryside and described themselves as gentlemen. Rhys Pritchard, for example, traded from Tenby, but owned a house in nearby Penally. It was common for merchants to have premises in several ports and their relatives were scattered across the towns of Wales and the West Country, particularly Bristol. It has been suggested that these close links allowed radical ideas to seep into the professional ranks of what was otherwise in Wales a conservative society.

4 Overseas Expeditions & Tax

In the autumn of 1625, one hundred exhausted, sea-sick men disembarked in Plymouth after a voyage from Pembrokeshire to join an expedition against Spain.[1] They were soon joined by other levies from across Wales. War had been declared and a great fleet was being assembled to attack Cadiz, with the aim of inflicting a defeat that would damage the prestige and military might of the King of Spain and his kinsman, the Holy Roman Emperor, Ferdinand II, then engaged in a war against Dutch and German Protestants. In addition, Ferdinand had driven King Charles of England's sister, Elizabeth, and her husband from their recently occupied throne of Bohemia. There was enormous public support in Britain for a military intervention to ensure their restoration.

The fleet finally sailed in October and by December, disease-riddled and storm-battered, it was creeping back into Plymouth with over half its compliment dead.[2] Welsh counties which had provided healthy men for the expedition now had to provide relief for the sickly remnants. Wales had sent over 800 men the previous winter for service in Ireland,[3] and then, in 1627, a second disastrous expedition took place, this time to the Isle de Rhé in France, where the nearby Huguenot port of La Rochelle was besieged by a French Catholic force.[4] Most of the Welsh counties were expected to supply 50 men, with 100 each from Glamorgan and Monmouth. The Deputy-Lieutenants of Pembrokeshire did not find it easy to recruit the required number and wrote to inform the Council of State of the fact: 'In pursuance of directions from the Lord Lieutenant of Wales. They have levied 50 men and have them ready to be sent to Plymouth. Pray that Milford Haven may be fortified and that on future occasions they may have power given to them to levy men in the town and County of Haverfordwest and other corporations in the county. Not having that authority they are obliged to impress such men as they are both sorry and ashamed to present'.[5] The other two south-western counties also encountered problems in fulfilling their quotas. Cardiganshire sent 47 men, whilst Carmarthenshire delivered 49, both shires receiving in return receipts once the levies had been delivered to Lieutenant Hugh Hookes for transport to Plymouth.[6]

Public enthusiasm for these wars may have been fuelled by expectations of an invasion, a belief particularly prevalent in communities along the Welsh coastline, where it was thought that the arrival of the Catholic powers was imminent. It was, however, not only armed forces which threatened the peace of Wales. In August 1628, the Justices of the Peace in Pembrokeshire wrote to the Council of State: 'Of late great numbers of Irish poor people have been landed in that county with passes. Being much pestered and burdened by them the writers have made a stay of a bark of ten tons, wherein were carried about 70 of these poor people. They were landed suddenly and some of them secretly in the night ... Submit that caution should be given to the Lord Deputy to restrain this confluence into this kingdom'.[7] Two months later the Justices wrote again, 'complaining of a great concourse of Irish people transported to this country, owners of barks make much gain by transporting at 3s a piece for young and old. The reason they allege for the coming are last year's dearth of cattle and dearth of corn ...'.[8] The problem was even worse during the spring of the following year, when within four weeks over 300 people were put ashore 'on rocks and in creeks' where the authorities could not find them in time to prevent a landing; the rate for a passage from Ireland had gone up to 5s per person.[9]

The impact made by these refugees in an area of small, scattered communities, where even the largest towns housed only a thousand people at most, can easily be imagined, especially when it is remembered that Wales had only recently emerged from three years of poor harvests and food shortages. To make matters worse, the majority of the refugees were Catholic and many Welshmen would have agreed with the view of Sir James Perrot, expressed in a letter to the Council: 'The dangers of Milford Haven are increased by the dwelling and resort thither of recusants'.[10] In addition, the seaborne trade of the Principality had suffered for decades from the activities of pirates, who occasionally launched raids on the mainland itself.

Preparations to defend the long and indented coastline of Wales were soon in hand. It was decided that Pembrokeshire in particular needed special attention because of the long and sinuous Milford Haven Waterway, historically recognised as an ideal landing place for invaders. The fortifications at Tenby were also to be put in repair and at least £3,000 was to be spent on the repair or building of forts at Dale Point, Rat Island and Stack Rock in the Milford Haven Waterway.[11] Work began fairly quickly, though enthusiasm soon drained away, as Sir James Perrot reported to Secretary Conway, who passed the news on to his masters in the government: '[Sir James] reports on steps taken concerning the fortifying of the Haven, there is a coldness, he will not say a carelessness, in most of those whom this service most concerns. Suggests a commission to inquire as to what money in hand in the adjoining counties [is] applicable to that purpose'.[12]

Meanwhile, the trained bands of Pembrokeshire, consisting of some 600 locals, were to be strengthened by a further 500 men, with similar additions to

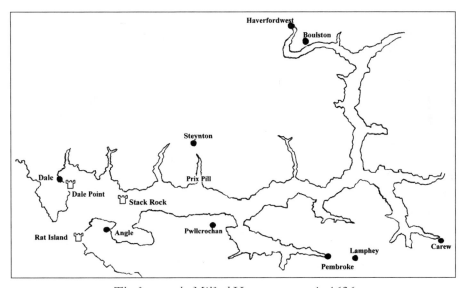

The forts on the Milford Haven waterway in 1626

the militias of other counties. A group of 84 experienced drill-serjeants was made available to train the new recruits and the pay of these old soldiers was doubled from six shillings to twelve. They stayed for three months and found ready employ in at least two counties, Glamorgan and Pembroke, where they gave daily instruction to the officers of the trained bands. Corporals were drilled in the finer points of musketry and there were twice weekly practices for the foot soldiers. Attempts to standardise weapons were less successful; the cost of up-to-date fire-arms even encouraged Glamorgan to consider equipping their men with bows and arrows.[13]

There was some opposition to the demand for funding for these measures. In July 1626, the Pembrokeshire Justices of the Peace declined on the grounds of poverty to give a voluntary grant of supply as requested by the King. The gentry, they explained, were short of cash due to poor harvests earlier in the decade and because of the burdens already placed upon them. The justices noted that it would have 'ministered no small comfort to their hearts' had the supply been voted by Parliament.[14] A few months later the Justices of Pembrokeshire found themselves unable to supply a pinnace demanded for the King's service, as their fellows in Cardiganshire had refused to share the cost. Caernarfonshire, Merioneth and Denbighshire also pleaded poverty, whilst Monmouthshire refused to pay any further subsidies unless approved by Parliament. Carmarthenshire was asked to supply a vessel of 30 tons, but the authorities begged to be excused on the grounds that theirs 'was an inland county with only a few creeks, in which there was no ship'. Some pressure must have been brought to bear, because in a letter dated 15 September they emphasised that they had no vessel of that size, but promised a sum equivalent to its value.[15]

Opposition was again voiced when a general loan was demanded. Commissioners were appointed in each county to assess what should be demanded from those able to pay. They were to ensure that the money was collected without trouble; no excuses were to be accepted and the names of the obstinate were to be noted. If anyone 'refused to assist with their purses, it is the King's pleasure that they should do so with their persons'. They were to report to the Military Yard near St Martin's-in-the-Fields in London to be enrolled in the King's service.[16] The Common Council of Tenby instructed their Chamberlain to pay from municipal funds subsidies which had been required of 'certain townsfolk' by the King, the inference being that the townsfolk could not or would not pay themselves.

Opposition was much more vocal in London, where a new Parliament had been convened in March 1628. Members were anxious to prevent the levying of more taxes without their agreement and drew up a Petition of Rights which had a threefold aim: taxes and loans could not be levied without the consent of Parliament; no subjects could be imprisoned without trial, as had happened to some of those who had refused to pay earlier demands; and soldiers should not be billeted on unwilling civilians. These proposals seemed to Charles to affect the royal prerogative granted to him by God. A number of hot-tempered debates now took place within the Commons, with the King only granting assent to the Petition upon receipt of subsidies to pursue the war against Spain and France (see p.23).

There were, however, still disagreements between the King and the Commons. The members, especially those with Puritan or strict Protestant leanings, viewed with suspicion the activities of William Laud, Bishop of London and subsequently, from 1633, Archbishop of Canterbury. An advisor to the King, Laud was anxious to restore the proper observance of church ritual; the celebration of the sacraments were to be observed, together with the strict adherence to the Book of Common Prayer. Clergymen who abandoned certain aspects of the service found themselves censured, particularly if they were of a Puritan bent. It seemed to some that these measures were a step to the restoration of Catholicism. The King's Catholic wife, Queen Henrietta Maria, was regarded with hostility because of her open proselytising at court and her encouragement of those willing to convert.[17] The very fabric of the Church of England might therefore be under threat.

Things came to a head in March 1629, when the King ordered Parliament to adjourn during a discussion on the royal right to collect customs duties. This was regarded as contrary to the Petition of Rights and members refused to obey the King's instruction. To ensure that the debate continued, the Speaker, Sir John Finch, was held down in his chair and Black Rod was denied entrance to the Chamber. In a fury, King Charles dismissed Parliament.

A period of personal rule by the King now began, during which political problems were compounded by a series of bad harvests and all levels of Welsh society suffered hardship. Prices of basic goods were pushed up, causing an industrial slump, with consequent unemployment. It was alleged that suffering was particularly severe because, despite shortages, corn continued to be exported to Ireland by some of the gentry. In addition, outbreaks of plague ravaged mid and south Wales and there was an increase in the activities of pirates in coastal waters.

Ship Money

Fear of pirate raids may have been one of the reasons why there was little opposition to the imposition of the Ship Money Tax. Originating in the Plantagenet era, this was a tax on property which had occasionally been levied on maritime communities on order to provide cash or ships for national defence. In 1634, anxious for funds to finance the fleet and without Parliament and its power to vote taxes, King Charles decided upon its re-introduction.

It was just one of a number of financial devices dreamt up by the King and his advisors to raise money, but proved to be one of the most controversial. First suggested by Charles in 1628, when a total of £173,411 had been demanded, public reaction had been immediate and hostile and the idea was dropped. Five years later, after several years of warfare, opposition was less vocal and money was collected without too much trouble. Encouraged by this, less than a year later Charles sent out a fresh demand for £218,500 and this time the tax was extended to inland as well as coastal towns.[18]

Wales and Monmouthshire were assessed at a total of £10,500. Pembrokeshire's share was £713 10s, with a further £65 due from the town and county of Haverfordwest. The other two south-western counties, Cardiganshire and Carmarthenshire, were also assessed, the former at £654, though £160 of the Carmarthenshire rate of £760 was uncollected.[19] The money was gathered in Pembrokeshire without opposition, but on about 1 February, during the journey to London to deliver it, the Sheriff of Pembrokeshire, John Scourfield of New Moat, was drowned with several of his escort at Eynsham Ferry. Of the money he carried, £43 sank to the bottom of the river with him.[20]

There was considerable resentment in 1636 when Ship Money was again demanded. By now it was clear that the levy was becoming an annual fixture and even supporters of the King questioned its legality. The main burden of collection fell upon the sheriffs, who were soon at their wits' end. Not only was there an unwillingness to pay, but people also refused to buy the goods which had been seized in place of money and then offered for sale.

In 1637, Richard Price, sheriff of Cardigan, reported to the Council that in 'endeavouring to levy the ship-money, he tried by all fair and gentle means, but could not receive one penny, so that he was compelled to distrain oxen, kine, horses, sheep, household stuff and implements of husbandry, the which petitioner can get no money for, nor anyman to offer for them one penny, though often set at sale'.[21] In the same year, Sir John Stepney of Pembrokeshire also experienced problems in collecting arrears, though these were 'in respect of men's poverty and not otherwise'. Things were no easier in Carmarthenshire, where in 1640 arrears were caused by 'the slackness of some few. The most part having already been paid, the residue will be recovered on the getting in of this harvest'.[22]

The amount of money uncollected grew each year. In 1635, Cardiganshire had paid all of its assessment of £654, but in 1639 not one penny was gathered in. Carmarthenshire, which in 1635 had paid all but £160 of its assessment of £760, was rated for the same amount in 1639, but managed to pay only £100. Pembrokeshire had paid all of its first tax, bar the £43 lost in the accident at Eynsham, but four years later produced only £450 of the expected £683 10s.[23]

The Bishops' Wars

To these financial and legal problems were now added a further crop of religious tensions. In 1637/38, King Charles attempted to impose a new version of the English Prayer Book on his Scottish subjects. Very little discussion had taken place to prepare the Presbyterian Church in Scotland for this innovation and as a result, rioting broke out in many areas. The Scottish assembly angrily adopted the National Covenant, which rejected any form of meddling with their religion.

The King prepared to suppress this disobedience. A levy of 700 men was raised in Wales for the royal army. The number was doubled in 1639, but the Exchequer was unable to provide the necessary funds and the number of men required fell to 600, with 150 coming from Pembrokeshire. The Council of State eventually decided that the levy was not needed, but by then the town of Tenby had been incensed by the demand. Its people 'would not assist this intolerable levy neither with men nor with money' and the following year the town magistrates would 'not respect the authority of his Majesty's commission of Lieutenancy'.[24]

Whilst there had been no actual fighting against the Scots in the so-called first Bishops' War, when the second Bishops' War erupted in 1640, matters were different. The King was still determined to stamp his authority upon Scotland and he issued writs to raise a larger army. Wales was expected to provide over 2,000 infantry.[25]

Once these preparations were begun, King Charles instructed the Earl of Bridgewater, President of the Council in the Marches, to call upon the deputy lieutenants of south Wales to place themselves under the authority of the Earl of Worcester.[26] This gentleman was a Catholic who, it was rumoured, had been entrusted by the King with a 'secret service'. What exactly this might have been was never specified, but the story heightened the fears of many who suspected Charles' religious intentions. There was a fresh burst of rumour when it became known that Charles had told the Earl of Pembroke that all his friends and tenants should obey Worcester's instructions. People began to wonder if England, not Scotland, was the King's intended target.[27]

The Scottish campaign did not go well. Newcastle was taken by the Scots on 30 August 1640, the English garrison having retreated from a city which their commander knew to be indefensible along its southern perimeter.[28] Fortunately for the inhabitants, the invaders had drawn up strict rules against looting.[29] Within a week, Northumberland and Durham were under Scottish control.

The King now commanded all the trained bands to move northwards. With Wales virtually undefended, there were concerns that an invasion was imminent. It was reported that a Papist army was 'to have landed, not in Scotland, but in Wales, where the earl of Worcester, a firm head of the Popish faction, had commission to receive them'.[30]

King Charles soon realised that he could no longer prosecute a war without a further injection of money and to achieve that he needed the support of Parliament. He had already convened what became known as the Short Parliament; meeting in April 1640, but it lasted for no more than three weeks. When he realised that it would vote the subsidies he required only after a discussion of concerns over royal policy, Charles dismissed it.

Now, in November, another session of Parliament was called and this, the famous Long Parliament, was to sit until 1653. There was a general hope and expectation that problems might be resolved and that there would be a return to the proper functions and balances of government that had occurred earlier in the century. At least 400 of the 493 Members of Parliament were in broad agreement that there should be no repeat of Charles' personal rule and that measures should be introduced to curtail the prerogative powers of the Crown.

The unofficial leader of this faction was John Pym, a Somerset lawyer and a passionate exponent of the rights of Parliament, who had developed a clear strategy for achieving those aims. Recognising the need to isolate the King from his unpopular advisors, Pym orchestrated the impeachment and execution of the Earl of Strafford and the imprisonment of Archbishop Laud. In addition to these measures, the ensuing months saw the passing of a bill forbidding the dissolution of Parliament without the consent of its members and another declaring Ship Money to be illegal. Further bills followed: one for the abolition of the Star Chamber, which had been used to enforce statutes and to prevent public disorder and which had come to be regarded as an instrument of tyranny; another for the ending of taxation without the agreement of Parliament; and one for the introduction of a three year period for Parliamentary sessions.

The suggestion that the King should only rely upon those councillors that 'Parliament may have cause to confide in' was seen by Charles and his supporters as particularly revolutionary and caused many reformists to reconsider their position.[31] Edward Hyde, later Earl of Clarendon, had formerly supported reform but could not stomach the idea that Parliament should dictate to the sovereign. It was, he later wrote, a question of whether the King was above Parliament, or was Parliament above the King? The answer, when MPs considered a bill giving them the right to nominate royal councillors, was clear enough; the reformists were victorious by over 150 votes, but attitudes on both sides were hardening.

To add to the gathering maelstrom of discontent, in October 1641 rebellion broke out in Ireland. Hundreds of mainly Protestant refugees escaped across the Irish Channel to the safety of Pembrokeshire and Anglesey, bringing with them tales of hideous atrocities. There were stories of French involvement in the rising and Wales once again braced itself to face invasion.

5   Simmering Discontent

On 13 January 1642, Parliament gave notice of a popish plot aimed at the kingdom. All county authorities were warned to prepare for invasion. Magistrates and sheriffs were to ensure that local magazines were stocked with arms, guards would be set and no stronghold would be delivered up without the authority of Parliament.[1]

On 28 January, Sir Hugh Owen, MP for Pembroke, laid before the House a report he had received from John Poyer, Mayor of Pembroke. Poyer had been busy examining refugees from Ireland, who warned him of French plans to aid the Irish rebels. Owen was one of several MPs chosen to report to the Commons on the progress of discussions with the House of Lords about the crisis in Ireland.[2] The members were concerned about sightings of suspicious vessels off Milford Haven and Aberdyfi, and fresh in their minds were the words of Sir William Jephson, a Munster landlord, who had informed them in December that he had proof that the Queen had approved of the rebellion, as it was a defence of the Catholic church.

Owen and three other Members were ordered by Parliament to instruct the mayors of Bristol and Pembroke to stay ships, persons and the good of merchants from Ross, Wexford and Kilkenny and, if possible, to seize the merchants themselves. On 30 January, alarmed by swelling numbers of Papists entering Britain from the rebellious areas of Ireland, the Commons ordered that they should be sent back. In a vain attempt to cut off supplies to the rebels, all shipments of arms and armaments to Ireland were banned.[3]

As rumours swirled across the country, tensions were added to by reports of events in London. The House of Commons was awaiting the King's reply to the Grand Remonstrance, which had been presented to him at the beginning of December. This document, drawn up in November 1641 by John Pym but actually based on the reports of earlier Parliamentary committees, catalogued the grievances of the past decade, rehearsed the measures taken to remedy them and set out proposals for the future, especially with regard to religion. Behind its high-flown protestations of loyalty to the King lay a carefully planned manoeuvre to ensure that the army, which had been voted into being to deal with the Irish rebellion, should not be used instead to squash the rebels in Parliament.

The demands set out in the Remonstrance outraged the King. He felt his prerogatives to be as menaced by the radicals of Parliament as they believed their hopes of reform were by him. He decided to remove the ringleaders as quickly as possible. Using as an excuse their contacts with the Scottish Covenanters, he ordered the arrest for High Treason of John Pym, Arthur Haselrig, Denzil Holles, William Strode and Lord Mandeville. On 4 January he went in person to the House of Commons to detain them.[4]

The five members had been forewarned and had gone to ground in the City of London. Charles, baffled and confused, withdrew. He had committed a colossal blunder which alienated public and Parliamentary sympathy. Over the next few days, fear and panic ran hand-in-hand through the capital. Fearing an attack by Royalist troops, the city gates were closed and the inhabitants began to arm themselves. Parliament issued a proclamation which declared as a public enemy anyone who breached its privileges and a Committee of Public Safety was formed.

Believing themselves to be in danger of assassination, the King and Queen took themselves first to Hampton Court Palace and later to Windsor. In a belated attempt to calm the situation, on 13 January, the same day as Parliament's warning of popish plots, Charles sent a conciliatory message to both Houses. It did little good. The size of the London trained bands was increased and when, on 22 January, the King asked for £100,000 to prosecute the war against the Irish rebels, Parliament refused. During the succeeding weeks, contacts between Charles, the Commons and the Lords blew hot and cold, by turns agreeable, procrastinating, reproachful and hostile. One of the main sticking points was the Militia Bill, originally intended as a way of raising county forces against possible threats to the nation. Fearing the uses to which the militia might be put, Charles refused to sign it.

News of these events increased the atmosphere of suspicion and distrust in west Wales. In February, John Poyer and John David, the Mayor of Haverfordwest detained a man named Hugh Molloy, a Catholic priest. At the same time they also arrested two further suspects, Captains Beale and Darcie, both Catholic officers who probably came from the Earl of Ormonde's army in Ireland. Their presence in Wales was regarded as highly suspicious, perhaps the precursor of invasion, for Ormonde's troops, originally intended to crush the Irish rebels, could easily be transported into Britain to deal with the King's enemies.[5]

Uncertain what to do with their prisoners, the two mayors wrote to the Speaker of the House of Commons for further instructions. Whilst awaiting a reply they received news that seven suspected papists, the survivors of a shipwreck at Llanina, near Cardigan, had arrived at Milford Haven and were seeking passage across the Irish Sea. Poyer had them all arrested.

On 31 March, the Commons sent a message of thanks to Poyer and David for their diligence. Molloy was tried for treason at the Great Sessions at Haverfordwest and, being found guilty, was sentenced to death. The presiding judge, Thomas Tourneur, delayed the execution until the views of the Commons were known. Shortly afterwards, the sheriff was ordered to convey all the prisoners to London; their subsequent fate is unknown.[6]

The presence in Pembrokeshire of so many suspected traitors can only have added to John Poyer's worries. He was clearly apprehensive about the state of the county's defences and its ability to meet an invasion. On 12 February 1642, he dispatched the following letter to Sir Hugh Owen:

> I have sent you here enclosed the examination of William Lurtine, master and owner of a ship of Liverpool, which confirms the former report of aid to be sent the Rebels in Ireland by the French, the Lord prevent them.
>
> Since my last letter, sent you the 18 January, there have been hundreds of poor English landed in Milford stript by the rebels, who do increase daily. If aid be sent to the Rebels it is very likely some of them may be driven or willingly will come into the river of Milford, where 500 or 1,000 armed men, as I conceive, may possess themselves of the whole country, and fortify Pembroke town with the Castle and other strong places in the said county which will not so lightly be regained.
>
> I desire you to move the House, that order may be taken that the Trained Bands and all other persons fit to bear arms in the town and liberties of Pembroke may be put in a posture of defence in these dangerous times, and that course may be taken with all persons that are rated at arms, and for providing of powder, lead and match in this town – for many are backward in the service. I desire that it may speedily be looked into. For the Trained Bands of the Town and County of Pembroke in general for want of exercise are not fit for sudden service, if they should be required. Their arms are much defective, for punishment is not laid on the offenders. I likewise certify your worship that I lately viewed the arms of the store of the whole county of Pembroke kept in the town of Haverford, I assure you that these arms on a sudden service will not arm 200 men – as I conceive – they are so defective. I have divers times desired the Deputy Lieutenants of the County to deliver me arms for forty or fifty musketeers with powder, match and lead out of the same store for the safeguard of the town of Pembroke, if occasion should be offered, but they have refused to deliver me any, notwithstanding that this town hath paid for the providing of the said arms, powder and lead, neither have they given any order or directions for watch to be kept in this town, either by night or by day. We have not in this brave river of Milford one piece of ordnance mounted, the Trained Bands are not exercised, arms provided or power granted for punishing of persons refractory in this service. I desire you to acquaint the House with these particulars.[7]

It is likely that the recommendations put forward in 1626 for the fortifying of the waterway had not been carried out, or if they had been, were not properly maintained. It is also odd that the Commons *Journal* for this period makes no mention of Poyer's letter being placed before the House by Owen. Perhaps, in the confusion of events, there was no time.

There is also no record of Poyer's movements during the next few months, but he can have had little time for leisure. Even if the number of refugees arriving in Milford had dwindled, there must still have been those who required temporary food and shelter and the £100 entrusted to Sir Hugh Owen by Parliament to relieve their hardships would quickly have been used up. The fugitives were questioned and, if they appeared suspicious, were detained. All of this Poyer and John David of Haverfordwest had to organize, as well as maintaining a watch along the coastline and at the county magazines and storehouses. That John Poyer continued to be diligent in his duties, perhaps too much so, is evident from an entry in the Commons *Journal* dated 27 June 1642.

> That the Mayor of Plimouth be required speedily to take into examination the commitment to prison of John Poyer, the Mayor of Pembroke: and if he find the cause thereof to be the arresting or staying of some ships that were bound with goods to Galloway a town in open rebellion: which he stayed by virtue of an order of this House: and was a special service done to the Kingdom therein: that he be forthwith discharged of his imprisonment: and Zidracke Pope, of whose suit he was arrested, to be brought up in safe custody to this house.

No other reference exists to this mysterious affair. It can be inferred that Zidracke Pope was a merchant who traded between Plymouth, Ireland and Milford Haven and whose vessel was detained on Poyer's orders. He may have been based in Devon, which might explain why the Mayor of Plymouth became involved. It is also possible that Poyer travelled to Plymouth to find out more about a man he regarded with suspicion and was arrested there. Frustratingly, the result of the Mayor of Plymouth's investigation is unknown, nor is there any clue as to exactly where or for how long Poyer was kept in prison. It is evident, however, that the Commons also had their suspicions about Pope, or they would not have ordered his conveyance to London for examination.

In London Parliament was struggling to persuade the King to sign the Militia Ordinance and Charles, well aware that to do so would transfer command of the militia to Parliament, adamantly refused. Frustrated by the lack of progress, on 5 March the House of Lords passed the Ordinance as a legally enforceable law without the Royal Assent. The recruitment and management of the county militias would now be under the control of the Lords Lieutenant of the various shires, who would themselves be appointed by Parliament.

In response, Charles issued a proclamation 'forbidding all his Majesty's subjects belonging to the Trained Bands or Militia of this Kingdom to rise, march, muster or exercise by virtue of any Order of Ordinance of one or both Houses of Parliament'.[8] In June, he issued opposing Commissions of Array, which nominated people to assemble and train militia to serve the Crown and began collecting money to finance his cause. Within days he also rejected the 'Nineteen Propositions' put forward by both Houses, which would have transferred supreme power from the Crown to Parliament.

In West Wales, the men nominated by Parliament to carry out the provisions of the Militia Ordinance were Richard Vaughan, Earl of Carbery, and Algernon Percy, Earl of Northumberland. Carbery was appointed as Lieutenant of Cardiganshire and Carmarthenshire and the town of Carmarthen, probably because his estates near Llandeilo gave him great influence in the locality, but he quickly declared his loyalty to the King. The choice of Northumberland as Lieutenant of Pembrokeshire and the town and county of Haverfordwest is harder to understand. He had no links with the area and may have been selected simply because of his known loyalty to Parliament. The three local MPs, Sir Hugh Owen, John Wogan and Sir John Stepney, were all named as Northumberland's deputy lieutenants. In addition, a number of other gentlemen were nominated by Parliament including Sir Richard Phillips of Picton, Thomas ap Rice of Scotsborough, John Eliot of Earwere (Poyer's nemesis), John Laugharne, the father of Rowland, Griffith White and Roger Lort.[9]

Richard Vaughan, Earl of Carbery
(Carmarthen Museum)

Over the next few months, these nominees all reacted differently to their appointments, which they well may not have sought in the first place. Owen remained in London until 22 August, when he was given permission by Parliament to travel to his home in Orielton; at about the same time Wogan was sent off to Pembrokeshire to persuade the county to support the Parliamentary cause, but his appeals were cold-shouldered by most of the gentry. Sir John Stepney made no attempt to enforce the Militia Ordinance and soon chose to throw in his lot with the King.[10] Phillips, Eliot and Roger Lort initially followed Stepney's example, but changed sides during the war, some of them more than once. Thomas ap Rice of Scotsborough near Tenby subsequently pledged £2,000 to the Royalist war effort, but took no part in the fighting. John Laugharne was to remain stout in his support of the 'Just Cause'.

A Committee of Public Safety was formed in July 1642, composed of Lords and Commons. A resolution was also taken on 12 July to raise an army of 10,000 men from London and its environs. Another Ordinance was issued to collect money from Parliamentary supporters in the capital. Finally, a Captain General was appointed to command the forces of Parliament. This was Robert Devereux, third Earl of Essex, who was given a commission from 'King and Parliament'. He was expected to secure the safety of the King, to ensure the defence of the Commons and the Lords and to preserve the true religion, laws, liberties and peace of the kingdom.[11]

Wales, like the rest of Britain, was now a nation teetering on the precipice of war. People looked fearfully into the future; many could not believe that a thing so monstrous as civil strife should come to pass. Portents of disaster abounded. A witch was seen walking on the waters of the Thames and visions of warring armies appeared in the skies.[12]

Even those who had a specific role in the warlike preparations prayed that the worst might not happen. On 19 May, the Earl of Northumberland, Lieutenant of Pembrokeshire, had written to Sir John Banks, 'God forbid that either king or parliament should by power and force go about to cure the present distempers for that course can produce nothing but misery, if not ruin, both to king and people'.[13]

Samuel Wood, the steward of Sir John Trevor of Trefalun in Flintshire, also put his apprehensions in writing. 'The lord show his mercy to us all of his kingdom and continue our peace, if it be his will ... our fears do daily increase here whether upon just grounds or not God knows'.[14] John Griffith of Cefnamlwch felt that the 'end of the world is not far off', whilst the puritan Morgan Llwyd was certain that the 'pillars of the world' were trembling.

For many people, the most terrifying thing of all was the choice that they must make – to support the King or to go against him. Looking back across the centuries to that distant summer of 1642, it may seem to us that the choice was simple – tyranny or liberty. The men and women involved in the struggle did not see it in so simplistic a way. Their world was a much more ordered and hierarchical one, where everyone's place in society was ordained. At the pinnacle of that pyramid stood the King, to many a semi-divine figure whose supremacy came direct from God. To challenge that was to call into question the whole fabric of the universe and if it was torn asunder, people felt that chaos would inevitably ensue.

The gentry were aware that they owed their position, their prestige and their landholdings to the goodwill and favour of successive monarchs. Even those who were deeply concerned over issues such as religion or the erosion of Parliamentary rights, still hesitated to come out against their sovereign. He was, after all, the King, divinely appointed and Welsh loyalty and pride in the Tudors had been transferred in some measure to the Stuarts. The biblical verse 'For who can stretch forth his hand against the Lord's anointed and be guiltless?' (1 Sam 26.9) was often quoted.[15] For most of those who took the cause of Parliament, it was not their intention to remove King Charles or to abolish the monarchy. They hoped that he could be persuaded to work with Parliament and allow it a due share in the governance of the kingdom. Indeed they went to war chanting the slogan 'For King and Parliament'.

Across Wales most families declared for the King, but with varying degrees of enthusiasm. The Marquess of Worcester was to spend a fortune in supporting Charles, and Sir John Owen of Clenennau became a mighty bulwark of Royalism. In Pembrokeshire, John Barlow of Slebech was so strong in his belief in the King that 'he was rather a pattern for the gentry of the county to wonder at, than in hopes to be imitated by them'.[16]

Some gentlemen, however, were so lukewarm in their Royalism that when the conflict was over, they seemed to their contemporaries to have been opportunists, waiting to trim their sails to the prevailing wind. The Lort brothers were two who changed sides: Roger was later described as 'of any principle or religion to acquire wealth', whilst as for his brother Sampson, 'any government, religion or office will suit him so it carries some lucre along with it'. Sir John Stepney, though he never deserted his Royalist principles, was thought of as no better: 'a habit of ease hath made his disposition not very inclinable to be very industrious to his own or the public affairs of his country'. John Vaughan proved to be 'one that upon fits will talk loud of monarchy but scrupulous to wet his finger to advance it'.

There remained one group whose convinced Protestant outlook placed it firmly in the Parliamentary camp. The Laugharnes, Owens, Meyricks, Powells and Cunys were united not only by family ties, but by their sympathy to the puritan and anti-papist views of the Earl of Essex.[17] When it became necessary, they aligned themselves quietly but firmly against the King.

All these families were based in the southern half of Pembrokeshire, within the 'Englishry', that section of the county which was English by tradition and custom and which had been heavily settled by the Norman conquerors five centuries before. This was the area which was to be the scene of most of the military actions of the war in west Wales. Across Wales, there were few other centres of Parliamentary resistance. Puritan enclaves existed along the Welsh border country, most prominently at Llanvaches and Wrexham. Some prominent landowners, such as Philip Herbert, Earl of Pembroke, Henry Herbert of Coalbrook and Sir John Myddleton of Chirk Castle, also declared against the King. Their views were not so much anti-monarchist as pro-Parliament, though Colonel John Jones of Maesygarnedd became a noted republican.[18] These, however, were isolated pockets of resistance and Wales as a nation, as represented by its gentry and leading citizens, was generally Royalist.

The views of the peasantry are harder to discover. Their opinions were not canvassed and they left no written record of their thoughts. Many marched out to support one side against another because they were following their landlord or squire, the traditional focus of local respect and influence. Others may have been caught up by the excitement of recruitment drives, taking the King's or Parliament's coin with no clear idea of what it might involve. Those who hoped to remain aloof from the conflict were to find it impossible. Rich and poor alike, town-dwellers and country-folk, merchants and labourers, all were about to be tipped into a conflagration which would consume them and change their world forever.

6 The Raising of Armies

As the summer of 1642 slipped by, the preparations for war grew more complex. On the Royalist side, between the end of July and late August, Commissions of Array were issued in the King's name to gentlemen in all the Welsh counties. Their main duty was to ensure a ready supply of cash for the Royalist war effort and they were expected to encourage donations and loans from the King's sympathisers. In addition to the moneys freely given, the King also began to levy regular amounts from his supporters, usually paid in a county tax, the rate of which was set by local committees made up of gentlemen and commissioners. Further amounts were raised by seizing the estates of Parliamentary supporters, which were then administered by nominees of the commissioners.[1] Towns across Wales were also expected to provide men and billets for the various regiments being raised.

Commissions were also granted to individual gentlemen allowing them to raise regiments on the King's behalf. Every estate could in theory produce a body of men, however small, drawn from its tenantry, the servants at the big house, the farm labourers, and the mineworkers and craftsmen. As each regiment was expected to field about a thousand men, the commanding officer resorted to recruitment drives to make up the number. He would also appoint a number of captains, who might be lesser gentlemen of his acquaintance, and these would provide their own companies for the regiment, each of about a hundred men. To begin with, these regiments were rough and ready, armed with whatever weapons their colonel could provide. It was not unusual to see a gathering of men dressed in an assortment of clothing, with antiquated war gear which might include scythes, axes and makeshift pikes as well as muskets and swords. Money to equip these men properly was sometimes provided out of the colonel's own pocket, but was usually received from the royal coffers or from local subscription. Once the regiment had joined the main army, its payment, training and equipping became the responsibility of the Royalist high command.[2] In this way, it was reckoned that during the first six weeks of the war, Wales provided at least six regiments for the King.

Carew Castle, which changed hands several times during the Civil War; the remains of a defensive earthwork, or ravelin, can be seen before the gate

Those gentlemen who were unable or unwilling to raise their own regiments set about fortifying their houses. In Pembrokeshire, Roger Lort prepared his house at Stackpole for war, as did Thomas Bowen of Trefloyne. Castles such as Picton, Manorbier, Roch and Carew were repaired as necessary and food stocks were laid in.

On 22 August, the King raised his standard at Nottingham. This was a clear declaration that, as all negotiation had failed, he would resort to arms to defeat his opponents. There was no going back. In September Charles left Nottingham and, travelling via Derby and Wellington, arrived at Shrewsbury. Recruitment in the Welsh Marches was in full swing and by the time the army set out for London on 12 October, it had doubled in size. An estimated ten thousand men followed their King, a very large percentage of whom were Welshmen.[3]

There was already sporadic fighting across England. On 7 September Portsmouth surrendered to Parliamentary forces under William Waller. Eleven days later, Prince Rupert arrived at Worcester and at Powick Bridge, just outside the city, he routed a troop of Parliamentary dragoons. Although only a skirmish, this encounter was the first serious clash between the two sides and the victory was a great morale boost to the Royalists.[4]

In south-west Wales, the King's supporters in Pembrokeshire, Carmarthenshire and Cardiganshire formed a Royalist Association under the leadership of the Earl of Carbery, now the King's commander in South Wales. Amongst those who joined it were Roger Lort, who was granted a commission by Carbery to raise a regiment, his brother, Sampson, and John Eliot.[5]

Meanwhile, on the Parliamentary side in the southern half of Pembrokeshire there were feverish preparations to meet a possible attack. At Tenby, the town's

Known today as the Five Arches, this was the West Gate of Tenby and was originally reached by a bridge over a moat

mayor, David Hammond, together with Devereux Wyatt, a former mayor, joined together to preserve the town for Parliament. Wyatt took charge of the watch, whilst Hammond busied himself in repairing the fortifications. He obtained guns and ammunition from the guardship *Lyon* in Milford Haven and paid workmen to make cartridges and to prepare a bolt for one of the carriages of the ship's cannon. He also purchased culm, sand, gravel and limestone, timber for bars and lintels, and iron to make chains, pins, bars, spikes, locks, bolts and staples. The North and West Gates were repaired, as well as the smaller Haven and Whitesands Gates, and 33 barrels of lime were used to make mortar for the rebuilding of ruinous sections of the town walls. A large elm was sawn to provide two pairs of wheels, perhaps for the cannon, and coals and candles were supplied for the use of the town guard.[6] A document preserved in the Tenby Corporation Order Book records further preparations and the expenses incurred:

> Wee whose names are underwritten hereby undertake that Mr Thomas Wyatt shall bee paid him for Gown powther and shott and match which he has bought for the use of the Towne by the 1st of November next ensuing being the sum of five pounds nine shillings and eleven pence.
>
> David Hammond, Mayor
> Abraham Bowen
> The 22 September 1642.

Defensive preparations at Tenby seem to have begun shortly after Charles raised his standard at Nottingham, but Pembroke was not long in following suit. At the end of September 1642, or early in October, John Poyer made his bid to hold Pembroke for Parliament. His period as Mayor ended at Michaelmas, but suspecting that his successor, Walter Cuny of Welston, either held Royalist sympathies or was hesitant to take sides, Poyer gathered together a group of like-minded townsfolk and usurped the office of mayor, holding it for the next six years.[7] According to John Eliot, Poyer's henchmen were 'a loose rabble of the meaner sort of the Town', who forced their way into the castle, and seized its store of arms. Eliot also states that several merchant ships anchored in the haven were detained by Poyer, who sold them and used the money to raise a company of foot soldiers and a troop of horse.[8]

In his reply to these charges Poyer presented a very different picture of events. He had been commander of the Trained Bands of Pembroke since 1633 and, by virtue of this office, he had the right to hold the castle. Furthermore, the inhabitants, whose love he had gained, were encouraged by a certain unnamed gentleman to help their ex-mayor in fortifying the town and castle for Parliament. The ships he had seized had actually been intended for Royalist service and Poyer had not received 'one penny by the sale of their goods', though he had raised a troop of horse, two of dragoons and three foot companies.

Whatever the truth of the matter, the castle was now firmly in the hands of Parliamentary sympathisers. How long Pembroke and Tenby could hold out in a county which was largely Royalist remained to be seen, especially as the situation at Haverfordwest appeared to be one of flux.

Perched on a bluff overlooking the Pembroke River and surrounded on three sides by water, Pembroke Castle was to prove a challenge to Royalist and Parliamentarian alike

The flow of events at Haverfordwest has divided historians. A.L. Leach was of the opinion that no definite action was taken in the town by the adherents of either side, but Sir Frederick Rees has referred to a letter written on 2 November 1642, the same day that members of the gentry were instructed to meet the Marquess of Hertford at Carmarthen to pledge their loyalty to the crown. The letter states that Haverfordwest, Tenby and Pembroke were all held by the local trained bands in the name of Parliament, a situation apparently confirmed by the King's proclamation of July 1643 (see p.45). The fact that Haverfordwest, like Tenby, was soon to switch allegiances may owe something to the condition of its ancient town walls, which were in no state to withstand attack.[9]

On 23 October 1642, the battle of Edgehill was fought, the first major confrontation of the war. The Parliamentarian army was commanded by the Earl of Essex and amongst the officers fighting on the right wing of his force was one John Gunter, probably a member of the Gunter family of Lamphey Palace in Pembrokeshire.[10] He was one of a large number of Welshmen present on the field that day, at least 1,200 of them in the Royalist army. Few of these men had received either proper training or adequate equipment and many fled the field, to be later described by Robert Evans as 'poor Welsh vermin, the scourings of the nation'.[11]

Although neither side scored a definitive victory, as a result of the battle the King had achieved one great advantage; Essex had withdrawn to Warwick, leaving the road to Oxford clear. Charles quickly established his presence in the city, which became the main centre of Royalism for the duration of the war, and then began an advance on London.

On 7 November, Essex entered the capital to a hero's welcome. Two days later he was ordered to take his troops out of London to bar the King's approach. On 12 November, Prince Rupert stormed Brentford, the prelude to a planned attack on the capital. The Parliamentary regiments of Denzil Holles and Lord Brooke suffered heavy casualties during the engagement, but having achieved victory, Rupert allowed his soldiers to sack the town. Lurid reports of the scale of looting and devastation circulated rapidly through the country and Londoners, next in line for an assault, made an even more determined effort to resist. An estimated 24,000 people, a mixture of infantry, mounted troops, the city trained bands, militia from the surrounding counties and thousands of London's apprentices, gathered at Turnham Green to face the approaching Royalists.

Supplied by foodstuffs brought out to them by their womenfolk in over one hundred carts, the citizen army constituted a formidable obstacle. A few shots were fired, but recognising the disadvantages of numbers and terrain, the Royalist army drew off and the King returned to Oxford.[12]

In south-west Wales there were no major confrontations during the first six months of the war, though the people of Pembrokeshire found themselves under

Lamphey Palace, occupied by the Gunter family, was the source of many of the supplies that fed Poyer's garrison at Pembroke

threat. The Royalist Association based at Carmarthen launched a series of raids on the communities of the Englishry. Cattle and other food supplies were stolen from farms and villages. In a raid on Lamphey Palace, the home of Thomas Gunter, Captain Crowe is said to have driven off over 700 head of cattle. The palace may have been targeted for two reasons; firstly because it was the property of the Earl of Essex, and secondly because the Gunters were supplying the garrison of Pembroke Castle with foodstuffs. Between 10 January 1643 and 16 September 1644, Mrs Gunter was to supply goods to the value of £208 10s to the castle garrison.[13]

Two other Royalists, Richard Morgan and his son Anthony, are also known to have stolen livestock which they passed on to George Oakley, a Carmarthen alderman, who sold it in Worcester and used the proceeds to buy pistols to arm his friends.[14]

In the meantime there were rumours that the Royalists were to build a fort on the shores of Milford Haven, which would give them a base through which troops could be brought from Ireland. During November 1642, John Wogan had written to the Earl of Stanford and to the Speaker of the House of Commons, warning them of the dangers threatening Pembrokeshire. The county could hold out only 'for some short time'. His letter to Parliament was discussed in the Commons and members requested the Navy Committee to consider sending a fleet under Captain Swanley to watch the Irish coast.

This did not satisfy Wogan who felt desperate enough to write another letter on 20 January 1643, this time to the Mayor of Bristol.

The desperate condition of the county requires me to apply to you for its relief ... the malignant parties have already plundered the estate of Capt. Gunter, in the very heart of our county, and driven away all his cattle by night under the conduct of Capt. Richard Crowe of the county of Carmarthen ... we have certain intelligence that my Lord Herbert of Ragland with the Earl of Carbery are suddenly raising a force of 8,000 men to make a strong invasion upon us ... I beseech you to be a means both by yourself and by moving the chief commanders ... in your noble city, that present supplies may be sent us from all parts ... it is most requisite that 300 or 400 be instantly sent us that we may make a defensive business of it till stronger supplies come. It is not our livelihood they aim at, so much as their surprise of our haven of Milford ... whereby a door may be opened to receive foreign forces to prejudice the troubled state more than themselves can.[15]

Wogan also requested that a copy of the letter should be sent to Parliament, but this was probably not done, as there was no reaction from the Commons. On 19 April 1643, John White, the MP for Southwark, received a letter from his brother Griffith White of Henllan outlining the dangers of allowing a stronghold to be built on the shores of the waterway. This he passed on to his fellow members, who took immediate measures to try and prevent a Royalist coup in Pembrokeshire. Sir John Stepney was deprived of his seat in the House, moves were made to impeach Lord Carbery whilst, more practically, the guardship *Lyon* or another suitable warship was to remain in the haven, its crew to help in the apprehension of two noted Royalists, Roger Lort and the elderly Robert Rudd, Archdeacon of St Davids.[16] Five weeks later, the Commons resolved that 'the Lord General be moved to send some force into Pembrokeshire' to retain control of the county and a committee of local gentlemen was named to oversee matters.

The King meanwhile had not been idle. On 19 July 1643 he offered 'his Majesty's Grace, Favour and Pardon to his subjects the inhabitants of the Tounes of Pembroke and Tenby in the County of Pembroke and of the Toune and County of Haverfordwest in the Dominion of Wales'. This proof of Royal condescension spurred 24 gentlemen in west Wales to issue their own declaration:

August 18. Declaration of the Gentlemen of Co. Pembroke and of the Town and Co. of Haverfordwest resolved on at Carmarthen at the Conference with Richard Earl of Carbery, Lord Lt. General of Cos. Pembroke, Cardigan and Carmarthen.

The gentlemen declare themselves loyal and faithful subjects to his Majesty: they will obey his authority committed to the Earl of Carbery: they will raise a considerable sum of money for his Majesty in token of their loyalty: they desire his lordship's protection against their ruin by sea or their being debarred of commerce: they are willing that his lordship shall secure Pembroke and Tenby and garrison them for his Majesty, the forces now in the county to be disbanded: his lordship to employ such commanders in the said towns in his absence as may be approved by the gentlemen of the county.[17]

Many of those who signed had been appointed as Commissioners for Parliament in the earlier Militia Ordinance (see p.35), but they now made clear where their loyalties lay, at least for the time being. Only a handful of those earlier Militia Commissioners did not put their names to the document: Sir Hugh Owen, John Laugharne, John Wogan, Arthur Owen, Griffith White and Thomas Price. It was only a matter of time before a conflict broke out between the two sides in Pembrokeshire.

7   Widespread Fighting

Across Wales, the Royalist cause seemed to be prospering. The flow of volunteers into the King's army was at first steady, enabling the Commissioners of Array to increase the number of armed garrisons dotted about the country. When, inevitably, the numbers began to dwindle, the commissioners resorted to impressments so that additional units of men could be sent to the defence of Chester or to take part in the sieges of Gloucester and Bristol.

Lord Herbert of Raglan had already pleased Charles by raising an army of 1,500 foot soldiers and 500 horse. In return, he was appointed regional commander and his father, who had spent a fortune in financing the Royalist war effort, was raised to the rank of marquess. The news of these advancements was not greeted with unanimous enthusiasm. Lord Herbert was a Catholic and 'the Welchmen ... would not rise in Monmouthshire because my Lord Herbert had the command of that country and professed that they had rather perish than be under the power of a papist'.[1]

In spite of this, in February 1643 Herbert felt confident enough to march on the Parliamentary stronghold of Gloucester. Amongst his troops were rumoured to be 140 women 'with knives neere half a yard long' which they were planning to use to dispatch the enemy.[2] Herbert's force moved through the Forest of Dean, where he defeated a Parliamentary unit at Coleford, taking 40 prisoners, and at last came to Highnam on the northern bank of the Severn. He remained there for the next month or so, controlling the road from Gloucester to Ross and Newent, whilst Prince Maurice harried the city from the north and east. Herbert may have hoped for reinforcements before closing in on Gloucester, but they did not come. Instead, on 24 March, the camp was attacked by the combined forces of Sir William Waller and Colonel Edward Massey, who forced a surrender on the following day. Over 500 of Herbert's men were killed and 1,442 common soldiers and 150 gentlemen were taken prisoner. They were marched into the city and were locked up in the churches of St Mary de Lode and Holy Trinity for ten days, and then were released upon the promise that they would no longer fight against Parliament. One of those who gave this promise and later disregarded it was Welsh Thomas, a Carmarthen lad of 16 or 17. Many years later, at the age of 90, he would recall that during his brief captivity, he and his companions had been fed on turnip tops, cabbage leaves and other scraps.[3]

Lord Herbert was in Oxford at the time of the battle, perhaps pleading for reinforcements, and his reputation was severely damaged. The Earl of Clarendon sneeringly referred to the defeated army as 'the mushroom army' and the whole campaign was regarded as a waste of time and money.

Five months later, Sir William Vavasour, with a Royalist army of 4,000 men, many of them Welsh, besieged the western side of Gloucester, whilst the King and his forces blocked the eastern approaches to the city. When the King toured the camp, he was greeted with enthusiasm, and was delighted when 'the Welshmen ... did throw their caps and hallow with much joy'.[4] However, this siege was abandoned on 6 September, with the approach of the Earl of Essex's army. Essex's entry into the city was received as enthusiastically as the King's tour of the camp had been. The garrison was almost out of supplies and was down to the last three barrels of gunpowder.

A cat and mouse game now took place. As Essex marched back towards London, the King set off in hot pursuit and after days of marching and counter marching, often in heavy rain, the royal army caught up with Essex at Newbury. On 20 September, the first Battle of Newbury was fought.

Facing the Parliamentary left wing were Sir William Vavasour's Welshmen, who launched a series of hard-fought attacks against Lord Robardes' regiment. They suffered heavy casualties, though without being able to budge the enemy. The battle lasted some 12 hours and over 3,500 men were killed, a slightly higher percentage of them Royalist.[5] Charles' army was running low on ammunition and had lost 25 officers, and on the morning of 21 September, it was marching towards Oxford.[6] The Earl of Essex, aware that the King had retired from the field with his purpose unfulfilled, resumed his march to London.

A few months earlier, there had been a resounding Royalist success at Bristol. The city, initially held for Parliament, found itself challenged by Prince Rupert, who, on 24 July, demanded its surrender. The governor, Nathaniel Fiennes, refused on the grounds that, having been 'entrusted to keep the town for King and Parliament, he could not yet relinquish that trust till he were brought to more extremity'. On the following day there was heavy fighting on the northern fringes of the city and on the 26th an assault began at dawn. There were severe Royalist casualties, but nevertheless by dusk Fiennes had been forced to ask for terms.

The news of the capitulation of Bristol was received with joy in Royalist circles, but in Pembroke there must have been dismay. Bristol had been a source of supply and encouragement to the castle's garrison, and amongst the prizes taken by the Royalists were a number of Parliamentary warships, including two armed merchantmen, the 28 gun *Fellowship* and the *Hart*, of 12 guns. These were immediately attached to the Royalist navy and at the beginning of August were sent to Milford Haven to secure the anchorages there and to help with the building of the fort.[7] Few who witnessed their departure could have imagined that their arrival in the Haven was to have an immediate and invigorating effect on Parliamentary fortunes within Pembrokeshire.

By 4 August, the *Fellowship* and the *Hart* had slipped into Milford Haven and anchored near the mouth of Castle Pill, then known as Prix Pill. They carried guns and ammunition to equip the fort that was under construction, and aboard the *Fellowship* were four captains: Barnaby Burly, Will Hazle, Richard Nelson and John Brooks, some of whom were intended to command the garrison of the fort.[8]

The fort was by then under construction on a headland on the west side of the pill, overlooking the Haven. Work had begun at some time in the spring or summer of 1643, though the exact date is unknown. King Charles was interested enough in the project to send from Oxford a man named Richard Steele, 'a great talker who pretended to be an engineer'.[9] The fortification he designed consisted of extensive square-shaped earthworks, the ramparts of which were built on a rubble or stone foundation.[10] Construction may have been almost complete by the time the two ships arrived in the Haven.

A fleet of Parliamentary warships was engaged in patrolling the waters between Wales and Ireland to prevent the movement of troops from Ormonde's army into England. The little armada consisted of nine naval vessels, augmented

The fort built by the Royalists at Prix, or Castle, Pill stood immediately behind the building in the middle of the photograph; it has now been built over

by twelve merchantmen contracted to the navy.[11] In command was Richard Swanley aboard the *Leopard* regis – a naval vessel titled 'regis' to distinguish her from the *Leopard* merchantman, also part of the fleet. Two of the other ships were the 36 gun *Swallow*, under Captain Will Smith, and the *Expedition*, Captain Joseph Jordan.

Whilst on patrol out of Kinsale, Captain Smith had come upon a boat carrying a cargo of timber from Strangford to Milford Haven. The captain of this ship told Smith that he had recently encountered the *Expedition*, then in pursuit of a vessel from Hamburg which, in addition to a cargo of salt and supplies destined for the Irish rebels, was also carrying a number of mysterious passengers. In fleeing from the *Expedition*, the Hamburg ship ran ashore near St Davids Head and the passengers, believed to be Jesuits, scrambled ashore and were now at liberty in Pembrokeshire.

Will Smith immediately put the *Swallow* on course for Milford Haven, where he expected to find Jordan and learn the whereabouts of the fugitives. He was followed by another Parliamentary warship commanded by Captain Wilkinson. They entered harbour about 7 August and discovered not the *Expedition*, but the Royalist ships *Fellowship* and *Hart*. On 17 August Smith wrote a letter describing what happened next:

> When I came before the harbour's mouth, a fisherman came on board, who told me that in Milford were two ships, men-of-war, one of which was the *Fellowship*, burthen of about 400 tons, of force 24 guns.
>
> The said captains had summoned on board the *Fellowship* all the gentry in these parts.[12]
>
> The gentlemen of the county had been assured that the King had taken Bristol and the war was over. They had also agreed to present a petition to the King 'in tender of their services to him and also to raise a sum of money to comply with his Majesty's occasions.

Smith's letter continued: 'There came off a boat from the *Fellowship* towards the *Swallow* and in it one Captain John Brooks, holding forth a white flag, who desired a parley upon condition that I would let him return aboard the *Fellowship* if we could not accord, to which I consented. Then he came aboard and leaping down into the waist he cried, "God bless King Charles" to which we all said "Amen" '.

Brooks twice requested a private conference with Smith, which was refused on the grounds that all the *Swallow*'s complement should hear what was said. Brooks next made a plea to the crew that they should take the ship to Bristol, upon which Smith ordered him to be silent.

Smith now demanded that the two Royalist ships should surrender and threatened that if they did not he would sink them or seize them as pirates.

The *Fellowship*, presumably with Captain Brooks back on board, and the *Hart* attempted to escape, but the *Fellowship* ran aground, surrendering as soon as the *Swallow* opened fire. The *Hart* was struck by a cannon ball which killed two men, the first known casualties of the Civil War in Pembrokeshire. She made a run upriver, perhaps in the hope of reaching the protection of Haverfordwest, but either because of the state of the tide or because Captain Wilkinson in pursuit was too close, was beached near Boulston.[13]

Dusk may have been falling by this time because it was the next morning before Wilkinson opened fire on the stranded vessel, taking possession of it. The *Hart's* crew, led by Captain Nesson, reached Haverfordwest where they were welcomed by the mayor. The town was now nominally Royalist, following a visit some months earlier by Lord Carbery, and the mayor entertained the fugitives and gave them £2 towards their homeward journey.[14]

However jubilant the Parliamentarians may have felt about their victory on the Cleddau, they were about to suffer a serious reverse. The King's sympathisers within Tenby were contacted by Roger Lort on behalf of Lord Carbery. The mayor was offered a security of £30,000 by Lort, with a further £20,000 from his brother-in-law Thomas Bowen of Trefloyne, if he and other councillors would acknowledge the King's authority. If this gesture was not made, then the town would suffer a blockade which would seriously threaten its prosperity. Faced with the carrot and the stick, many of the aldermen agreed to sign a declaration of loyalty in which 'they would obey the King's commands and submit to the authority placed in Lord Carbery: they would contribute to his Majesty's service to the best of their abilities: they would not receive into their town any rebels under the name of forces of "King and Parliament" but would welcome any forces which Lord Carbery should send to garrison Tenby for the King's service'.[15]

Among the 32 signatories to this document were Rice Prickard, Richard Jewell the puritan minister of St Mary's Church, the ex-mayor David Hammond, and the brothers Richard and Thomas Wyatt. Thomas is said to have delivered up the keys of the town to Carbery. The incumbent mayor of Tenby, Abraham Barrowe, did not sign. Another who refused to do so was a John Poyer. This cannot be John Poyer the mayor of Pembroke, who was obviously not a townsman of Tenby, but it has often been stated that it was his son. It is unlikely. No existing account mentions that Poyer had a son of this name and, furthermore, at the time of his execution in 1649, he is described as the father of four young children, not adult ones.[16] The name Poyer was not uncommon in Pembrokeshire at this time and several other Johns are known. For example, a tanner named John Poyer was living in Tenby in 1643 who died in 1648, his will being proved that August; he might well be the Poyer whose signature is appended to the declaration.

The loss of Tenby was a direct challenge to the Parliamentary presence in Pembrokeshire and plans were swiftly drawn up to regain the town. One of those proposing to lead the attack was Rowland Laugharne. This is the first time that his presence is mentioned in Pembrokeshire during the war. When or why he arrived is not clear, though he is said to have been sent to the county by the Earl of Essex. He may have been in London for the first ten months of the conflict, though there is mention of a Major Lanchane or Lauchane who was present in north Wales at about that time.[17]

Laugharne's army was not large enough to take Tenby and he seems to have faced considerable local opposition – warning beacons are said to have been lit on the hilltops as he approached the town – so he withdrew his forces. Captain Swanley did not give up quite so easily.

He brought eight of his ships, the *Leopard* regis, the *Swallow, Prosperous, Leopard* merchant, *Crescent, Providence, Fellowship* and *Hart*, the last two presumably pressed back into Parliamentary service after the Cleddau action, and ranged them offshore before opening up a heavy bombardment of the town. Over one hundred shots were fired, the cannon balls thudding into the seaward-facing defences of the town or punching through the roofs and walls of the houses, whilst the inhabitants huddled in whatever shelter they could find or attempted to escape through the gates of the town. The gun batteries in the town and on Castle Hill gave as good as they got. One of the cannon supplied to Mayor Hammond by the guardship *Lyon* in the autumn of 1642 'shot one of the best ships through and through' and the fleet was forced to give up the attack and sail away.[18]

The Earl of Carbery now moved to consolidate his hold on Pembrokeshire. He appointed a Carmarthenshire man, John Gwynn, as Governor of Tenby and in September went in person to Haverfordwest. He was greeted by the ringing of bells and the members of the council and certain unnamed leading inhabitants signed a declaration of loyalty to the King. A few weeks later a troop of Royalist soldiers from Carmarthen, under the command of Sir Francis Lloyd, arrived to garrison the town.

Carbery now appointed his uncle Henry Vaughan to command the King's forces in Pembrokeshire. A financial encouragement was also received; in late September King Charles awarded £250 towards the expenses of raising men for the Royalist Association in west Wales. As a result, enthusiasm for the war effort was redoubled. When Sir John Stepney arrived in October to assume the post of governor, he was welcomed with pealing bells and was entertained at a banquet.[19]

On 18 September, at Haverfordwest, 47 members of the gentry signed what became known as 'The Protestation of Pembrokeshire'. This document set out a scheme of action by which it was hoped to bring the town of Pembroke to obedience to the King. There would be no help given to the garrison of Pembroke and the victualling of ships manned for 'King and Parliament' would be opposed. Moreover, the surrounding countryside was to be protected from the incursions of sailors from the ships and the soldiers of Pembroke.

Royalist newspapers trumpeted the supposed effects of the Protestation. The inhabitants of Pembroke, according to the erroneous reports, were so alarmed that the Town Council begged Lord Carbery to hold the town 'wholly for the king's use'. An issue of the Royalist broadsheet *Mercurius Aulicus* published on 26 September boasted of the surrender of Pembroke and named as signatories to the Protestation not only the puritan Griffith White and William Laugharne, but also Sir Hugh Owen. That the first two signed is unlikely, but Owen may have had no choice. It is possible that he had gone to Haverfordwest in the hope that, as an MP, he could negotiate with Carbery's representatives, and was then arrested. He was certainly a prisoner in the town in February 1644, when the Royalists abandoned it.[20]

Despite the propaganda, Pembroke had not surrendered. Even if a section of the population wished to do so, Poyer and Laugharne ensured that the town remained resolutely Parliamentarian. The two men had by now joined forces and had raised a strong enough force to feel confident of holding off the Royalists, at least for a few months. They faced considerable odds. Not only was the new Royalist fort at Prix Pill nearing completion, but many of the great houses and castles in the vicinity of Pembroke were held in the King's name. Within a radius of eight miles, five or six armed garrisons had sprung up. Stackpole House had been put into readiness by Roger Lort. Lort's brother-in-law, Thomas Bowen,

The ruined shell keep of Wiston Castle and its surrounding earthworks are said to have housed a Royalist picquet during the first Civil War

the owner of Trefloyne House at Penally, had gathered together some 150 foot soldiers and 50 mounted troops. Carew Castle, the nearby fortified rectory and Manorbier Castle were all garrisoned and Tenby was still commanded by Governor Gwynn. To the north of the Haven, Roch Castle, Haverfordwest, Haroldston Hall, Prendergast House, Boulston Manor, Picton Castle and the ancient shell keep at Wiston all housed the King's men. Only Lamphey Palace, defended by a small contingent of musketeers, was held for the 'righteous cause'.

Ringed in as they were by a chain of enemy bastions, Laugharne and Poyer looked to the sea for aid. If the Parliamentarian ships patrolling the Irish Sea could bring in supplies and ammunition, then Pembroke could hold out indefinitely, but with the new fort rapidly taking shape at Prix Pill, nothing was certain. Help was urgently needed, but would it come?

8   The Position in Pembroke

As the winter of 1643 wore on, the garrison of Pembroke received news that must have disheartened them. On 18 November over 2,000 troops of the Marquess of Ormonde's army landed near Mostyn on the Dee estuary. Within a month the whole of north Wales was firmly in their grip and the Parliamentary forces led by Colonel Brereton and Sir Thomas Myddleton had retreated across the Dee at Holt. It must have seemed only a matter of time before a similar army came ashore in Milford Haven.

A firsthand account of the Mostyn landings could well have been given to Laugharne and Poyer by Simon Thelwall, MP for Denbigh, who arrived in Pembrokeshire on about 15 December. Although some authorities have described him as a refugee from north Wales, he may have been sent to Pembrokeshire by Parliament to examine the military situation. Whatever the truth of the matter, it is thanks to a letter that he wrote on 15 March to the Speaker of the House of Commons, and another written by Captain Smith of the *Swallow*, that we have a clear description of events in west Wales during the early months of 1644.

The King's supporters exulted in the news from Mostyn. Some of Lord Carbery's soldiers, few of whom were local, had continued their raids into southern Pembrokeshire and issued blood-curdling threats against anyone suspected of rebel sympathies. Carbery was supposed to have said that after the harbour was fortified 'he would plunder the town of Pembroke and the houses of the gentlemen who adhered to that party and that their persons should be put to death by cruel tortures'.[1] His men promised to 'kill the dogs and ravish the bitches and root them out in the third and forth generations'.[2] John Poyer was to be thrust into a barrel and rolled down the cliffs into Prix Pill. These threats certainly caused consternation amongst the more prominent burgesses and gentry of south Pembrokeshire, and a deputation of wives and children was sent into Tenby to plead with Lord Carbery. Amongst them was Mrs Elizabeth White, the wife of Griffith White of Henllan, and a sister of Roger Lort. She was described as

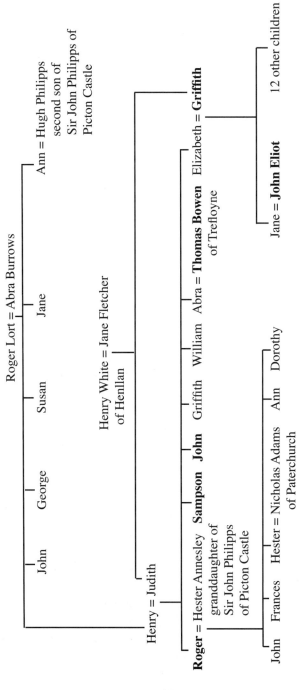

The relationship between the Lort and White families

a revered, aged gentlewoman … who had in her house eight sons and eight daughters, who were virgins and four small grandchildren, in all 20 in number, with divers servants, both male and female.[3]

This gentlewoman pressing his lordship to commiserate her sad state, in case her house should be plundered, desired his protection, assuring his lordship that, whensoever he pleased to give her husband leave to wait upon him, she did not doubt her husband would give his lordship ample satisfaction in all his lawful demands. His lordship replied that he would find a time to speak with her husband but as for protection he would give her none.

The gentlewoman, with tears in her eyes, desired his lordship to look upon her children, who in point of honour he stood engaged to protect, as also the chastity of matrons and virgins, the which, without his Lordship, she said, must undoubtedly be violated, and her family perish. To which his Lordship answered with divers reproaches and some jests that it were better her children and family should perish than that the King should want means to perfect his design. To which she said, the King would not want, if his Majesty would be graciously pleased to be content with what God and the laws of the land have provided. At which his Lordship flung out of the room, leaving the gentlewoman with tears in her eyes and so she departed to her house, full of grief and pensive thoughts.

With the publication of a second protestation, the problems of the Pembroke garrison seemed to worsen. The document reminded its readers that, contrary to the hopes expressed in the first protestation, Pembroke Castle still had not been delivered up to the King. The second protestation went on to say that 'Lord Carbery having informed them that large forces hostile to the king would shortly invade the county of Pembroke they, the undersigned, would resist any such forces. They think that Lord Carbery should employ the trained bands and raise a body of horse (in addition to the 100 horse already maintained) to reduce Pembroke: such forces not to be maintained after Pembroke Town and Castle had submitted to his Majesty's authority'.[4] The signatories again included Sir Hugh Owen, Sir John Stepney, Sir Richard Phillips and John Eliot.

In an attempt to warn the Lord Admiral of the Parliamentary fleet of the plight of the Pembroke garrison, John Poyer sent out one of his own ships, armed with eight guns. Shortly after leaving the Haven, it encountered the Royalist warships *Globe* and *Providence*, which were inward bound for the fort at Prix Pill. Poyer's vessel and its crew were taken prisoner and forced back to the Haven. The *Globe* and *Providence* were carrying guns for the fort: two culverins (15 pounders), two demi-culverins (9 pounders), two sacres (5½ pounders), and two minions (4 pounders). Some of their own guns were also unloaded and added to the defences of the fort. Poyer's ship was taken up to Haverfordwest where its cannon were unshipped and given to the town's garrison.[5]

By the beginning of 1644, the men in Pembroke Castle may have been running low on supplies. The normal method of feeding hungry soldiers and topping up their stock of food was for foraging parties to scour the surrounding countryside, availing themselves of any cattle or foodstuffs they came across. It was probably for this reason that Rowland Laugharne, with a small company of horse and foot, left Pembroke in late December or early January and moved towards Carew.

He would have been aware that Carew Castle was held by about 50 Royalist musketeers under the command of Lieutenant Jones. Barely a quarter of a mile away, probably in the Old Rectory, a fortified medieval building near Carew Cheriton church, was another small band of soldiers. As Laugharne and his men dispersed to find food, they came under attack from a body of musketeers led by Lieutenant Jones. With considerable presence of mind, Laugharne drew together seven of his mounted troopers and charged the enemy, capturing 20 of them, including Jones, and scattering the rest.[6]

On 23 January, the fortunes of the Pembrokeshire Parliamentarians were given a boost when a fleet of warships under the command of Captain Richard Swanley arrived in Milford Haven. Swanley had been appointed Admiral of Parliament's ships in the Bristol Channel. He seems to have been a hardened seaman who, to judge by his subsequent actions, harboured a virulent hatred of papists. In addition to his own ship, the *Leopard* regis, Swanley's fleet at Milford consisted of the *Swallow, Crescent,* the *Leopard* merchantman and the *Providence;* confusingly, this Parliamentary warship had the same name as the Royalist vessel accompanying the *Globe.* Within three days of their arrival they were joined by the *Prosperous* and two other ships from Liverpool.

As soon as Swanley's ships were spotted, the two Royalist vessels, the *Globe* and *Providence*, took shelter in Prix Pill where, with other small barques, they lay under the shelter of the guns of the fort. As the Pill was narrow and tidal, Swanley anchored his ships offshore and for the next few days exchanged shots with the fort.

On 24 January, Poyer and Laugharne, accompanied by some local gentlemen, clambered aboard the *Leopard* regis for a conference with Swanley. They warned him of the perilous state of affairs in the county; without aid the Protestant and Parliamentary cause in Pembrokeshire would fail. Swanley immediately promised two hundred seamen, backed by a demi-culverin, a sacre, a brass falconet and all the necessary powder and shot for use against the Royalist garrisons within the county. Laugharne, with only 60 foot-soldiers and 30 mounted troopers at his disposal, delightedly agreed.[7]

Before mounting a campaign, Swanley sent out a letter to all the gentlemen of Pembrokeshire, requesting them to submit to 'King and Parliament' and encouraging them to drive out of the county 'that malignant rout, who seeks to enslave this nation under the yoke of the Anti-Christian beast'. There was no answer. It is difficult to imagine what other response Swanley expected, for the men within the fort continued their harassment of his fleet. At dawn on 27 January, the look-outs on the ships realised that during the night, their opponents had placed a gun on a nearby hill, probably the high ground on the opposite side of the Pill to the fort. This opened fire on the *Swallow* and might have done some damage had it not burst from its own charge. The weather was also deteriorating and the *Swallow* and the *Leopard* regis were forced to take shelter in Angle Bay, a circumstance that encouraged the Royalists to claim that Swanley feared the power of their guns. The Admiral, in a letter dated 2 February, clarified his intentions towards them:

> To the Commander-in-Chief of the Forces at Prickspill under the command of the Earl of Carbery, dated 2 February 1644.
>
> Gentlemen, I understand you have reported that you have fright-ened me away with the noise of your guns, assure yourselves had I been acquainted with the Channel, as I make no doubt but I shall be afore I go hence, I had tried which had been strongest, my ships' sides or your mud walls, and having some other business now in hand I refer that to a fitter opportunity. I came not hither to build Castles in the aire, nor in any hostile manner, to make a division in this Country, but only for Peace, which at this time I am willing to proffer to you, and if you please to send a man or two to treat upon Propositions which shall tend to the glory of God, the honour of the King and the happinesse of the subject ... If you desire a friendly parley I promise you upon the faith of a Christian and the word of a Commander that you shall as safely return as come, of which if you doubt, I will send Hostages of such quality as you send to me.[8]

There seems to have been no reply. The *Prosperous* and *Leopard* merchant-man had remained at their anchorage and upheld Swanley's honour by indulging in a desultory exchange of shots with the fort. One of the Royalist guns scored something of a triumph, for one of its balls smashed through the side of the *Leopard* and wrecked the captain's empty bed. Swanley meanwhile had managed to land a demi-cannon on the south shore of the Haven which, placed within the shelter of a temporary earthwork, was able to fire directly into the fort.

In the meantime, plans for a campaign against the Royalist garrisons that ringed Pembroke had rapidly advanced. Laugharne had realised that these strong-holds, scattered as they were and with small garrisons, could expect little help from Carbery if attacked, as he had split up the forces at his disposal to man them and consequently could field no strong army. Accordingly, Stackpole House, the home of Roger Lort, was the first to come under fire. On 30 January, Laugharne marched out of Pembroke with a combined force of seamen and footsoldiers numbering about 300 and with a body of mounted troops plus artillery. Local legend has it that John Poyer accompanied them, though none of the written accounts mention his presence.

The ancient house, overlooking what was then a narrow tidal creek through which ran a stream, was an imposing structure with thick walls. The 60-strong garrison put up a vigorous defence and even though under constant fire from small arms and artillery, managed to hold off their attackers for eight hours or more. Eventually Laugharne's troops, with the loss of two men, stormed the outer defences and with pickaxes and crowbars made a breach in the main wall, forcing the garrison to surrender.[9] The defenders had suffered several killed and wounded, but of Lort there was no sign. He may already have defected to Parliament, though according to legend he was hiding in a cave known afterwards as Lort's Hole.[10] Every trooper who had taken part in the action was allowed to appropriate whatever he chose in the looting of the house. Poyer was later to remark, 'What was taken by the soldiers in the heat of blood cannot be imputed to our dishonour'.[11]

Laugharne marched his victorious troops back to Pembroke, leaving a small garrison to man the shattered house. A few days' rest was allowed before setting off for Trefloyne House.

Trefloyne, the residence of the Bowen family, stood just outside Penally on the banks of the Ritec, then a wide tidal creek to the west of Tenby. A causeway crossed the creek close to the point where the stream issued into the sea. The house was garrisoned with a stronger force than Stackpole for, as mentioned earlier, Thomas Bowen had gathered together about 150 footsoldiers and 50 mounted troops, all well armed and prepared.[12] As Laugharne's men approached, Lord Carbery led a force of horse and foot from Tenby towards the village of St Florence, but when the Parliamentary guns opened up, he promptly turned back and withdrew into the protection of Tenby's walls.

The Trefloyne garrison was not disheartened by Carbery's flight. Captain Swanley described in a letter how they 'played their parts warfully, by playing their small shot and using all material endeavours in matters of defence and opposition ...'.[13] Despite a storm of fire from the windows of the house, Laugharne's men marched forward, seizing the outhouses. One of the artillery pieces had knocked a breach in the defences and, seeing the hopelessness of their position, the Royalists requested quarter, which was granted 'and honourably performed'.

Laugharne had lost two men killed and six wounded. Forty saddled horses were found in the stables, as well as a cannon and all the arms and ammunition of the footsoldiers. The walls of the mansion were slighted to prevent further use as a stronghold and Laugharne withdrew his troops to Pembroke.

With Stackpole and Trefloyne no longer a threat, Laugharne paused to consider his next target. Tenby was a possibility, especially as Carbery 'like a valiant commander, with twenty horse and four field pieces ranne away, telling the rest of the Commanders that he rode into the adjacent county to raise more forces and that he would return'.[14] But Laugharne knew that the real problem was Pill Fort, for if troops should arrive from Ireland he would find it difficult to oppose their landing with the forces at his command. A second conference was held aboard the *Leopard* regis and it was decided that all the resources of the Parliamentarians should now be used to destroy the enemy stronghold.

Early on the morning of Friday, 23 February, a determined force of men and artillery assembled near Pembroke Ferry and were transferred to a fleet of small boats belonging to Swanley's ships, including 'a great gabbard that God sent accidentally out of Ireland'.[15] This was used to transport many of the 250 foot soldiers, half of them seamen, under Captain Willoughby, and 60 horsemen across the Haven, their passage guarded by the *Crescent* frigate. Five small field-pieces, a sacre and a demi-culverin were also ferried across. Accompanying Laugharne was his father, John, 'a good, hearty old gentleman ... who had long before left his country habitation and with his whole family, a few servants excepted, betaken himself to the Town of Pembroke. His interest and fair, noble carriage had always engaged unto him the affections of many in that part of the county we were to set upon, called Roose'.[16]

By eight o'clock the men were coming ashore somewhere in the vicinity of Newton Noyes, to the east of Prix Pill. Any qualms they may have had about

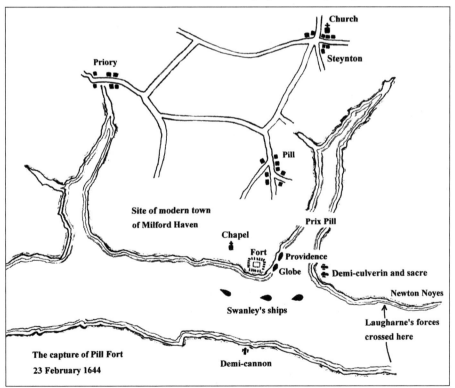

The capture of Pill Fort, 23 February 1644

During the attack on the fort at Prix Pill, Rowland Laugharne placed a troop of musketeers in the tower of Steynton church to halt any advance from Haverfordwest

their reception by the local people were quickly dispelled, for they received help in dragging their two heaviest guns up to the high ground on the eastern side of Prix Pill, overlooking the fort. In the late afternoon, these two guns began a bombardment of the Royalist position. The fort was also under fire from units of Swanley's fleet. The *Prosperous* and the *Leopard* merchantman were anchored to the east of the fort, while the *Leopard* regis and the *Swallow* lay offshore to the west, and all four began pounding at the earthen walls topping the headland.

As veils of gun-smoke drifted downwind and the crash of the cannon echoed along the length of the Haven, Laugharne sent a detachment of mounted men inland around the head of the Pill to block the approach of reinforcements from the Royalist garrison at Haverfordwest. Twenty musketeers were placed in Steynton church, the tower of which provided a clear view of the surrounding countryside. A few stray Royalists, probably messengers from the fort bound for Haverfordwest, were rounded up and placed under guard in the church. Then, late in the afternoon, movement was seen on the road northwards. Sir Francis Lloyd, with about 60 horse and some foot, was approaching from Haverfordwest. The musketeers in the church tower watched as they 'descended a hill from Johnston but being fearful of our artillery, they never touched the ascent of Steynton, where our Horse were drawn but retreated to Haverford'.[17]

The gathering darkness put an end to the bombardment of the fort and Laugharne's men huddled round their camp fires in the bitter cold, or attempted to sleep in the shelter of the hedges. As dawn broke the following morning, the cannonade began again. A shot from the *Swallow* crashed into the fort and 'took off the head of one man and the posteriors of another of which he dyed the next day'.[18] One of the *Swallow*'s sailors was killed by a shot from the *Globe* but this was caused by 'his own folly'.[19]

Laugharne meanwhile had moved his troops southwards from Steynton towards 'an Ambuscado the enemy had placed in a hedge a little distant on the Stainton side from Pill, and having divided ourselves into three parts, the Horse furiously and disorderly charged upon them and routed the whole, took officers and most of the soldiers, the rest fled into the fort; hereupon we presently possessed the village of Pill and the ruines of an ancient chapel that stands above the Fort'.[20]

What followed is in dispute. In his account, Leach states that Laugharne's men followed so close on the heels of the retreating Royalists that they stormed the gates of the fort before they could be slammed shut. Simon Thelwall, writing shortly after the event, says that 'while we were in preparation of a violent Assault, the Gentlemen in the Fort hung out a Flagge of Truce, by which they obtained quarter, in rendering us possession of the Fort and themselves prisoners'.[21] Amongst those prisoners was John Barlow of Slebech, 'Master of the Ordnance and Captaine of a Troop of horse, a Church papist', as well as Captain William Marychurch, a member of another prominent Pembrokeshire family, and between 240 and 300 soldiers. All their weapons were also taken, including 18 great guns, and the two ships *Globe* and *Providence*, which had been unable to escape.

News of the capture of the fort caused consternation in Haverfordwest. As soon as he heard that Laugharne had crossed the Haven, Sir Henry Vaughan had sent Captain Steele under a flag of truce to discuss peace terms, but by the time Steele arrived on the scene, the fort was already under attack.

Steele returned to Haverfordwest with the ill tidings and Vaughan, vowing to be avenged 'on the round-headed Parliament dogs', gathered together 450 of his troops and prepared to march towards Prix Pill. In the meantime Sir John Stepney, the governor of the town, 'like a prudent overseer, went into the churchyard to see if he could discern [Parliament's] forces approaching towards Haverfordwest'.[22] Unfortunately for Stepney, a grazier named Wheeler was keeping a herd of cattle on a hill to the south of the town and these, possibly frightened by the distant cannonade at Pill, stampeded down the slope towards Haverfordwest. Mistaking them for the approaching enemy, Stepney and his men were thrown into a panic and ran about shouting 'God's wounds! The Roundhead dogs are coming'. In the confusion, most of the Royalist troops fled the town, dropping in their haste various articles of clothing, whilst the boys of the town managed to relieve them of over 60 muskets. Even Sir Hugh Owen was hustled away. Held in custody in the town since the first Protestation against Pembroke he was 'unbreasted and in his Pantables preparing for bed ... where Sir Henry Vaughan, and another man with a Mountier drawn over his face, takes him by the shoulders and calling him a dissembling traitor, some Musketeers having presented their Muskets at him, compelled him downstairs, and then on horseback, not permitting him time to put on his boots, nor his virtuous lady (a Character justified in her pious resolution, to share hard fortune, and declines with her husband) suffered to have a pillion to ride upon behind him'.[23]

Hardly any of the Royalist officers at Haverfordwest appear to have acted with any coolness of purpose, but one who did was Lieutenant-Colonel Butler of Scoveston near Steynton, who with 80 men marched straight to Tenby to join the garrison there.

On 25 February Rowland Laugharne entered Haverfordwest. He discovered a hundred new red coats left behind by the fleeing soldiers, stocks of food and ten pieces of ordnance. Two days later, Roch Castle surrendered. Nothing is heard of the tiny garrisons placed in Picton Castle, Wiston, Boulston and the other fortified houses; it is likely that they abandoned their posts and retreated towards Tenby or Carmarthen.

Laugharne was now undisputed master of most of south Pembrokeshire. Only Tenby awaited his attention.

9   Further Successes

On Tuesday, 6 March, Laugharne set out for Tenby 'to extirpate and root out the anti-Christian malignant party out of the ... county'. He commanded a force of 600 horse and foot that included all of the seamen who could be spared from the ships, as well as Swanley's master gunner who was in charge of a brass demi-cannon, a demi-culverin and a sacre, plus powder, shot and match. Before Laugharne arrived before the walls, Tenby was blockaded on the seaward side by *Swallow, Prosperous* and *Crescent*, all anchored in the Caldey Roads.

As soon as the ships dropped anchor, an exchange of letters took place between Swanley and the authorities within the threatened town. Both Governor Gwynne in the castle and the Mayor in the Council Chamber received separate notes summoning them to surrender and neither could have been in any doubt about the menace that lay behind the polite phrases. The letter to Mayor Wyatt and the council read as follows:

> Gentlemen,
> In a former letter unto you, wherein was presented the late Declaration of the Honourable Assembly of Parliament: Wee the Commanders of His Majesties ships, desired your Resolutions whether you would comply in the contents thereof, and joyne with us in the preservation of the Gospell, the Kings Honour, and the Kingdomes Safetie, to expell the Forces brought into the Counties by the Earle of Carbery, but receiving no answer, Wee are nowe come to your Towne, to let you know that unless you yield obedience thereunto, Wee shall use our best endeavours to force it. In which, if it shall please God to deliver you into our hands, you must expect no other favour than what is due to Traytors both to God and their Country: wherefore I advise you seriously to consider, and wisely to provide for your present and future safety, and let us receive your speedie Answer, that by your timely adhering to us, you may prevent the demolishing of your Towne by the battering it about your eares with our Ordnance, and hoping you will preserve it as also the effusion of much blood by your sweet complyance, Wee reamaine and rest

*The keep, Tenby Castle; in March 1644, the Royalist Governor of the town, John Gwynne,
and his garrison came under heavy bombardment from Parliamentary warships*

As you may give us cause, your faithfull friends to protect you

Postscript

We further declare that if the Commanders and Souldiers shall joyne with you in the surrendering of your Towne that they shall have quarter for their lives to go whether they please, or continue and be received into the service of the King and Parliament.

The letter to Governor Gwynne was shorter and to the point:

Gentlemen

These are to require you, that upon sight hereof, you immediately yeild up the Fort to the use of the King and Parliament: and so doing you shall be received into the protection of that Assembly and injoy the benefit of Loyall Subjects. But in case you shall continue in your Rebellion you must expect to be proceeded against as Traytors to your King and Country, and enemies to God and the Protestant religion: for if you shall make one shot at the King and Parliaments Ships, not one of you shall escape for his life if it shall please God to give us the Victory. Consider of it and let me receive your Resolutions, in which if you please you shall find me

Your faithfull Friend to preserve

Wm Smith

Exactly how much consultation there was between Wyatt and Gwynne over their answers and how long their deliberations took is uncertain. They must have agreed some time before on a defence of the town, knowing as they did that it was only a matter of time before the Parliamentary forces appeared before their

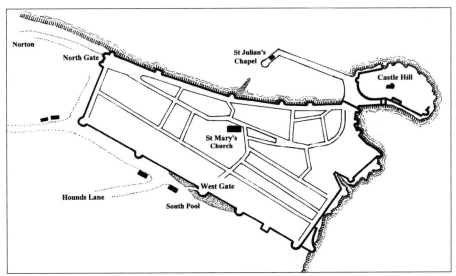

Tenby during the Civil Wars

walls and Gwynne would certainly have been mindful of his oath of loyalty to the King. The delay in replying probably lasted no longer than it took to concoct and write the letters, which were soon being rowed back to Swanley's flagship.

> Gentlemen,
>
> Yours we formerly received, with a Declaration their [*sic*] inclosed, which was required from us before we could peruse the contents thereof, which was the cause of our not returning any answer thereunto, yours of the present we have received; wherein you desire us to complye with you for the preservation of the Gospell, and His Majesties Honour, which is the worke we have vowed to maintaine with our lives and fortunes; and so doing, we hold ourselves true Subjects to God, our King, and Country. And whereas you threaten the demolishing of our Towne, which is not ours to dispose of, but His Majesties, all which we pray you to take into your serious consideration, as also the cry of the effusion of much innocent blood: for Answeare from the Commanders and Souldiers, we referre you to the Letter you shall receive from the Governour of the Towne and Fort. Thus with our best respects we take leave and rest
>
> Your loving Friends if you please
>
> Tinbie, 6ᵗʰ March, 1643
>
> Richard Wyett, Maior   Francis Longe
>
> David Hammond   Richard Prickard
>
> John Rogers

The letter from the castle referred to was as brief as Swanley's demand had been:

> Gentlemen
>
> This Towne we hold as loyall Subjects to the Kings Majesties use, for defence thereof we have his Majesties gracious Commission, which we will endeavour to maintaine with the hazard of our lives and fortune against all opposers, by what colour or pretence soever. This is the resolution of
>
> John Gwynne
>
> David Gwynne
>
> Thomas Botler

Having considered these replies, Swanley sent a further message into the town, proposing that Gwynne should allow all non-combatants, especially women and children, to leave before the attack commenced. From the evidence available, it seems that this humanitarian suggestion was not followed up.[1]

By the afternoon, Laugharne was within two miles of Tenby and from the high ground Swanley's ships could be seen at anchor in Caldey Roads. Unaware of the correspondence between the Admiral and the Governor, he sent a message out to the *Swallow* requesting that efforts should be made to obtain a surrender. On receiving copies of the letters, he set up camp in the fields around the town.

At about 8 o'clock the next morning, the guns of the warships commenced a bombardment, shooting 'very thick upon the town'. Laugharne had moved his men closer to the walls; their demi-cannon was placed on a hill 'within musket shot', with the demi-culverin much closer. As they approached, the Parliamentary forces drove off the Royalist pickets which had been sheltering behind the hedges bordering the roads. They also captured a solidly built house near the town wall.

There next followed a lull in the action. To the sound of a trumpet, Laugharne made a final bid to obtain the submission of the garrison to 'King and Parliament'.

A 17th-century culverin (top) and saker at Tenby Castle

The request was turned down in no uncertain terms by Governor Gwynne. There were now no options left for either side and at about one o'clock on the afternoon of Thursday, 7 March, the land guns opened fire on the town.

Tenby at this time was still completely encircled by its ancient defensive walls (see map, p.67). Two main gates gave access into the town from the landward side: the West Gate, known today as the Five Arches, and the great North Gate, which led to the North Town or Norton, a suburb existing to the north of the town beyond the walls. Lapping the walls around the West Gate was a moat, the South Pool, the gate being reached by a wooden footbridge. The walls continued along the cliff tops overlooking the South Beach, and turned northward above the North Beach, with the Whitesand and Haven Gates leading out to Castle Hill and the harbour. A series of some 14 towers and turrets punctuated the walls at regular intervals.

Both sides in the siege concentrated their efforts on the North Gate. Governor Gwynne, realising that the defences there were in a rickety state, had ordered a mixture of dung and refuse to be rammed in layers against the inner stonework, where it had hardened off to a solid consistency. The outer face of the gate itself was protected by great baskets called gabions, made of tightly woven branches of willow or hazel and filled with stones and earth to deaden the effects of cannon fire. A narrow passage had been left between the baskets, allowing only a single file approach to the wicket in the main gate.

The bombardment continued for three days, during which time a number of the defenders were killed and wounded and numerous houses were damaged, but the walls and North Gate remained standing. It was becoming clear to Laugharne that the siege was dragging on for too long; the weather was cold and his men had already spent three nights in the open without adequate protection. The morale of the naval contingent was regarded with special concern – they were thought to respond best to 'a hot and sudden action'.

It was therefore decided that an attempt should be made to storm the town that evening. The fire of the muskets and the field guns had been concentrated on the North Gate and its defending outworks. One of the cannon scored a lucky hit, smashing in a strong door in one of the breastworks, a solid construction of 'stone and lime within a small distance of the gate', whilst further shots wrecked the wicket in the main gate.[2] The foot soldiers were ordered to advance towards the Norton, driving back the defenders who held the hedges and the houses lining the approach road. As they moved forward they took possession of a turnpike that blocked their way. With this achieved, the horse were able to gallop forward, their progress marked by the sound of trumpets and the cheers of the infantry. The fight was fierce and the attack might well have failed had not the Royalists suffered two losses which sapped their morale. Governor Gwynne, leading out a contingent of musketeers to face the onslaught, was shot and mortally wounded.

Minutes later, their master gunner was in the act of training his cannon, loaded with grape shot, on the advancing horsemen and had just remarked to his gun crew, 'You shall see me make a slaughter of these Roundheads', when he was shot in the head.[3]

Laugharne's men now pushed forward and within a short while Captain Peter Whittie, with a company of seamen, had forced his way through the shattered North Gate. Hot on his heels was Lieutenant Colte with a contingent from the *Swallow* and immediately behind them were Laugharne's mounted troops.

The garrison quickly surrendered. As well as the dying governor and his brother David, there were taken prisoner Lieutenant-Colonel Butler, Captains Lewis, Metholl and Pritchard and over 300 soldiers; eight guns were captured. Archdeacon Rudd, who had been described as 'a malignant priest', was also taken into custody.[4] A certain amount of looting was said to have taken place in the aftermath of the siege, though it was probably limited to the possessions of the captured Royalists, as Laugharne would not have wanted to alienate the townsfolk of Tenby, many of whom had never supported the Royalists.

On the following day, a Sunday, John Poyer appeared before Carew Castle to demand its surrender. The garrison was quick to accept terms and the men were allowed to march out with their weapons and baggage.

Parliament was now supreme in Pembrokeshire. Not one of the houses which had been held by the King's men at the beginning of the year was still garrisoned in his name. Laugharne was perfectly well aware, however, that danger threatened from beyond the county borders. The Royalists of Cardiganshire and Carmarthenshire might yet strike against him.

He wasted no time in issuing a demand to the Committees of both these counties that they should submit to the authority of Parliament. The Cardiganshire men refused point blank and the Carmarthen soldiery, consisting of 150 horse and 300 foot, prevaricated. Their commanding officers might have preferred to resist, but they knew their men to be ill-equipped and that the defences of the town amounted to no more than an earthen wall. Whilst they dithered, Laugharne gathered together an army of 400 foot and 150 horse on Colby Moor, a traditional gathering place for musters, some five or six miles east of Haverfordwest. The burgesses of Carmarthen took the hint and signified their willingness to submit to Parliament. The garrison was already marching out, heading northwest to Lord Carbery's castle at Emlyn (Newcastle Emlyn). Yet another Royalist stronghold had been neutralised.

On 27 March, the *Globe* sailed out of Milford bound for Bristol. On board was Simon Thelwall, who passed the tedious hours of the voyage in writing a long and detailed letter to the Speaker of the House of Commons describing the campaign that had just taken place in Pembrokeshire. The document reached Parliament before he did and by 8 April it had been placed before both Houses, together with letters from Swanley and Captain Smith. As a result, some very strange behind-the-scenes manoeuvrings seem to have taken place. There was no vote of thanks to Laugharne in recognition of his services, nor was his name mentioned in the published reports of Parliament's deliberations. A report by the Earl of Essex, dated 8 April and printed in the Common's journal merely noted that:

> It had pleased God to give us good success in Pembrokeshire by the care and valour of Mr XXX, a servant of the Earl of Pembroke, to whom his Lordship gave a commission at the beginning of these troubles, whereby these places have been preserved for the Parliament. He was in his whole strength sixty Foot, thirty Horse, till of late he was assisted by captain Swanley with some of the seamen, who have done brave service.[5]

The substitution of XXX for Laugharne's name has mystified historians ever since. There is no apparent reason for it, unless Essex had a grudge against him. As has been mentioned earlier, this seems likely, though we have no idea of the cause. Essex was a notoriously touchy individual and his rancour against Laugharne seems confirmed by his nomination of a Colonel Davies to be commander-in-chief in west Wales. This idea may have met with some opposition amongst MPs, as a few days later a Mr John Gryffyth suggested himself as commander and not Colonel Davies. The whole business was referred to a committee of the House for consideration, but nothing more was heard of either proposal, perhaps because by then the scrupulously fair-minded Thelwall had spoken in person to the House about events in Pembrokeshire. He may also have had a number of private conversations with members in which he set the record straight.

After hearing Thelwall's report, the Commons recorded its thanks for his services in Pembrokeshire and made evident their confidence in him by asking him to draw up recommendations for administering Pembrokeshire 'to the best advantage of the Parliament'. On 20 April he was granted the enormous sum of £1,000 with which to purchase arms and ammunition for its defence.[6]

We do not know what Laugharne's thoughts were on the lack of gratitude shown to him by Parliament. If the Commons and Lord Essex imagined that he would retire into obscurity, the tide of events was to prove them wrong.

10   Parliament in Control

Following his successful campaign in west Wales, Rowland Laugharne moved eastwards across the coastal plains of Glamorgan. Swansea refused his call to surrender, but there was better luck at Cardiff, where he was able to install a garrison in the castle. It must have seemed, albeit briefly, that all of south Wales might soon be in Parliamentary hands, for in January a force from Gloucester had raided the Royalist stronghold of Chepstow, seizing loot and prisoners.[1]

It was possibly during Laugharne's absence from Pembrokeshire that Richard Swanley committed one of the worst atrocities of the Civil War. Details of the incident are sparse and are recorded mostly in the broadsheets of the time or in private correspondence. It appears to have occurred in April 1644, and may have been the latest and worst in a string of similar events. Swanley's ships had been patrolling the Irish Sea for some months, seizing any vessel they suspected of ferrying Royalist troops from Ireland, but large numbers were slipping through the net, perhaps because many of the Parliamentary seamen were involved in Laugharne's land campaign. Up to 2,000 Royalist soldiers had been landed from small convoys at harbours along the north Wales coast and the balance of military strength seemed generally to be tipping in the King's favour.

The Parliamentary press described these men as responsible for the murder of Protestant settlers in 1641, though most of them were in fact English and Welsh levies who had been sent to Ireland to put down the rebellion. The propaganda was widely believed, however, and the King's supporters in north Wales pleaded with him to stop further landings. The situation was not improved when the captains of the transport ships demanded large quantities of supplies from the ports where the troops came ashore.

To add to the fear and confusion, it was also reported that further detachments of men were to be sent from Ireland to Bristol. In April, a Captain Anthony Willoughby set sail from Dublin in command of 150 men, but soon afterwards they were intercepted by ships of Swanley's fleet.[2] Attempts were made to persuade the Englishmen amongst the troops to take the Covenant and enlist in the service of Parliament. Some agreed and were said to have been subsequently absorbed into Laugharne's own regiment. The Irish soldiers and any others who refused to change sides were barbarically treated. Swanley decided 'to try whether they could tread the seas as lightly as their Irish bogs ... and binding them back to back, cast them overboard to swim or drown'.[3] In this way, at least 70 men and two women were cold-bloodedly murdered, though the Royalist news-sheet *Mercurius Aulicus* suggested that in fact all 150 soldiers had been killed. The editor also claimed that the prisoners had been brought back to Pembroke before being drowned in the waters of the Haven on 23 April, St George's Day.[4]

Swanley and his fellow captains may have carried out further atrocities. Royalists were in no doubt that he made a habit of drowning any Irish soldiers he found aboard captured vessels. There were copy-cat murders, too. Two years later, in August 1646, Major-General Thomas Mytton's army captured the Royalist-held town of Conwy. Some of the Irish defenders managed to escape into the castle, which continued to hold out, but those unlucky enough to be taken prisoner in the town were ferried out to sea, tied back to back and thrown overboard.

The massacre at Milford Haven sent shock waves through the ranks of the Royalists, nowhere more so than in Ireland. Few men were willing to chance the voyage to England. The Marquess of Ormonde warned a correspondent that many soldiers 'were very fearful to venture upon this voyage ... soe that until these seas be cleared ... Anglesey can expect little (indeed noe) succour out of Ireland'.[5]

As King Charles needed to swell the ranks of his armies one way or another, he now demanded more recruits from Wales. Each of the Welsh counties was set a quota, to be met by impressments, and the wealthier members of society found themselves yet again being milked for money. Viscount Bulkeley of Anglesey was expected to cough up £120, and similar amounts were expected from other landowners in England and Wales.

It was not surprising that a feeling of malaise began to spread across the country, a certainty that no more could or should be done. When Colonel Gerard arrived in Glamorgan and expected extra men to be made available to him, he was told by the Commissioners of Array that they could not 'apprehend any possibility how or where to find any further numbers of men as are required from hence' .

This disquiet seemed to affect all areas of the country and all classes. In Royalist Chepstow, the governor felt that he could no longer trust the towns-people with arms.[6] The activities of the King's commanders in north Wales so alienated the locals that they were regarded as grasping intruders, causing one contemporary writer to report that the inhabitants 'love not a stranger longer than he can tell them the news'. Such was the lack of co-operation and the sense of distrust that Captain Thomas Dabridgecourt wrote to Prince Rupert, 'if your Highness shall be pleased to command me to the Turk or Jew or Gentile, I will go on my bare feet to serve you; but from the Welsh, good Lord deliver me'.[7]

Some of this ill feeling may have been partly rooted in the ancient rivalries between the Welsh and the English, but there was a growing perception that Welshmen were being used as cannon fodder by the Royalists. The Parliamentarian writers were keen to emphasise this aspect of the war as it helped slow Royalist recruitment in Wales, but a number of private diaries and letters also mention it. When Cirencester was seized by Prince Rupert in 1643, the puritan minister John Corbet noted that the Welsh amongst his troops 'were reported to suffer the greatest slaughter, who in that army were a continuall sacrifice to the sword'. At the storming of Leicester in 1645, the King's infantry, most of them Welsh, were said to have been driven forward by their own cavalry to attack the defences, and many were killed.[8]

There had also been a change of policy regarding Welsh troops on the part of the King. In the first year of the war he had allowed the formation of Welsh regiments commanded by Welsh officers, but following the defeat of Lord Herbert at Highnam, there had been a re-structuring of local organizations. South Wales became part of the Association of the South Marches and Welsh soldiers were combined with English troops recruited from the border counties. At a later stage of the war, much of the recruitment in south Wales was being overseen by English officers, who then escorted the soldiers to their regimental bases.

There were also questions about the commitment of the Welsh soldiers. Some did not wish to serve far from their native country. When a force of Roundheads from Gloucester attacked Tewkesbury, the Welsh amongst the garrison 'partly repining for want of pay, fell into a desperate mutiny ... hasted over Upton Bridge and did scarce look back till safe in their own country' .

The King was deeply angered over this desertion, which he did not forget or forgive. When, in March 1644, Prince Rupert sent 1,200 footsoldiers from Wales to Oxford, they were armed only with clubs and were escorted by two regiments of horse, who might have been intended to ensure their arrival as much as to protect them. When the King inspected them, he told them that they were likely to run away and they were given proper weapons only when they had promised to the contrary.[9]

It was not, however, only the Royalists who were experiencing difficulties with their recruitments. The officers of the Parliamentary army were also finding it hard to persuade some of the County Militias to serve outside their own shires. Many men feared for the safety of their families should they be called away. Oliver Cromwell had found a way round this by forming some of the counties of Eastern England into military associations. This allowed groups of counties to raise bands of local men for mutual defence and peace-keeping duties. The idea was successful enough for the Commons to apply it in other areas and an ordinance for associating the counties of Pembroke, Cardigan and Carmarthen was consolidated by the Commons on 20 May and was adopted by Parliament on 8 June 1644. It gave the three shires the right to appoint a Committee to raise a force of men with all the necessary arms and ammunition to defend west Wales. Contributions of money towards the project were to be repaid at an interest of eight percent. The Committee was to put into execution all Parliament's ordinances for sequestering and selling the estates of malignants, delinquents and papists. It could also administer the Covenant to all who ought to take it. Most importantly, perhaps as a result of Simon Thelwall's intervention, the Earl of Essex was required to grant a commission to Rowland Laugharne to act as commander-in-chief of the combined forces of all three counties.

The local committee consisted of 30 members nominated by Parliament. They included stalwarts such as Rowland Laugharne, his father John, Rice Powell, John Poyer, Walter Owen, Simon Thelwall and Captains Swanley and Smith. Also appointed were Roger and Sampson Lort, Sir Richard Philipps of Picton, John Eliot of Earwere and Griffith White, all of whom except White had previously declared for the King and who now had changed sides with the flood of the Parliamentary tide. Some, like Eliot, were to shift their allegiances more than once and became known as 'the West Wales Weathercocks'. Howell Gwynne of Glanbran perfectly summed up their attitude when he declared, 'Heigh God, heigh devil, I will be for the strongest side'.[10]

The Association was most effective in Pembrokeshire; Carmarthen and Cardigan were too Royalist in their sympathies for it ever to have succeeded within their borders.[11]

Laugharne's appointment as commander-in-chief may have soothed whatever wounded pride he had, but the Commons showed even greater favour to Swanley and Smith. On 4 June they were summoned before the bar of the House where they were awarded medals to be attached to gold chains worth £200 and £100 respectively. Swanley's reputation rose even higher when, on the same day, a letter was received from Parliament's Lord Admiral. Enclosed with it was a request for supplies from Captain Moulton of the *Lyon* at Milford Haven, and another from the Pembroke County Committee pleading that Swanley might be appointed their commander-in-chief. The Commons, concerned that Pembrokeshire might lie open to attack, ordered Swanley to return to Milford as soon as the *Leopard*, *Swallow* and *Providence*, then at Plymouth for refitting, were ready.

11   Royalist Revival and Retreat

In an effort to restore Royalist fortunes in south Wales, King Charles had dismissed Lord Carbery as his commander in the area. Ever since the attack on Trefloyne in February 1644, Carbery had been lurking on his Carmarthenshire estate. His failure to defeat the enemy was attributed by some 'to a suspected natural cowardice, others to a design to be overcome'. Suspicions of his motives only deepened when it was learned that he had been in correspondence with some of the Parliamentary sympathisers in west Wales. In his place the King appointed Colonel Charles Gerard, a professional soldier whose conduct was to gain him a reputation for ruthlessness and savagery, but whose military skills were to overturn all of Rowland Laugharne's achievements.

Gerard crossed the Severn from England at the beginning of June, landing at Black Rock on the Monmouthshire bank. He brought with him a large group of soldiers who had crossed from Ireland to Bristol, probably during the previous November, and who might well have been eager to avenge the murder of so many of their fellows by Captain Swanley in April.

Within days Gerard had driven out the garrison installed by Laugharne at Cardiff. Despite the reservations over recruitment voiced by the Commissioners of Array, he seems to have gathered a number of men who were eager to face the rebels of Pembrokeshire. By the second week of June, he was pushing into Carmarthenshire, where Cydweli, Carmarthen and Laugharne all fell before him. He then turned northwards, traversing the Pembroke/Carmarthen border to take Newcastle Emlyn and then Cardigan, where his men killed or took prisoner 200 rebels.[1] Pembrokeshire, regarded by Royalists as 'the most seditious county of all Wales', was now isolated.

Hoping to halt his advance, the County Committee of Pembroke summoned all able-bodied men between the ages of 16 and 60 to gather on 14 June with arms, horses and enough provisions for six days.[2]. It is unlikely that many answered the call, as no attempt seems to have been made to block Gerard's progress. From Cardigan, he struck south-westwards, marching across Pembrokeshire to seize Roch Castle, where some 300 head of cattle and 1,500 sheep were confis-

*Roch Castle was used as a gathering point
for cattle intended to feed Laugharne's troops;
it changed hands several times during the
Civil War*

cated. They had been originally intended to feed Laugharne's men and their seizure was part of a deliberate scorched earth campaign practised by the Royalists as they marched through the surrounding countryside. Indeed, Gerard's actions were remembered with bitterness for many years. A contemporary account described how 'the barbarous and cruel enemy drive away our cattle, rifle our houses to the bare walls. All provisions of victuals, where they come, carried away or destroyed. Divers villages and county towns, being neither garrisons nor any annoyance to the enemy, burnt to the ground. The standing corn they burn or destroy. All sexes and degrees are stripped naked by the enemy – aged and unarmed. Persons inhumanely murdered in cold blood and others half hanged, and afterwards stigmatised, and their flesh burnt off their bodies to the bare bones and yet suffered in great torture to live'.[3]

Even before the capture of Roch Castle, Captain Moulton aboard the *Lyon* had recognised the situation as potentially disastrous for Parliament. In a letter written to the Lord Admiral, he warned that 'unless there is a speedy sending of good commanders, a faithful committee and an enlarged commission to Col. Rowland Laugharne, these parts are like to be lost to Parliament'.[4] As it was, Haverfordwest was already blockaded by units of Gerard's column and Laugharne's troops were boxed into Tenby and Pembroke. If Gerard's unstoppable progress continued, these towns might also be lost.

During this time, Rowland made no move to challenge his opponents. He may have been short of supplies and ammunition (nothing is known of what happened to Thelwall's £1,000), or perhaps he considered the Royalist force to be superior in numbers and ability to his own. Moulton's letter indicates something of the sort, but if Gerard did have an advantage, he had no time to profit by it.

On 2 July, at Marston Moor, near York, Prince Rupert was defeated and the whole of northern England was lost to the Crown. Three weeks after the battle, Gerard received orders recalling him to the King's side. He marched towards England, leaving behind a detachment to continue the blockade of Haverfordwest.

It was a stroke of luck for Laugharne, for not only had he been facing a formidable opponent, but the naval support on which he had previously depended was also at risk. Swanley's two principal warships, the *Leopard* regis and the *Swallow*, were still at Plymouth undergoing a refit, and three other units of his fleet, the *Lyon, Crescent* and *Entrance*, desperately needed repair. Only the merchant ships contracted to the navy still remained on station at Milford Haven and their continued presence depended on the renewal of the contracts between their owners and the navy. Even the maintenance of the guard ships at Tenby was proving too expensive at £1,250 a month.

Eventually, the Lord Admiral ordered Swanley back to Milford, where his fleet was to be permanently based, and Laugharne's land forces were augmented by 140 men sent into Pembrokeshire by the Earl of Essex. There was also an improvement in the quantity of supplies available. The County Committee purchased food, iron, cloth and canvas to the value of £557 from the owners of the *Gillyflower*, which was engaged as a guardship at Tenby for £150 a month.[5]

With Gerard's departure and a fresh infusion of supplies, Rowland Laugharne felt justified in taking to the field once more. There was, however, an early setback. His brother Thomas took a troop of horse towards Haverfordwest to challenge the Royalist blockade and was captured with his entire force. On 22 August the Parliamentary force holding the town decided that their position was untenable and retreated to Pembroke. If this retreat led to a Royalist occupation of Haverfordwest it was a brief one, as the King's troops seem to have quickly withdrawn to Carmarthen, leaving Laugharne considerable room for manoeuvre.

His plans may have been delayed by bad weather which affected south Wales during August, but if so, the storms also brought him some good luck. A detachment of infantry commanded by Colonel Beale and Colonel Carter were en route for north Wales from London when their ships were forced to take shelter in Milford Haven. The voyage was abandoned and the men remained in Pembrokeshire until plans could be made to march them northwards to link up with Sir Thomas Myddleton's forces.

In October the *Leopard* arrived in the Haven carrying £991 worth of arms and ammunition. This enabled Laugharne to put into the field an enlarged force consisting of his own men and Colonel Beale's (no mention is made of Colonel Carter's whereabouts), to which was added a detachment of seamen and one of the *Leopard*'s demi-culverins.

The first target of this army of about 2,000 men was Laugharne Castle. By Monday, 28 October they were encamped about a mile to the north of the town

*Laugharne Castle held out for a week in the autumn of 1644,
before surrendering to Rowland Laugharne*

and early the next morning Rowland Laugharne moved his men to the vicinity of
Glan-y-mor where an ancient earthwork overlooked the castle from the north-
east. From this vantage point, the cannon began a steady bombardment of the
defences, with little effect. On 30 October, Laugharne decided to move 200
of his musketeers and his heavy guns to Fern Hill to the west of the castle,
where they could fire directly on to the front of the outer gatehouse. Later that
same night a detachment of troops stormed the town gate and several of the
Parliamentary guns were dragged forward to a spot where they could pound the
gatehouse of the castle at close quarters. The bombardment lasted throughout
the Thursday and Friday. At 11 o'clock on the Saturday night, under a starlit sky,
200 men moved forward and after a sharp fight captured the battered remains
of the outer gatehouse. This left just the inner bailey to capture. The thickness
and height of its walls were formidable and a direct assault might have resulted
in a considerable number of casualties. The defenders, however, can have been
in no doubt about the hopelessness of their position. At about three o'clock on
the morning of Sunday 3 November they began calling out of the windows of
the castle, requesting a parley. By seven o'clock, they had surrendered.[6]

About 10 of Rowland's men had been killed, with some 30 wounded. Of the
castle garrison, numbering some 200 men under the command of Lieutenant
Colonel Sir William Russell, 33 had been killed. The officers were allowed to
march away, most of them heading for the safety of Carmarthen. Parts of the
castle were demolished to prevent its use as a fortress, though this destruction
may not have occurred until much later.

From Laugharne, the Parliamentarians moved on to Clog-y-fran House near St Clears, from which they evicted the Royalist garrison. They then marched northwards towards the Cardigan border, trouncing the enemy yet again in a skirmish at Merthyr, west of Carmarthen. Nothing now prevented them from joining up with Sir Thomas Myddleton, who was advancing south through mid-Wales, and the two forces duly met at Llanbedr in Cardiganshire. By 27 November they had reached Machynlleth where, just outside the town, they encountered a Royalist troop commanded by Major Hookes and Sir Richard Price. A running fight through the town ensued, with Hookes' men falling back over the Dovy Bridge. On the far bank the Royalists made a desperate stand, holding out for as long as their ammunition lasted and finally scattering in disarray. Machynlleth was given over to plunder 'without mercy' as some of the Royalist broadsheets put it. A day or two later, Myddleton's troops arrived at the mansion at Mathafarn, about 5 miles east of Machynlleth, where they killed two men and set fire to the building.[7]

As Mathafarn went up in flames, Rowland Laugharne may have been on his way south to Cardigan. He clearly did not wish to leave a Royalist garrison on the northern borders of Pembrokeshire and when he reached the town shortly before Christmas the burgesses quickly surrendered. The castle proved to be a different proposition. Major Slaughter, in charge of the garrison, refused to give up the ancient fortress and Laugharne was forced to embark upon a siege.

Slaughter had managed to obtain ordnance from the frigate *Converse* which had been wrecked on the coast not far away. These guns proved more than a match for Laugharne's artillery and it was not until a large brass cannon had been unloaded from the *Leopard* (whether the merchantman or naval vessel is unclear) that he was able to make any progress. After a three day bombardment a breach

The besieged garrison of Cardigan Castle was saved after one of its members swam across the river during the night, carrying a message to Rowland Laugharne

was opened up in the castle walls and the order was given to storm the building. As they scrambled over the shattered masonry, the storming party discovered that the enemy had hastily thrown up a crescent-shaped earthwork behind which they were crouched with their great guns loaded with case shot. If these had been fired, Laugharne's men would have been decimated, but the Royalists seem to have been paralysed with shock, for 'as men bereft of all sense, having not the power to give fire to their guns, although the linstocks were in their hands ready lighted, [they] cast down their arms and cried for quarter, the which was granted'. Although most accounts agree that the castle was taken by storm, some Royalist broadsheets claimed that it fell because of the treachery of a sergeant who had been bribed to open a sally port.

A few days later, Captain William Smith described in a letter the haul of weapons and prisoners taken at Cardigan: 'Major Slaughter and wife, Captain Vaughan, with their lieutenant and ensign, one Doctor Taylor, a Divine, with about an hundred common soldiers, six great guns, a hundred and fifty arms, a quantity of powder, ball and other provisions, and this was done the 29 December last'.[8]

Laugharne did not bother to celebrate his triumph. Leaving Rice Powell as governor of Cardigan, he set out in pursuit of the remaining elements of Gerard's force, which were still lurking in various corners of Pembrokeshire. These he drove out of the county after defeating them on or about 14 January 1645 at an unknown location somewhere on the Carmarthen side of the county borders.

It was around this time that Gerard returned from England. No evidence exists for the date of his arrival in west Wales, nor of his exact whereabouts, but he is mentioned in several accounts as leading the attack on Cardigan which now took place. Learning that Powell's men had few provisions left, Gerard gathered together a column of 1,300 foot and 1,200 horse and set off for the town. As he approached Cardigan along the banks of the Teifi he intercepted several boats loaded with provisions for the castle and after taking possession of the town on 4 January, demanded Powell's surrender. This was refused; Powell had already managed to send a message to Laugharne urgently requesting help and he was determined to hold out for as long as possible.

Gerard gave orders for the destruction of the bridge across the Teifi, but this was only partially done. Drawing up his artillery before the castle, he commenced a steady pulverising of the ancient walls, punctuating the barrage with assaults launched upon the weakest points of the defences. Powell's men must have put up a fierce resistance, for it was reported that the Royalists lost more than 150 men in these attacks.

On receipt of Powell's message, Laugharne hastily collected together a force of 300 foot soldiers, including 120 of Swanley's men, and 600 horse. As they approached Cardigan they encountered a second messenger from Powell. This was a soldier who had left the castle during the night hours and had swum across the river to the south bank. He carried with him a warning that the garrison could not hold out for more than eight days. Their most desperate need was for provisions without which they would starve.

A rescue plan was quickly put into operation. A boat was found which was filled with supplies and to it were lashed other boats, four on each side. Two of these were manned with musketeers and the whole makeshift raft was used to ferry food supplies across the river. A heavy fire was directed at it from about 300 of Gerard's soldiers lining the river bank, some of whom were picked off by the musketeers in the boats. Despite the musket balls whipping about their ears, Laugharne's men managed to land all the supplies and carry them into the castle.

Gerard then received information that Sir Thomas Myddleton was hurrying down from north Wales to join up with Laugharne. Unwilling to be caught between the two armies, he decided to march north to challenge Myddleton before he could reach Cardigan. Leaving a token force to continue the siege, he set off around 19 January, but had covered barely 20 miles when he discovered that Myddleton was still in north Wales. It is not known if Gerard had picked up a genuinely false rumour or if it had been deliberately planted by Laugharne, but the latter had taken full advantage of Gerard's absence. On 22 January Powell had already been warned of the impending attack by the relieving force; an arrow had been fired over the castle's walls tied to which was a note requesting him to launch a sortie through the castle gates as soon as Laugharne's men had gained the north bank of the river. The ruined bridge proved to be no obstacle to determined men. Laugharne's engineers easily repaired the damage using faggots of wood and planks and the troops were able to cross it with ease to link up with Powell's men now issuing from the castle. The Royalists were driven out of their first and second barricades and then 'out of their main guard which was at the market place and

Rowland Laugharne
(National Library of Wales, Aberystwyth)

then out of the church, where our forces took two brass demy-culverins which Gerard brought from Bristol ... and following the enemy, beat them all out of town and so we are now masters both of the town and castle. Of the enemy were slain in the place 85, besides those that were slain before the castle; 100 prisoners were taken'.[9]

Accounts of what happened after this victory are confused. The Royalist broadsheets insisted that Gerard counter-attacked, regaining many of his guns and releasing the men who had been taken prisoner. Unsurprisingly, the Parliamentarian papers report that those Royalists who escaped from Cardigan took refuge at Newcastle Emlyn. Gerard himself was said to have been in Carmarthen on 21 February, where he took part in a recruiting drive. After this date he moved on to north Wales, but his exact movements are unknown.

Rowland Laugharne's whereabouts are also unclear. It is likely that he marched his men into mid-Wales, but nothing is sure until April when he began a siege of Newcastle Emlyn. Powell presumably remained at Cardigan.

John Poyer, who had not taken part in any of the campaigns described above, was probably still at Pembroke, where he was responsible for the safety of the town and castle. If he or any of the townspeople imagined that they were now to enjoy a period of relative quiet, they were soon to discover otherwise.

12   Ebb and Flow

Whilst Laugharne was absent from Pembroke, John Poyer, left in charge of the town and castle, found himself beset with problems. They originated in his strained relationships with members of the County Committee, some of whom looked upon him with an antipathy bordering on hatred.

The Committee included John Eliot, Sir Richard Philipps and Roger and Sampson Lort, all of whom had abandoned their former loyalty to the King and were awarded positions of authority within the county by Parliament. Poyer, who later claimed to have spent a large part of his own fortune in Parliament's cause, may have viewed these 'West Wales Weathercocks' with suspicion, even contempt, and was in all likelihood too hot-tempered and dogmatic to have hidden his feelings. For their part, the Lorts and John Eliot were quick to take offence at Poyer's over-bearing, self-confident manner. Sensitive concerning their adoption of new loyalties and anxious to maintain their influence and prestige, not to mention their estates, in the uncertain atmosphere in which they now found themselves, they probably regarded Poyer with distaste. He was, after all, of humble ancestry, yet with the agreement of Parliament he had risen to a position of authority which might otherwise have been filled by someone of their own standing. It is noticeable that whilst their utterances against Poyer are venomous, their remarks concerning Laugharne are expressed in much more measured terms.

The antipathy between Poyer and the Committee became public early in 1645. Poyer had appealed directly to Parliament for supplies to meet a perceived threat to Pembrokeshire from elements of the Marquess of Ormonde's army. He feared invasion and on 27 March wrote to the Speaker of the House of Commons detailing rumours of an Irish landing on a scale which could not be repelled without help. He included with the letter a petition signed by himself, his brother David, Walter Cuny and about 120 inhabitants of Pembroke and the surrounding area. This document reminded the Commons that the signatories had maintained the garrison of Pembroke at their own expense, but now needed money to pay the Pembroke soldiery and the garrison at Carew. Lastly,

Poyer enclosed a list of supplies urgently needed at Pembroke, which gives an insight into the practicalities of garrison life at that time:

> The Particulars the Garrison in the Towne and Castle of Pembroke greatly
>   wants this present March the 27 ...
> Imprimis our monthly pay for 250 soldiers with theire officers.
> Item. A Surgents chest furnished for 250 soldiers.
> Item. Twenty barrels of powder.
> Item. 400 great shott for demi-culveringe, Saker, and minion.
> Item. 12 mouldes to cast musketts and carbyne bullets.
> Item. 2,000 li. Of match.
> Item. 50 saddles, 2 bridles and furniture for 50 horse.
> Item. 50 cases of pistolls or 50 Carbynes.
> Item. One hundred musketts.
> Item. 200 firelocks.
> Item. 300 Swordes, Beltes and bandeleroes.
> Item. 4 drums with an Ensigne for the Castle.
> Item. One tunne of vinegar.
> Item. 2 tunnes of Iron for making portcullises, chaynes and other uses.
> Item. Some corse cloth to make Clothes and Canvas for Shirts with shooes
>   for the Souldiers.[1]

The Commons made no answer to these appeals.

For his part, Poyer may well have written without the sanction of the County Committee because on 1 April its members fired off their own broadside. In a letter addressed to the Commons, they gave vent to their frustration and anger by describing the wrongs done to Sir Richard Philipps, 'a person of integrity in public and private consideration', who held the lease on Carew Castle. They claimed that Poyer was guilty of using for his own purposes the stock and profits of the demesne lands of the castle to the value of £300 and that he had also spoiled the timber and lead in the castle. Outhouses had been demolished without Sir Richard's agreement and Poyer had also refused to give up the building when requested to do so by the Deputy Lieutenants and by Laugharne. Furthermore, there was considerable discontent amongst the local gentry who resented Poyer's actions to such an extent that they would not contribute to the Committee's funds.[2] The letter was signed, not unexpectedly, by the Lorts, Griffith White and John Eliot. Poyer might have been able to dismiss it as an act of malice, had not the document also contained the names of Captain Swanley and Captain Smith. This alone was enough seriously to damage his reputation with Parliament and from this moment onward there was a steady erosion of confidence in him.

There may have been an element of truth in some of the charges. Following the surrender of Carew to Poyer on 10 March 1644, he had taken over the management of the demesne estate, but he never rendered to Parliament an accurate account of what he had done with the profits from rents and other dues. He might have used the money to equip or feed the garrison of Pembroke and it is also possible, though never proved, that he had re-imbursed himself for the expenses he had already incurred.

Poyer seems to have been aware of the hostility building up against him, for at about this time he arrived in London. The reasons for his visit are unknown, but it may have been an attempt to clear his name. The County Committee took the opportunity to send another letter to the Speaker of the Commons, dated 23 April, requesting that Poyer be detained in the capital until such time as the charges brought against him could be investigated.

In all probability he was arrested, for he was still in London on 13 September, when Rowland Laugharne was forced to intervene. He wrote to the Commons, explaining that 'Mr Roger Lort, in our greatest exegencie, deserted us and in contempt of my commaunde for his staie shipped himself off to London, there, as I understand, makeinge Mr Eliot his faction, bestowed himself in disgorging private ranckor and malice against those whose meritt will endure the test ...'.[3] Laugharne's support resulted in at least a temporary change of attitude towards John Poyer. He was allowed to return to Pembrokeshire, but if he thought that his release marked the end of the campaign being waged against him, he was mistaken.

If John Poyer's reputation was beginning to suffer, Rowland Laugharne's was in the ascendant. During 1644, Parliament had shown its faith in him by sending extra troops to west Wales – some 1,200 foot and 300 horse. He had also been appointed commander-in-chief of the Association of Pembroke, Cardigan and Carmarthen. On 15 January 1645 he was publicly thanked by the House of Commons for his services and five days later the members approved a proposal to send him a further 1,100 dragoons and 50 barrels of powder. On 6 March he was rewarded with a personal gift of £500 and was promised 1,000 muskets and 500 pikes; a further increase of 50 more barrels of powder was voted on 24 March. In addition, the Commons decided to raise an extra £3,000 for munitions for his forces. In June, a tense month in west Wales, as Gerard was again marching through the area, a hasty resolution was passed that 100 barrels of powder, two tons of match and 10 barrels of bullets should be sent to Pembroke. Rowland's skills as a military commander were about to be put to their most severe test.

The Royalist garrison holding the castle at Newcastle Emlyn were dismayed when, on 12 April 1645, they looked out over the battlements to see a large force of Parliamentarian soldiers erecting a siege camp before the walls. In command of the operation was Rowland Laugharne, attempting to reduce one of the last remaining garrisons holding out for the King in west Wales. After the fall of Cardigan on 22 January, Rowland's whereabouts are uncertain. Some reports place him in Shropshire, where he was supposed to have aided Colonel Mitton in

The remains of the castle at Emlyn, showing the ravelin constructed before the gates by the Royalist garrison

the taking of Shrewsbury. There are also rumours of his presence in north and mid Wales, but nothing can be confirmed until his arrival at Emlyn.

Shortly after Laugharne's appearance before Newcastle Emlyn, a Parliamentary newspaper reported that Charles Gerard had been ordered back to Wales specifi-cally to deal with him. As in his earlier campaign, Gerard behaved with 'great strictness in forcing the country along with him and [he] not only sweeps away the men but all the cattle, horses provisions and what he can find out, before him'.[4]

Despite rumours that Gerard's force had been attacked en route, he is said to have made a forced march of over 100 miles from England in a week.[5] On Sunday 27 April, without warning, his men launched an attack on the unprepared camp outside the walls of Emlyn Castle. As a contemporary pamphlet reported, the Royalists 'suddenly and secretly fell upon our men, slew and took most of our foot companies, besides many horse ...'.[6]

Laugharne was forced into a humiliating retreat, during which many were killed and taken prisoner. Reports put the number of dead at between 150 and 400, though the higher figure may have been an exaggeration. Nevertheless, the pursuit of the defeated army stretched out over seven miles of countryside, with '486 prisoners taken, with 20 commanders besides inferior officers, 120 good horse, one piece of ordnance ... almost 700 arms'.[7]

Laugharne and the remnants of his army managed to find refuge in south Pembrokeshire, but Gerard followed up his advantages by marching on Haverfordwest. Astounded by news of the defeat at Newcastle Emlyn, the garrison immediately evacuated the town. According to one description 'they no sooner decried his Majesty's forces at one end of the town, but the rebels ran out at the other in such strange confusion that very many of them were taken prisoner'.[8] In their haste to escape they left behind stocks of provisions, ammunition and ordnance.

The men holding Cardigan Castle reacted to the news in much the same way. Having set fire to the buildings within the fortifications they embarked on a fleet of small boats and set sail for Pembroke.

With his foes penned up in Tenby and Pembroke, Gerard was free to roam across the northern half of Pembrokeshire, mopping up any resistance that remained. On 30 April he made a night attack upon Picton Castle, capturing the two daughters of Sir Richard Philipps, their brother Erasmus, heir to the estate, as well as £500 in cash, 12 trunks of silver plate, 150 arms and a supply of powder. A legend, well known in Pembrokeshire, grew up as a result of this episode. The story relates how the attacking Royalists requested a parley, which was agreed. A group of mounted troopers rode up close to the castle walls in an attempt to persuade the garrison to surrender and whilst the negotiations were taking place one of the soldiers noticed a nursemaid eavesdropping at one of the windows, with the baby, Erasmus, in her arms. Sidling his horse directly beneath the window he stood suddenly upright in the saddle and pulled him from her grasp. Other versions state that the trooper was carrying a letter containing the suggested terms of surrender and when the nursemaid leant out to receive it, the trooper snatched the infant from her. To prevent the baby from being put to death the castle was surrendered. Over the years the story has changed in many of its details. Some versions describe the attackers as Parliamentarians, but if there is any truth to the legend, it must have occurred in 1645, when the young Erasmus was amongst those taken prisoner by the Royalists.[9]

Gerard now set up a garrison in Carew Castle and invited a group of merchants from Bristol to guard Milford Haven in the King's name, as he mounted a blockade of Pembroke. A battery was constructed above the Pembroke river to try to prevent supplies or reinforcements from reaching the town.

The next 11 weeks proved a time of almost unendurable hardship, which few people in the area ever forgot. Stores of food and cattle were seized by the Royalists, buildings burnt or looted and innocent people imprisoned. Laugharne reported that the enemy did not hesitate to 'imprison and plunder, and abuse the well-affected townsmen, range everywhere about the country, pillage and destroy that which should be [the] present and future livelihood of our army, and have given us a sure testimony that they will leave nothing undone that mischief and violence can invent against a distressed county'.[10]

There are other testimonies to the sufferings inflicted on the population, though they are all written by Parliamentary supporters. John Poyer was later to petition the Commons that 'General Gerard at the time when he beleaguered the ... town of Pembroke, caused divers of the Dwelling houses, Barns and Reeks of corn to be fired belonging to such persons that your Petitioner had borrowed monies of for the services aforesaid and their cattle and household goods did plunder for their utter undoing'.[11]

Some of the documents give a glimpse of the desperate measures taken to preserve Pembroke and its garrison from starvation and capture. At Lamphey Palace, Mary Gunter, the widow of Major Thomas Gunter, was continuing to ransack the estate to find enough food to feed her Parliamentary neighbours. In addition to the supplies provided during the initial stages of the war, she had also sent into the castle provisions worth a further £720 16s 8d, as testified by a Public Faith Bill signed by Laugharne, Poyer and five others on 30 April 1645. It is interesting that Mrs Gunter had obtained this receipt, which could theoretically be redeemed for cash, shortly after the defeat at Newcastle Emlyn. She was making sure that, should Pembroke fall, she still had proof of what she was owed.[12]

There were others who were prepared to sacrifice even more than cattle to protect the town. Thomas Powell, a gentleman of Pembroke, watched as several of his houses were demolished 'for the better serving of the town of Pembroke' All his cattle and sheep were taken as provision for the garrison. At his own expense Powell was also maintaining two of his sons as soldiers, the eldest of whom served under Sir Thomas Fairfax.[13]

Another document, presented to Parliament during the interval between the first and second Civil Wars, was drawn up by William Adams of Paterchurch, who declared 'that out of his affection for Parliament he had served at his own charge under Major-General Laugharne ... when the enemy were in the county, voluntarily gave way for firing of divers of his houses in the suburbs of Pembroke ... Afterwards obliged to take refuge with his wife and child in Pembroke and the enemy then fired his houses and corn and drove away all his cattle. He subsequently came by ship to London and has there remained above twelve months. He has been plundered of all he has, is much indebted and prays the House to give him some assistance in rebuilding his house'.[14]

The houses owned by Adams and Powell probably lay within a musket shot of the town walls, perhaps in the vicinity of the East Gate, and were demolished to prevent their occupation by the enemy and to provide a clear field of fire. Although no date is given for their destruction, it is likely to be after 1643, following Laugharne's arrival in Pembrokeshire and definitely before 28 May 1645, when Laugharne and Poyer signed a certificate attesting to the losses suffered by Adams.[15] Efforts to improve Pembroke's defences had been going on since the outbreak of war but, given the date of the certificate, it is possible that the burning of the buildings took place in 1645, shortly before the signing of the document, at a time when Gerard menaced the town. Archaeological work carried out in Pembroke during the 1980s would seem to confirm that everything possible was being done to create an impregnable fortress. Excavations at the South Quay, just below the castle, revealed the foundations of a wall, estimated to have been about seven metres in height, which probably dated to the seventeenth century.[16] A gap in the medieval defences existed at precisely that spot, as shown by contemporary maps of the town. In a petition to the military court which tried him in 1649, Poyer specifically mentioned his part in the repair of the town walls and it is tempting to wonder if the new wall was built to meet the threat from Gerard.

The Houses of Parliament were considerably alarmed about the turn of events in Pembrokeshire. A flurry of commands and instructions emanated from the Committee of Both Kingdoms, directed at those best able to send help to the garrisons of Pembroke and Tenby.

On 26 May an order was sent to the committee of Plymouth. 'We cannot send those [at Milford] any supplies which could reach them in time, we therefore earnestly recommend it to you to send thither 500 men if with any safety to your own town you can possibly do it; till we [are able] to provide for more'.[17]

At the end of June, the Committee of Both Kingdoms sent an urgent dispatch to the Committee for the Navy. 'The garrisons of Pembroke and Tenby being in great want of ammunition, the Commons have appointed that 100 barrels of gunpowder, with match and bullets proportionable, should be delivered for their use ...'.[18] The order further instructed that as the public store of munitions was very low, the Navy should provide what was needed.

Three days later, Sir Thomas Fairfax, then preparing to raise a siege of Taunton by the Royalists, was informed that the Committee of Both Kingdoms had 'received diverse informations of the distressed state of Pembrokeshire, the whole county with the exceptions of the garrison towns of Pembroke and Tenby being reduced under the power of the enemy. If those be lost, Milford Haven would thereby be in the enemy's power, available for landing there the Irish forces and for all foreign correspondent hitherto by reason of the distance of those parts from all our forces. We have been unable to give them the relief they have desired. When you have relieved Taunton, send to Pembroke and Tenby 200 or 300 men with provisions that they preserve those places and the harvest there, till more effectual supplies can be sent them'.[19]

The situation was indeed desperate but, just as in 1644, a distant battle was to prove the salvation of Laugharne and Poyer. On 14 June at Naseby, the King's forces were heavily defeated and Gerard was urgently recalled to England.[20]

Captain Moulton aboard the guardship *Lyon* described what followed in a letter to the Lord Admiral Warwick at Plymouth, news which was hastily passed on to the Committee of Both Kingdoms: '... the enemy is withdrawn about 10 miles from Pembroke, that Colonel Gerard and all the strangers with 500 foot are gone out of the country, that the Parliament forces are taking the field again ... that the people of the countryside are much divided amongst themselves and not likely to be reduced without the introduction of extraneous forces'.[21]

Warwick's dispatch to the Committee was recorded in the Calendar of State Papers on 1 August 1645, the same day on which Roland Laugharne achieved his greatest victory in west Wales.

With Gerard gone, Laugharne realised that he must re-establish the authority of Parliament in Pembrokeshire. There was still a large Royalist garrison at Haverfordwest, containing some of the men left behind by Gerard, and smaller groups at Carew, Manorbier and Picton. A rumour was also circulating that the Haverfordwest force was about to march out to burn the cornfields in the vicinity of Narberth, to prevent a vital grain supply from falling into Parliamentary hands.

Accordingly, on 29 July, Laugharne left Pembroke with 250 foot, 200 horse and dragoons and two small guns and marched northwards towards Canaston Wood, two or three miles from Narberth, at a spot where the road from Carew crossed the eastern arm of the Daugleddau River.[22] They surprised there a scouting party of seven men from Haverfordwest, killing one and taking the remaining six prisoner.

Near the same spot Laugharne made a rendezvous with a party of seamen from the frigate *Warwick*, commanded by Captain William Batten, who had recently arrived in Milford Haven in order to relieve Captain Swanley of his post. Swanley had been ordered to London to answer a number of charges before Parliament; exactly what they were is unknown, but he was acquitted and subsequently returned to his command. In his letter to Speaker Lenthall, Batten says he supplied Laugharne with 200 men, though Laugharne himself, in a subsequent report to the Commons, puts the number at 130. However strong the reinforcements, the Parliamentarians numbered little more than 1,000, possibly much less.

During the next two days, Laugharne's men crossed the Daugleddau River to occupy the village of Llawhaden with its ancient, dilapidated castle. Llawhaden straddled what was then the main road from Haverfordwest to Carmarthen, which ran a mile or more north of the present A40, winding its way through the tiny settlements of Crundale, Wiston, Llawhaden and Robeston Wathen towards the county borders. Laugharne would have known the area well and would have realised that anyone coming out of Haverfordwest to challenge him would have to follow this route. He had no doubt placed scouts ahead of his main force to report any movements along the roads and they would have warned him that a Royalist picquet armed with field guns was stationed in the ruined twelfth-century shell keep perched on a high earthen mound opposite the church in Wiston.[23]

On Friday, 1 August, Laugharne received word that the Royalists were marching out of Haverfordwest. Their troops were led by Major-Generals Stradling and Egerton and consisted of 450 horse and 1,100 foot with four large guns, and as they lumbered their way through the narrow, twisting lanes towards Colby Moor, Laugharne had a distinct advantage; he had already chosen his spot.

Today Colby Moor is farmland, traversed by minor roads dotted with farm buildings set amongst trees and hedgerows, but in 1645 it was open moorland, which had for generations been the traditional gathering place for musters of the County Militia. Towards the eastern edge of the Moor the land rises gently up into a long plateau which runs back towards Llawhaden. Although contemporary records of the battle are brief and give no indication of exactly how or where the Parliamentary army was deployed, it is likely that Laugharne placed his men on the upward slope and along its crest.[24] As Egerton and Stradling hurried their men, already dusty and tired from the march out of Haverfordwest, into position on the moorland, they would have seen their enemy drawn up less than half a mile distant.[25]

The battle began at about six o'clock in the evening when, as Laugharne reported, 'a small party of our horsemen, hoarded on both sides with 150 musketeers, charged their whole body.' The fighting continued 'very fierce and doubtful for near an hour', with volleys of musketry flashing out across the moorland until Stradling's mounted troops began to waver. A chaotic retreat now took place, with men casting aside their weapons and abandoning their heavy guns in an attempt to save their lives. The Parliamentary cavalry pursued them through the narrow lanes, cutting down the footsoldiers and chasing the mounted troops almost into Haverfordwest. The little picquet at Wiston is said

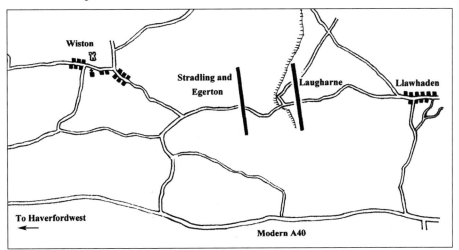

The Battle of Colby Moor, 1 August 1645

Colby Moor, looking westwards from Laugharne's probable position towards the area held by Stradling and Egerton

to have fired off its cannon in an attempt to hinder the pursuit, but was soon overwhelmed. A desperate band of men took refuge in the ancient earthwork known as the Rath overlooking Crundale, but by late evening they too had been slain or captured. Laugharne's victory was complete. The Royalists had lost 150 men killed and over 700 taken prisoner, including Lieutenant-Colonel Price, two majors, seven captains, 22 lieutenants and 'inferior officers'. Also taken were four guns, five barrels of powder, 800 arms and all the carriages and provisions.

That night the victors camped out in the fields to the west of Haverfordwest, rather than attempt an attack on the town in the darkness. At some time before dawn the Royalist horse slipped away and headed for Carmarthen, a move Laugharne probably expected, for he noted in his report 'the night then approaching we might not beset the town to keep in their horse'.[26]

The Iron Age earthwork at Crundale saw the last desperate stand of Royalist troops fleeing Colby Moor

On the next day, Saturday, Haverfordwest was occupied, though the castle still held out. Sunday was observed as a day of rest but on Monday 4 August a bombardment of the castle commenced. The medieval walls, perched massively on a bluff overlooking the river, resisted all efforts to breach them and it was decided to mount a full-scale assault. The storming party pushed its way through the area known as Castle Back, where the narrow streets still preserve their medieval layout, and under fire from the battlements, set alight the gatehouse and scaled the walls. Within minutes they had seized every part of the castle, taking prisoner 120 soldiers and some 20 officers, a cannon, 120 arms and 'some pillage to the soldiers beside the provision'.

In the actions at Colby Moor and at Haverfordwest Laugharne had lost only two men dead and 60 wounded. His haul of prisoners was now more than 800 strong. Those taken at Colby Moor were sent to Captain Batten who placed them aboard the ships anchored in the Haven, where some 450 agreed to take the Covenant and were sent across to Ireland to assist in the defence of Youghal. There is no word as to the fate of the others, but they were probably kept prisoner until such time as it was safe to release them. Their officers also took the Covenant, except two who remained under guard.

Friday 8 August was observed as a Day of Humiliation and Thanksgiving at Haverfordwest, Tenby and Pembroke. The next day, Laugharne wrote to the Speaker describing the victory at Colby Moor, mentioning that 'on this day we drew our force of horse and foot before Carew castle and are drawing up our ordnance to plant them before the castle, calling upon the Lord of Hosts for a blessing'.[27]

Carew soon capitulated, but Picton proved a more stubborn prospect. The garrison there held out for three weeks, finally surrendering on 20 September. Manorbier offered little resistance, so that by the end of September there were no Royalist strongholds left in Pembrokeshire.

Word of the victory at Colby Moor was received in London with celebration. A delighted Parliament awarded £10 to the messenger who brought the news, whilst it was agreed that 28 September was to be observed in the capital as a Day of Thanksgiving for the recent successes. It was also resolved by the Commons that Laugharne should be thanked for his services by means of a special letter signed by the Speaker, though financial rewards were not forgotten; the rich estate of Slebech, sequestrated from the Royalist and catholic John Barlow was settled on Laugharne and his heirs 'for ever'.

There were still some loose ends to be tied up before Laugharne could count his duty as done. On Pembrokeshire's north-east border Newcastle Emlyn was holding out for the King, as did Aberystwyth further north. Colonel Lewes was sent to Emlyn to deal with the castle there – it surrendered in December – and Rice Powell was dispatched to Aberystwyth, the capture of which proved to be no easy matter. Built by Edward I during the 1270s to protect the town, it was concentric in design, with two wards, one within the other, and a third, outer, ward on the north-western side. In 1637, on King Charles' instructions, a mint had been established within the decaying walls. This was withdrawn to Shrewsbury shortly after the war began and the building was garrisoned by Colonel Whiteley, who maintained it as an important bullion store, as well as a base for Royalist raids into the surrounding countryside.

Aberystwyth Castle had come under attack on several occasions during the war, but it was not until November 1645 that a serious effort was made to reduce it. Many of Powell's troops were said to have come from Cardiganshire and he was assisted by Colonel John Jones of Nanteos and by John Vaughan of Trawscoed.[28] The latter may have been regarded with some suspicion because of his Royalist sympathies; though not active in the King's cause, he was believed to have offered help to Powell in order to win favour.

As the siege dragged on, food supplies became a problem and the Parliamentary soldiers began to pillage in all directions, seizing not only victuals but prisoners. Their raids caused panic and bitterness amongst the people of the area:

> About the 8 December, Colonel Jones of Nanteos and about twenty soldiers came by night to Peniarth and there took Lewis Owen of Peniarth and Mr Francis Herbert of Dolguog (who did there sojourn for fear of the Parliamenteers) in their beds, and carried them to Cardiganshire.

> Jan 2. Cardiganshire men came over to Merionethshire, as far as Barmouth and on Saturday night, being the third [January], plundered that village and so went away in their boats.

Complaints were made to Rowland Laugharne, who issued strict instructions against pillage and who then wrote to reassure the frightened populace:

> These are to certify, whom it may concern, that what inroads were by my soldiers made in Montgomery and Merioneddshires were without orders and commands from me, and was done in my absence. Therefore, I desire a free and usual intercourse and correspondence to be carried on between the counties of my association and the said Counties of Montgomery and Merionedd: promising that if hereafter any of my men commit the like offences they shall be exactly punished according to the law of war.
> Dated 4 February 1646.[29]

The trials of the inhabitants of Aberystwyth came to an end early in 1646, when the garrison of the castle entered into negotiations for surrender. A letter from Laugharne's headquarters, signed only by 'E.L', described the final capitulation:

Sir,

Though we have lain long before Aberystwyth Castle, which is a place of great strength, yet it hath pleased God at last to give it into our hands. I have sent you enclosed the copy of the Articles of Agreement between Col. Rice Powell and Col. Ro. Whitney [*sic*] for the surrender thereof. When you read them you will find we have gained good terms for them, so that now we are ready to be put into a capacity for further service, either for Carnarvon, or to assist against Raglan, or what other service shall be thought meet, if the soldiers have but money.[30]

The articles of surrender were signed on 12 April and allowed the Royalist officers to march out with their swords by their sides. The foot soldiers could not carry arms as they left and many of them took the road to Harlech, eventually moving on to Denbigh.[31] Colonel Whiteley and five of his officers were given safe-conducts to go wherever the King might be.[32]

Nearer to home, Carmarthenshire remained a problem. There were an estimated 700 Royalists dotted about the county, of whom about 400 possessed firearms. Their mounted troops numbered about 200 under the command of Major-General Stradling, whilst the militia were armed with no more than pitchforks and clubs.[33] It was clear to many of the leading citizens of Carmarthen that the town could not hope to mount a successful defence should there be an attack. Therefore, on 5 September 1645, the Commissioners and Gentry of Carmarthen addressed a letter to Laugharne and to the Committee of Pembrokeshire. They explained that they had taken into consideration 'the unhappy effects ... that war may produce between the County of Pembroke and the neighbouring counties of Carmarthen and Cardigan ... the preservation of which you and we equally pretend, namely our religion, loyalty and laws, though we have been hitherto so unhappy as to endeavour the preserving of these by destroying one another'.[34] They went on to suggest a treaty between the three counties that would produce a better effect than war and asked for a meeting of representatives under safe conduct.

Laugharne was as anxious as they were to avoid further bloodshed. On 25 September he informed them that he would accept a treaty if full declarations were made of obedience to the King and Parliament. The Royalist horse should be detained or delivered direct to him and four representatives of the Carmarthen committee should be sent to negotiate with him at Haverfordwest. He added that 'we shall be ready upon your compliance to protect the common people and such of the gentry as we shall find capable of protection and refer the exempted to Superior Jurisdiction'.[35]

There seems to have been a hiccup in the proceedings at this point for no meeting had taken place by 2 October, and after a delay of eight days the Carmarthen committee wrote anxiously that they had heard that he was advancing into Carmarthenshire, 'which makes us send this bearer to receive your command, which shall be performed by us who profess and declare ourselves to be for the King and Parliament and will, with the best assistance we can, aid you with our lives and fortunes in anything that may conduce to the Parliament's service'.[36]

On the same day, Laugharne wrote from St Clears requesting a meeting there. This provoked an immediate response from Carmarthen, assuring him that there were 1,500 men in the town who were ready to support the King and Parliament. 'Tomorrow four of us will not fail to wait upon you. We desire you not to march till then. The castle we have not as yet, but it has been promised to us tomorrow; which with the hazard of our lives we shall keep for the King and Parliament.'

A number of conditions were requested by the Carmarthen committee, some of whom were ex-Royalists. Their objections may have centred on the demand that they take the oath of the Covenant. On 11 October, Laugharne made it clear that to refuse the Covenant was 'an open profession of enmity to king and Parliament;[37] acceptance was the only way of bringing peace to the area. This veiled threat resulted in a declaration in which the leading citizens gave repeated assurances that with their lives and fortunes they would assist the forces raised by Parliament. It was signed by the mayor, Thomas Griffiths, and by 31 other gentlemen. They may have been spurred into action by the sight of 2,000 Parliamentary foot soldiers and 600 horsemen gathering in the fields around the town. The evening before the formal surrender was spent in the interchange of parleys, which ended at about 11 o'clock at night. On the following day, so Laugharne informed William Lenthall, the speaker of the Commons, 'at nine o'clock in the morning 1,500 club men of the county marched out at one gate and I entered at the other'.[38] The garrison of Carmarthen Castle retired to Newcastle Emlyn, which was not at that point under siege, and Laugharne was able to take complete possession of the town and its fortifications.

The First Civil War was now coming to an end in west Wales. The people of the area must have hoped that the bloodshed was finally over and that they could resume the normal, half-forgotten rhythms of their lives. Perhaps it was the expectation of peace that prompted John Poyer to present gifts to the churches of Pembroke. He is said to have given chalices to both St Michael's and St Mary's, though only the latter has survived. Known as 'Poyer's Pot', it is now in the safe-keeping of the National Museum of Wales. Around the bowl of the chalice can be read the inscription 'The Guift of Captayne John Poyer Governor of the Towne and Castle of Pembroke to the parish church of St Marye in Pembroke Anno domini 1645'.

If the chalices were intended as a symbol of peace, it was a premature one. Laugharne, Poyer and Powell were about to enter a period of personal difficulties which would be every bit as turbulent as their military campaigns had been.

13   Poyer's Troubles

Following his return from London in the autumn of 1645, John Poyer resumed the governorship of Pembroke Castle. His personal finances, however, seem to have been in a precarious state, for towards the end of November he addressed a heartfelt petition to Parliament:

> During the last four years he has been Governor of Pembroke; he had prevented Royalist forces, first under Carbery, afterwards under Gerard, from seizing Pembroke Town and Castle: he had spent all his own money, together with £2,000 borrowed from well-affected inhabitants of Pembroke and its neighbourhood, in repairing the walls and gates of the town and supplying its garrison with money, arms, ammunition and clothing.
>
> When Gerard's forces were beleaguering Pembroke, they burned dwelling-houses, barns and corn-ricks and stole household goods and cattle from people who had lent him money for the services of the Parliament.
>
> He prayed the House to grant him, out of delinquents' estates, a sum of money sufficient to enable him to discharge his obligations to those who lent him money in the service of the Parliament.[1]

The petition was received by the House of Lords, which recommended it to the Commons on 3 December. No immediate action was taken, perhaps because Parliament had many other matters to consider, though the members may have been waiting to hear from Poyer in person. At some time in December, Poyer travelled from Pembrokeshire to London 'on the special service of Parliament'. He had been called to appear before a committee which had been established to investigate the charges laid against him in April by the Pembrokeshire Committee. Almost as soon as he arrived he was arrested because of two actions-at-law initiated by Captain Swanley. The accusations clearly mystified and shocked Poyer, because on 8 January 1646 he wrote from the Bailiff's House in Westminster requesting Parliament to order his release and to discover why Swanley had caused him to be detained.

The House of Lords decided that the whole matter needed further investigation and resolved that both Poyer and Swanley should appear before the members to plead their cases. On 16 January, Rowland Laugharne wrote to the Speaker from Haverfordwest, pointing out that 'Mr Lort and Mr. Eliot, the Committee agent, are so taken up with the prosecution of private malice that they can spare no thought for the public good ... I perceive Capt. Poyer is molested by some gentlemen who in our distress were our greatest enemies and whom only success induced to profess our friendship'.[2]

The Commons was unmoved by this plea, perhaps because on 3 February another petition was received from John Eliot who believed that the Governor of Pembroke had further charges to answer. Eliot pointed out 'that Poyer has applied to the House for the payment of £400 alleged to have been borrowed and expended by him in the service of the State, whereas he has in his hands money and goods of great value and unaccounted for, he prays that Poyer may be summoned to attend the Committee of Accounts, there to answer the petitioner's charges and show particulars of his disbursements'.[3]

Shortly after receiving this document, the Commons requested Simon Thelwall, chairman of the committee examining Poyer's petition for relief, to tackle 'the business of Mr John Poyer, late Mayor of Pembroke'.[4] Thelwall was given a week in which to prepare a report, but there is no record that he actually did so, or submitted it to Parliament.

John Poyer remained in London for a long period, for unless documentary evidence to the contrary has been lost, it appears that he did not return to Pembrokeshire until June 1647. Exactly why he was detained for so long is also unclear, unless some sort of bail bond had been set, which he and his friends were unable to meet.

In the meantime, the Commons granted Poyer £200 for his support whilst in London, a large sum for the time, but it must have quickly evaporated. As well as food and clothing, there were lodgings – or jail expenses if he was kept in custody – to find for himself and his wife Elizabeth, who had joined him. There were probably also legal fees to pay, as Poyer prepared a defence in answer to the charges brought against him. There is certainly no doubt that by 1647 the Poyers were living in great poverty. Their situation was so difficult that Elizabeth in desperation appealed to Ann Laugharne for financial help. Her brief letter is undated and is addressed to the 'most honoured' Madam Laugharne: 'Thanks for your unspeakable favours to me and especially since I came to this place, without which undoubtedly I should have starved. Prays the loan of 5s, I have not the wherewith to shift me, neither shoes to go out ... your pardon for my presumption and humblemost your servant. Elizabeth Poyer'. (In petitions presented to Charles II after the Restoration, Elizabeth makes it clear that she had left her four young children behind in Pembroke in order to be at her husband's side.)

Whilst Poyer was detained in London, events elsewhere continued to move at speed. Following his defeat at Naseby, King Charles had marched westwards with the remnants of his army to Hereford, which he reached on 18 June. After a brief stay he moved into Wales, entering Abergavenny on 1 July and two days later arriving at Raglan Castle, the splendid home of the Marquess of Worcester, one of the most committed of his supporters. Whilst at Raglan, strenuous efforts were made to divert the King's attention from his burden of cares. So successful were they that Sir Edward Walker, secretary of the Royalist Council of War, felt that it was as if 'the genius of the place had conspired with our fates, we were there all lulled to sleep with sports and entertainments; as if no crown had been at stake, or in any danger to be lost'.[5] But reality did insist on intruding. It soon became clear that the traditional loyalty of the Welsh towards their sovereign had been eroded. This was in part due to the fact that, after the defeat at Naseby, Charles' secret correspondence had fallen into the hands of the Parliamentarians. Amongst the vast trove of correspondence, cabinet books and other documents that were taken, there were letters which proved that he had sought to obtain further reinforcements not only from Ormonde in Ireland, but also from the Catholic Duke of Lorraine. Once Parliament had published the correspondence, it deepened the fears held by many people that the King intended a restoration of Catholicism and was willing to involve foreign princes and their troops in the pacification of his realm. There was also considerable resentment amongst the Welsh people over the numbers of English troops who were garrisoning Welsh strongholds such as Cardiff Castle. The nation was still expected to supply large numbers of men for the Royalist war effort and excessive amounts of money to equip and feed them were being demanded from communities already shattered by years of warfare. In Glamorgan and Pembrokeshire in particular, the wholesale looting carried out by Gerard's troops had not been forgotten.

A movement grew up which aimed to resist further military depredations, one of several such which arose more or less spontaneously in areas which had suffered particular hardships. Known elsewhere as the Clubmen Associations, in Glamorganshire it was called the Peaceable Army and its members were not only drawn from the ranks of the Glamorganshire levies who had been pressed into military service, but also included Royalist gentlemen and those with more Puritan beliefs, such as Edward Pritchard of Llancaiach and Miles Button of Cottrell, Rowland Laugharne's brother-in-law. When, at the end of July, it seemed that the levies would be required to march out of Wales to face a Scots army threatening Hereford, the men mutinied and refused to move. Within days, the Peaceable Army had attracted new recruits, some sources putting the eventual number at 10,000, a possible exaggeration. Its members were determined to prevent a repeat of the plundering which had marked earlier troop movements through the country. Whilst they expressed no opposition to the Royalist cause, they acknowledged their obligations to defend Glamorgan from attack and demanded a face-to-face meeting with the King to present a list of grievances.[6]

This took place on 29 July at St Fagans with, according to one report, 'the gentlemen on horseback and the levies drawn up in battle array'.[7] When the King asked them why they had gathered together, he was told that it was for 'the preservation of their county'. Charles assured them that he too wished for that and asked what else they wanted. The articles of grievance were then presented to him. They included demands that the English garrison at Cardiff, which was particularly resented, should be sent away and the present governor, Sir Timothy Tyrell, replaced by a Welshman; the £7,000 in arrears demanded earlier in the year by Charles Gerard should be remitted; and all papists should be driven out of the county.[8]

The meeting was adjourned until the next day and when it reassembled at Cefn Onn, north of Cardiff, the King had no choice but to agree to the demands. It was a humiliating experience for him; as Arthur Trevor, a Royalist supporter, noted in a letter to a friend, to negotiate with the King before obeying his commands might signal the end of the monarchy.[9] In addition Charles dismissed Sir Charles Gerard from his command in South Wales, replacing him with Sir Jacob Astley; Sir Timothy Tyrell was replaced by Sir Richard Bassett of Beaupre and the question of the arrears was dropped.

King Charles, disillusioned and despairing of being able to raise sufficient troops, moved on to Brecon. Within a few days, the Peaceable Army issued a proclamation denying that its members held anti-English views and stating that 'wee understand it to bee generally bruited that our present beinge and joining together is to make a nationall quarrell betweene us and the English here among us, naming them English doggs'.[10]

In early September, the Scottish army retreated from Hereford, but on the 10th Prince Rupert surrendered Bristol to a Parliamentary army led by Sir Thomas Fairfax. With the enemy now poised to the east and with Rowland Laugharne triumphant to the west, Charles had no choice but to leave south Wales. On the 13th, he departed, never to return. The situation he left behind was far from settled. Sir Jacob Astley found Glamorgan to be in such a disturbed state that he had no hope of supporting the King with more troops. In a letter to Prince Rupert he gave vent to his frustrations: 'It must be power to rule this people and not entreaties with a cap in hand to such as deserve the halter'.[11]

After his departure from Raglan on 13 September 1645, King Charles had moved northwards to Ludlow and then on to Chester. On 24 September, at Rowton Heath, two miles from the city, his army suffered another defeat. Whilst the King watched from the Phoenix Tower on the city walls, the troop of horse which had loyally followed him since Naseby was cut to pieces.[12] Rather than be trapped in the city by the victorious Parliamentarians, Charles headed for Denbigh, where he took refuge for three days in the castle. Whilst there, he learned of yet another disastrous defeat at Philliphaugh, where on 13 September, the Marquess of Montrose's army was decimated by the forces of David Leslie. Whatever hopes Charles may have had about joining up with Montrose were now in tatters. From Denbigh, the King made for Newark, which he reached on 4 October, remaining there until the beginning of November.

The war was slowly winding down. The last Royalist strongholds in the Midlands and the West were falling one by one and in Hampshire and Wiltshire Cromwell was dousing the final embers of resistance. Sensing defeat, some of the King's most ardent supporters were fleeing abroad or were attempting to reach an agreement with Parliament.[13] Amongst those heading for the Continent were Prince Rupert and a group of his followers, made bitter by the King's angry treatment of the Prince after the surrender of Bristol and by the dismissal of Rupert's friend, Sir Richard Willes, as governor of Newark.

With few options left open to him, Charles returned to Oxford, but as the autumn turned to winter, the situation steadily worsened. Basing House (near Basingstoke, Hampshire), a bastion of royalism, fell in October, as did Tiverton (Devon), to be followed not long after by Bolton Castle in Yorkshire and Shelford House in Nottinghamshire, where 140 of the defenders were slaughtered. Newark was besieged and Hereford, its Royalist garrison making only a token resistance, fell to Colonel John Birch. At the beginning of 1646, the Prince of Wales left the West Country for a temporary refuge on the Isles of Scilly.

There was a brief glimmer of hope for Charles when, in early February 1646, Edward Carne of Ewenni in Glamorgan, a particularly vocal critic of the new Puritan regime in Cardiff, declared for the King. Gathering together a force of like-minded men he marched on Cardiff and summoned Edward Pritchard, who had replaced Sir Richard Bassett as governor at the further behest of the Peaceable Army, to surrender the castle. Pritchard refused to do so and sent an urgent message to Rowland Laugharne requesting help. To the Parliamentarians it was obvious that this rebellion, unless nipped in the bud, would lead to renewed fighting. Carne was expecting help from the Royalists of Monmouthshire under Sir Charles Kemeys and Rowland Laugharne prepared to march from west Wales 'with about 250 of his own horse and foot and some others of the country that rose and joined him'.[14] By Monday, 16 February, Laugharne was drawing close to Cardiff. The Parliamentarian Vice-Admiral Crowther, learning of his approach, sailed his ships close to Cardiff, and 'shot off one piece of ordnance and then another and so six pieces were shot off to let them know at the Castle relief was then at hand'.[15] As Laugharne approached, backed by the troops of Bussy Mansell, a former Parliamentary Commissioner of Array who had been appointed Colonel-General in Glamorgan, Colonel Carne marched his men to the heathland a mile north of the town where they joined forces with the troops of Sir Charles Kemeys. The fighting began almost immediately, the Parliamentary troops behaving, as it was later reported 'with such gallantry that we routed them [the Royalists] and made them fly several ways. Carne himself stayed not to keep them together, but like a vagabond ran up and down, bemoaning himself, and glad he was that he had a nimble horse, not to charge, but to fly'.[16]

This description was probably propaganda. Carne was still on hand on 19 February to negotiate the articles of surrender, by which his followers escaped harsh punishment. Carne himself was imprisoned and fined, the ordinary soldiers were allowed to return to their homes, whilst the officers withdrew to other Royalist garrisons within a 50 mile radius. The articles ensured that the use of the Common Prayer Book would not be proscribed, an important concession to the committed Anglicans of Glamorgan. That Laugharne was prepared to agree to this is not so surprising, as his puritanism was not of an extreme variety. He had already shown a willingness to compromise by forming alliances with the gentry of Brecon and Radnor and had reached a private understanding with Lord Carbery by which the latter enjoyed his protection.[17]

Unfortunately the newly achieved accord at Cardiff was wrecked the day after it was signed. On 20 February, as Carne's men were withdrawing from Cardiff, some sort of disagreement arose between the two sides and fighting again broke out. The details are unclear, but Laugharne's men pursued the enemy for seven miles before the action was over. In the two days of fighting, Carne's men suffered heavy casualties, some 250 being killed and over 800 taken prisoner.

As a reward for his services, Rowland Laugharne received the thanks of the House of Commons and was appointed commander-in-chief in Glamorgan. A peace of sorts had been achieved in south Wales, though Raglan Castle was under siege and did not surrender until 19 August.

Elsewhere, on 21 March, Sir Jacob Astley surrendered the last Royalist field army at Stow-on-the-Wold. Exeter opened its gates to Sir Thomas Fairfax on 9 April. It was clear that the target of the Parliamentary army would soon be Oxford. Determined to evade capture, King Charles left the city on 27 April. Disguised as a servant and in the company of John Asburnham, a loyal follower, and Michael Hudson, one of his chaplains, he made his way towards Newark, following a circuitous route to avoid capture. Royalist Newark was now under siege, but its real attraction for Charles was that it was encircled by a combined English and Scottish army. Knowing the Scots to be war-weary and suspicious of the English Parliamentarians, he hoped that by reaching an agreement with them, he could checkmate any further moves by his enemies. He had in fact been in secret negotiations with the Scots for some weeks and by sending Hudson in advance of his arrival, he managed to obtain a promise that they would not force him to do anything against his conscience and that they would support him if Parliament did not restore his rights and privileges.

On 5 May, Charles entered the Scottish camp at Southwell, a few miles to the north of Newark. His arrival was 'a Matter of Much Astonishment', as Leven, the

Scots commander, assured the Committee of Both Kingdoms. With so valuable a pawn in their grasp, the Scots were in no mood to heed Parliament's demand that the King should be sent to Warwick Castle. On 7 May, they struck camp and retreated northwards, taking Charles with them. If nothing else convinced Charles of the foolishness of his escapade, the treatment he now received surely did so. He was a prisoner and his ride from Oxford had been his last real taste of freedom.

After six days of steady marching, the Scots army arrived at Newcastle on 13 May. This was to be the King's place of detention for the next seven months and during that time he entered into a series of negotiations with Parliament. As a result, in July he received a deputation of commissioners who brought with them a list of proposals known as the Nineteen Propositions, which they hoped he would accept. A rehash of suggestions made on a number of previous occasions, the Propositions demanded amongst other things that Charles should take the Covenant, that he should relinquish control of the militia for a period of 20 years, that there should be an abolition of episcopacy and that heavy penalties should be levied upon all Royalists. Furthermore, Parliament was to nominate all important officers of state.[18]

The King gave no direct answer to these suggestions, writing to Queen Henrietta Maria that 'all my endeavours must be the delaying my answer'. So successfully did he prevaricate that months of negotiations ensued, whilst at Westminster members of both Houses grew steadily more frustrated with a sovereign who seemed to them deceitful and untrustworthy.

There was still no stated policy within Parliament of deposing the monarch, but amongst soldiers of the New Model Army a different consensus was growing. Many of its officers saw the victory over the Royalists as an opportunity to establish a more egalitarian and godly society. Richard Baxter, one of the Model Army's leading chaplains, became aware of this growing radicalism when he visited troops shortly after Naseby. The belief that Charles was a tyrant was openly voiced and Baxter realised that there was a determination to bring him down and even execute him if necessary.

The New Model Army had been created in November 1644, after fierce debate amongst the Parliamentary leaders over exactly how the war should be prosecuted and what the long term aims of victory should be. A completely new military force was called for and was quickly formed: a national standing army, its members disciplined, well-equipped and well paid under the leadership of a unified and independent command. This truly revolutionary army consisted of 21,400 men, divided into ten regiments of horse, each of 600 men, 12 foot regiments of 1,200 men each and a regiment of 1,000 dragoons. They wore a uniform coat of red and were commanded by Thomas Fairfax, a man of limited military experience but known for his devotion to the Parliamentary cause and his ability to inspire the troops. Within a year of its creation the New Model had destroyed the King's army at Naseby, leaving the Royalist cause in tatters.

Now, with the winding down of hostilities, there was a widespread demand for a reduction in taxation, with a corresponding decrease in Parliament's military forces. Opposition was particularly strong in 'the turbulent county of Glamorgan', where the continued levying of contributions in order to support Laugharne's forces was biting deep. On 4 August 1646, in an attempt to head off possible trouble in south Wales, the Commons proposed to disband all the Glamorgan troops except Bussy Mansell's horse. Five companies of foot would be stationed at Cardiff and Swansea, though the disbanded men would be offered service in Ireland on the promise of a month's pay, over and above what would be paid to those who chose to leave the army.[19] A Parliamentary committee also reported that a troop of 200 horse placed in the three south-western counties of Wales should be enough to ensure quiet. Laugharne may well have protested about these moves to Parliament, for no obvious reduction of his forces took place. The report, however, added the following recommendations:

> If Tenby and Pembroke are to be kept as garrisons it is much to be desired that two commanders with their companies may be sent down to these garrisons out of the army of Sir Thomas Fairfax, that the county of Pembroke may not suffer, as it now does, by the oppressions and tyranny of the Governor.[20]

Once again John Poyer had been targeted by his enemies, but as before, no immediate action was taken against him.

During the winter of 1646, an event occurred which disturbed Rowland Laugharne sufficiently for him to write directly to the House of Commons to assure the members of his continued loyalty. In a letter dated 29 December, Laugharne, backed by several members of the Pembroke County Committee, informed the House that a communication had been received from Michael Hudson, the royal chaplain who had escorted King Charles to the Scottish camp outside Newark.[21] Hudson's letter assured Laugharne of the 'great value his Majesty has of him, desiring his assistance, with his other friends, to restore him to his rights, telling him ... that if the Parliament should not bring up the King with honour and safety before new Year's Day, all his Majesty's friends should declare for him'. Accompanying Hudson's letter was a copy of a further note apparently signed by the King, which requested Hudson to let his supporters know that he would grant any demands which would result in a Royalist rising. Laugharne explained to the Commons that he had immediately sent all the correspondence to Parliament, and that the man who had delivered Hudson's letter was safely under arrest.

It was a strange incident, which raised some unanswered questions. Why should Rowland Laugharne, a noted Parliamentarian, have been contacted by the

Royalists? In the event of a rebellion, did the plotters hope to bring in rein-forcements through Milford Haven? There is no evidence one way or the other and none that indicates Laugharne's involvement in any kind of plot, but doubts about his loyalty had already surfaced amongst MPs at Westminster.

In February 1647, Parliament, which from the outset had been doubtful of the political neutrality of the New Model Army, decided to press ahead with the thorny problem of disbandment. It was decreed that 10,000 foot and 6,000 horse should be dismissed and that a new army of 12,600 men should be formed for service in Ireland. A small field army would remain garrisoned at various loca-tions across England and Wales. No more than six weeks arrears of pay would be given to disbanded men, even though the foot soldiers were owed 18 weeks and the horse 43 weeks. Furthermore, non-Presbyterians and Members of Parliament were not to serve as officers.

These terms were greeted with hostility. The army issued a declaration which requested full payment of arrears, pensions for war widows and disabled soldiers and guarantees against future conscription. When Parliament refused to consider the declaration and again ordered a disbandment, the troops, now concentrated at Newmarket, refused to do so. Many believed themselves to have been betrayed and began to look for a way of forcing the Commons to grant their aims.

If the measures for troop reductions were met with anger within the New Model Army, they were welcomed with relief by the civilian population of south Wales. A garrison of 150 men was to be retained at Pembroke, with a force of 100 each at Tenby, Haverfordwest and Carmarthen. On 25 March, the Commons decided that the castles at the last two towns should be disgarrisoned and the buildings themselves rendered unusable.

In spite of all John Eliot's efforts, it was also resolved that John Poyer should continue as governor of Pembroke. Rice Powell was confirmed as governor of Tenby. Less than a fortnight later came a ruling which reflected the doubts now entertained about Rowland Laugharne by some at Westminster. A vote was taken in Parliament on 8 April 'that 100 horse and 100 dragoons shall be kept for the safety of south Wales under Major-General Laugharne to be commanded in chief by that general as other Horse are'. Fifty-five members voted for the motion, but a substantial number, 53, were against it. As a result, it was further resolved that command of the dragoons should be assumed by Colonel Okey. Although Laugharne thus remained nominally in charge of the forces in south Wales, he cannot have missed the point implicit in Okey's appointment. He no longer enjoyed the complete trust of Parliament and his actions were to be monitored by an experienced officer of the New Model Army.[22]

Four months later, in June 1647, Laugharne had the opportunity to make clear where his loyalties lay. King Charles had been handed over to Parliament by the Scots on 30 January and in February he was taken to Holdenby House in Northamptonshire. The leaders of the New Model Army, realising that he would be an invaluable bargaining counter in their dispute with Parliament, sent a detachment of 400 horse to Holdenby to remove the King. Charles was taken to Newmarket, where officers of the Army Command, including Oliver Cromwell, were awaiting him.

As news of this new detention of the monarch spread abroad, it gave added impetus to the unrest swirling through the country. In Glamorgan a group of discontented gentlemen, including members of the Stradling, Bassett and Merrick families, decided that it was time to topple the local Parliamentary Committee, which had done nothing to reduce the amount of monthly assessments or to remove radical puritans from office. The ringleaders called upon the High Constable of the Hundred of Miskin to summon all able-bodied men to gather at Cowbridge to support King Charles. This hastily assembled group then marched on Cardiff and upon reaching Llandaff, sent a message to Edward Pritchard, the governor of the castle, challenging his authority.

Laugharne wasted no time in responding to news of the rising. On 17 June he wrote from Carmarthen to the Speaker of the Commons:

> I am drawing up my forces hitherwards to suppress the Insolency; and find my soldiers, I thank God, very cheerful and inoffensive [sic] when they came, not capitulating for any conditions. I shall (God willing) never desert my first principles for the Parlt of England. The issue of this insurrection, probably, will occasion speedy and frequent records of this address by him who is, Sir
>
> The State's and Your loyal servant.[23]

Four days later he was in Cardiff and was able to inform the Speaker that the principal ringleaders, about 50 in all, had already fled the country. As a result of his prompt action, Laugharne received an acknowledgement from Sir Thomas Fairfax of his 'acceptable services to the Kingdom'.

At about the same time, John Poyer's long detention in London came to an end. There is no record of the outcome of the investigation into his conduct (see pp.99-100) which had commenced in December 1645. The only clue is that Poyer was later to claim that he had been sent back to Pembroke to assume command of the garrison, which might indicate a not guilty verdict. John Eliot, typically, was able to supply an entirely different reason for Poyer's departure from the capital. 'He was served with a warrant from the Committee of Accounts to answer certain charges that more than £6,000 had not been accounted for to the State by him ... but the day he was served with the warrant ... he took horse and went out of Towne and never appeared there since'.[24] If this charge was true, then Poyer, by his flight, gave every appearance of guilt.

No sooner had he arrived in Pembroke than he allowed himself to be drawn back into the old feud with the Lorts, this time with an added intensity. Whether there was some new cause for animosity or whether he was paying off old scores is unclear, but within weeks Roger, Sampson and John Lort were imprisoned in Pembroke Castle. Poyer claimed that his life had been in danger; the three men had apparently attacked him on the highway and had even attempted to assassinate him in church.

Months later an anonymous writer, possibly Eliot again, described the event in a letter written from Windsor, and gave another explanation: 'Poyer imprisoned Roger, Sampson and John Lort, solely in an attempt to squeeze money out of them: on one occasion when he kept them for forty-four hours in an open space of ground, without even bread and water, they had to lie on the bare ground, not even straw being provided for their relief'.[25]

The affair quickly became known throughout Wales and even beyond its borders. In August 1647, Sir Edward Perceval received a letter from Hereford, which informed him that 'the Lortes were imprisoned by the Mayor of Pembroke upon pretence of some plot against him but he declares not the particulars'.

News of the Lorts' predicament eventually reached the authorities in London, for in September Poyer received and ignored a direct order from his military superior, Sir Thomas Fairfax, who had been appointed general of all the Parliamentary forces on 19 July 1647, instructing him to release his prisoners. It took the guile of the Assize judges at Haverfordwest to achieve what Fairfax had not; they summoned Poyer to Haverfordwest under promise of protection and kept him there until he agreed to release the prisoners.

Poyer was now guilty of military disobedience, as well as his disregard of the warrant from the Committee of Accounts mentioned by Eliot. He must have known he would be called to give some explanation of his actions, but he might still have saved himself, even at this late stage, had he not stubbornly refused to co-operate with further directives issued by Parliament. An Ordinance of 24 December 1647 allowed for two months pay in cash to be made to members of disbanded units, with debentures or bonds for the remainder of their arrears, provided that they had been in service before 6 August of that year. If they had enrolled after that date they were to receive bonds only. An indemnity was to be granted to all soldiers for their actions during the war. Furthermore, all claims were to be made through the Commissioners for Monthly Assessments in each county. The Pembrokeshire Commissioners included Roger and Sampson Lort, Sir Richard Philipps and John Eliot. By the time the Ordinance was received in Pembroke it is likely that Colonel Fleming, an officer of the New Model Army, had already arrived in the town. He carried with him a commission from Fairfax appointing him as governor of the castle, together with an order that Poyer should present himself at Windsor to explain his conduct.

Incredibly, Poyer again refused to co-operate and barred Fleming from the castle. There is no rational explanation for this piece of folly and Poyer never gave one, though he must have been aware of the likely consequences. If Laugharne had been present in Pembrokeshire, he might have been able to persuade Poyer to back down, but he was at Windsor, receiving instructions for the disbanding of his own forces. No one else amongst Poyer's associates or his family is known to have tried to reason with him, but if they did, he ignored them. Perhaps he was too blinkered or too stubborn or too distrustful of the machinations of his enemies to think clearly. It is probable that he feared an inquiry into his financial dealings, particularly in regard to the revenues of Carew Castle.[26] If he thought his chances of a fair hearing were slim, he may have seen no alternative to defiance. One charge which was not levelled at him at that particular moment was that he was plotting with the Royalists, though a movement to restore the King with the aid of the Scots was widely rumoured.

News of Poyer's intransigence quickly spread across the country. It was already known in Windsor on 12 January, when the anonymous letter quoted on the previous page was written. The author of it was in no doubt about what motivated Poyer.

> He was not above thirty-six men strong in the castle but now he is gotten to be about 200 as it is reported. He is so desperately guilty and owns neither house nor land and it is well known that he is neither for the King, Parliament or Army, but his own interest of free-booting…
>
> He is seldom or ever sober but constantly drunk in the afternoon and a great swearer and a stiffe maintainer of the Book of Common Prayer…
>
> He hath within this three weeks taken prisoner Mr. William Hinton, Mayor of Pembroke last year and one Mr. Matthew Bowen who was elected Mayor this year but the said Poyer deposed him and all the ablest men in the town hoping to get monies out of them or to make them turn to his party…
>
> He breaks open people's houses in the Town and Country and takes out what provisions he pleaseth and brings it into the Castle. He hath drawn all the Catell of that part of the Country within shot of the Castle and kills them at pleasure for provisions for the Castle.

If this striking picture of what was happening at Pembroke is true, it suggests several possibilities. The first is that Poyer was frantically provisioning the castle against military action; the second that he was a man driven to extremes by the reality of his situation; and the third that he had become ruthless in his attempts to preserve his grip on the town and castle.[27]

The question of sending troops to deal with Poyer had already been discussed by Army leaders. Their decision seems to have been commonly known, because the Windsor letter ends with the following words: 'Forces are shortly to go down and its hoped he shall have no quarter … but is left to the Law to receive condigne punishment upon the Gallows'.

14   The Second Civil War

In November 1647, King Charles was being held in confinement at Carisbrooke Castle on the Isle of Wight. On 17 November, he sent a letter to the Commons asking for a resumption of talks and offering a number of concessions, including the suggestions that he should give up control of the militia, grant a number of free pardons and become a Presbyterian for three years. No answer was made until, following a further approach from the King, Parliament drew up the Four Bills. The main points of the Bills repeated some of the Nineteen Propositions: that there should be no royal control of the militia for 20 years and that episcopacy should be abolished. The Bills further proposed that the Book of Common Prayer should be banned, that leading Royalists should be put on trial, and that funds should be made available to pay the New Model Army. Furthermore, Parliament was to meet whenever and wherever it thought fit and all honours granted since the beginning of the war were to be annulled.[1]

The Bills were presented to the King not as a basis for negotiation but as legislation needing his signature. He was given four days to consider the matter, but at the end of that period he refused to sign. Charles believed that to do so would be to surrender his prerogatives to an authoritarian Parliament.

The deputation which presented the Bills to the King may well have wondered at the presence at Carisbrooke of three representatives from the kingdom of Scotland. The Earls of Lanark, Loudoun and Lauderdale had arrived on the Isle of Wight hoping to achieve an accord with Charles which would check the growing power of the Army.

There were fears that the religious radicals within the military would achieve control of the political agenda and that as a result the Presbyterian Church of Scotland would be under threat.[2] Accordingly, from mid-1647, the three earls had begun discreet negotiations with the King and now had arrived at Carisbrooke to suggest to him that, in return for military assistance to deal with the New Model Army, he should accept state Presbyterianism for three years and outlaw some of the more extreme religious sects.[3] To these proposals Charles acquiesced and he and the earls signed a secret pact known as the Engagement, his copy of which was placed in a lead casket and buried in a secret place in the castle garden. Charles entered into the Engagement on 26 December, whilst he was still considering the Four Bills. Once news of his refusal to sign the Bills became known in Parliament, the members passed the Vote of No Addresses (3 January 1648), which broke off all negotiations with the King and made it a treasonable offence for anyone to make contact with him.

The mood within Parliament was now hardening against Charles. Already, during an Army Council debate at Windsor in December, there had been a proposal that he should be tried as a criminal. In the discussions over the Vote of No Addresses, Cromwell had accused the King of being 'so great a dissembler, and so false a man, that he was not to be trusted'.[4] Others, more radical at this point than the man who was to replace Charles as Head of State, were already discussing the possibility of a republican form of government.

In the atmosphere of distrust and uncertainty which now prevailed at Westminster – and indeed nationally – it is not surprising that rumours of plots and counter-plots flourished like maggots in rotten meat. One such tale which surfaced in the middle of January 1648 was that discontented Royalists intended to seize Gloucester and other towns as part of a plan to restore the King's authority. Some 80 officers were said to be involved in the plan, along with various malcontents from London, and they were to receive the assistance of Rowland Laugharne and his troops.

At this time Laugharne was still at Windsor and he now came under the scrutiny of the Derby House Committee. Named after the London mansion in which it met, it had been set up in October 1646 and, as part of its remit, was entrusted with drawing up proposals for the reorganisation of the military establishment. In a letter of 22 January the Committee instructed Sir Thomas Fairfax to prevent Laugharne from leaving for Wales until it had been ascertained how deeply, if at all, he was implicated in the rebels' plans. Two days later, Fairfax was ordered to send the prisoner to London. This was apparently at Laugharne's own request, probably because he wanted to answer his accusers face-to-face.

On 25 January, Laugharne having arrived in London, Parliament resolved that 'Major General Langhorne be desired to pass his word that he will not go out of the town without leave of this Committee, there being divers things under examination of great concernment wherein he is named. Accordingly he passed his word and saith his lodging is the Spread Eagle in the Strand'.[5] He was to remain there for at least two months, though whether he was investigated by the Derby House Committee is unclear, for his name does not appear again in the Committee's minute books.

On the same day that Laugharne was sent up to London from Windsor, the Derby House Committee received information from John Eliot that Poyer had refused to surrender Pembroke Castle to Colonel Fleming. Fearing a general revolt in south Wales, the Committee passed on the letter to General Fairfax, with a covering note:

> By the enclosed petition you will see what information we have received concerning the state of Pembroke Castle, which besides the mischief to the well-affected of the Town thereby, for the present, may give beginning to a greater inconvenience. We therefore recommend it to your care and desire you to give order to some such forces for the reducing thereof as you yourself shall judge fit.[6]

Fairfax immediately ordered Sir William Constable, who commanded the garrison at Gloucester, to send 200 foot to Pembroke to reinforce Fleming. His action was backed by the Commons, which sent Poyer a letter personally signed by the Speaker, setting out Fairfax's original instructions concerning the transfer of the castle to Parliament's authority. When this arrived in Pembroke, Poyer refused to leave the castle to receive it. If the news-sheets of the period are to be believed, a note of farce now entered the proceedings. Fleming was allowed into Poyer's presence under a safe conduct and handed the documents to him, hoping for an immediate response. Poyer, presumably with a straight face, explained that he was unable to answer them before ten o'clock the next morning, due to 'illiterateness'. Disappointed, Fleming returned to his headquarters in the town, but in the morning, and for many mornings thereafter, no reply was received.

Poyer was no doubt aware of the feeling of widespread dissatisfaction amongst the troops awaiting disbandment in south Wales and he may have hoped that this would give him extra leverage in his dispute with the authorities. His chance came in mid-February, when Parliament appointed Commissioners for Disbanding the Supernumeraries in South Wales. This impressively titled body was to be assisted in their duties by local county committees and the money to pay off the soldiery was provided by Parliament.

On 22 February, Poyer at last wrote to Fleming:

> Sir,
> The soldiers in this Garison returns answeres to your demands thus, that if theire areares be paid they will lay downe theire Armes, and march forth presently, but they refuse to muster foorth of their quarters, if you are pleased they will wait for you in the Castle Greene to be mustered by you att your pleasure: theire Indempnitie they demaunds, And for my owne part my willingness shall not be wantinge, to obey the Comaunds of the Parliam(en)t and his Excellencie:
> S[i]r the soms you proffer foorth of my areares is to little to fitt me for my jiorney, besides the time is uncertain, how longue my stay may be untill my return, and you knows that in travell it is chargeable: I covet noe mans goods, his howse or castle, muchles any man's life, as mine is thirsted after,

by men of bloude, my Desire is to live [?quietly] my owne shall give me content, and hee that gapeth after the [sweate] of my labours, and to take the bread foorth of my wife and Childrens mouthes in my opinion is but of a verie colloric complection. S[i]r I have not else to trouble you w(i)th at p'sent but to continue in yo[u]r good opinion to be S[i]r

    Yo[u]r most humble Servant

    John Poyer

Fleming was not taken in by the conciliatory tone of this reply, recognising it as a further piece of stonewalling on Poyer's part. The payment of indemnities had already been guaranteed by Parliament, so there was no need for Poyer to have insisted upon it. The real cause for his defiance becomes apparent towards the end of the letter, when he assured Fleming of a desire for a quiet life and describes the 'colloric complection' of those who would steal food from his wife and child. He is surely referring to his feud with John Eliot and the Lorts; Poyer's obsession with the charges they had brought against him had turned to paranoia and he clearly believed that the only way to safeguard his life, if not his reputation, was to avoid an appearance before a court of inquiry.

News of Poyer's defiance appeared in the news-sheets of the day. *The Kingdome's Weekly Intelligencer* reported that he had even resorted to imprisoning market stallholders in an attempt to ensure a steady supply of their goods. There were also rumours that Poyer intended to declare his support for the King. It is possible that he had already been in touch with Royalist agents, though no proof exists of a contact this early in the year. The real problem, as far as Parliament was concerned, was that Poyer's belligerent attitude seemed to be encouraging discontent in other areas of Wales. There was alarming news from Glamorgan, where some of the disbanded troops attended a meeting with known malignants. Amongst the 800 strong crowd were those who wished to make contact with the rebel Governor of Pembroke, but this suggestion was shouted down by a group of officers loyal to Rowland Laugharne. In the event they preferred to draw up a petition which was forwarded to Sir Thomas Fairfax.

This document began by reminding Fairfax of the long and faithful service of the signatories in the Parliamentary cause, to the 'great loss and injury of their private estates', and noted that their pay was now two-and-a-half years in arrears. The officers made it plain that they were willing to disband upon the conditions laid down by Parliament, but they could not complete their accounts as the absent Laugharne still held the receipts of whatever pay they had received. They were 'aggrieved at the malicious aspersions cast upon the honour of [the] Major General and his forces as being ready to join Poyer in holding his castle against the Parliament – a false accusation could not be devised.' In conclusion, the officers charged John Eliot with delinquency in executing the King's Commission of Array and also with defrauding the Army of provisions provided by Parliament. Above all, they pleaded that Eliot should not be given custody of the arms gathered in after disbandment.

Fairfax passed this petition on to the Speaker of the Commons with a covering letter requesting that the demands contained in it should be granted. Parliament seems to have ignored both the petition and the letter, as no further action was taken, even though John Eliot was now accused of crimes similar to those he had laid against Poyer. There was obviously a strong dislike of Eliot amongst the soldiery, but the tide of opinion within Parliament was now turning against Laugharne and his associates and their loyalty was suspect.

On 23 February, the day after he had received Poyer's reply, Colonel Fleming wrote a letter to the Speaker which was also signed by Walter Cuny and the Lort brothers. They informed the Commons that:

> These remote parts are now in much distress by reason of Poyer's endeavours to begin a new war: he had refused to surrender the castle to Col. Fleming: was fortifying and victualling it, summoning the country … to his assistance, attempting to draw off these parts from the Parliament: and expecting to receive help from the disbanded soldiers of Major-General Langhorne [Laugharne].
>
> They [presumably local gentlemen] ask for 200 or 300 musketeers and desire the issue of speedy orders for the reduction of Pembroke that thereby these parts now … may remain under Parliament's protection. Milford Haven was lying open to any foreign forces which might decide to aid Poyer.

Shortly after receiving this missive, Parliament issued another Ordinance:

> Poyer hath refused to deliver up the castle of Pembroke according to the direction of the General … though required to do so by a letter from the Speaker and an order from the House: he hath continued to hold the castle and to victual and strengthen himself therein.
>
> The Lords and Commons now order that within twelve hours after notice he is to deliver the castle with all arms, ammunition etc., otherwise he and his adherents are declared Traitors and Rebels and the General is required to reduce the castle and bring him and his adherents to justice.[7]

This was the final warning. Troops were put on standby and all shipping at Milford and in the River Severn were to deliver guns, ammunition and men to help Fleming capture Pembroke. Some reinforcements had already reached the town. The 200 men dispatched from Gloucester by Sir William Constable had arrived at the beginning of March, enabling Fleming to occupy the town and blockade all approaches to the castle. Immediately upon receiving the Ordinance, which had been delivered by special messenger from London, Fleming sent it to

Poyer by a drummer with a 12-hour deadline for a reply. Eventually, long after the deadline had passed, a reply was received.

> Sir,
> The order and letter I read before your drum to the soldiers; they return this answer. That the officers and soldiers be paid part of their arrears according to the proportion of others, and sufficient security for the rest. Second. That £1,000 be paid unto me, which I have disbursed: and my arrears as the other officers according to my place and time of service. This granted we are ready to surrender the Castle and all that we have in our possession; if not we are resolved with the assistance of the Almighty to hold the Castle for the King and Parliament, according to the Covenant by us taken, until such time as our arrears, disbursements and indemnity be assured us. Our trust is not in the arm of flesh, but our hope standeth in the name of the Lord, and if bloud be spilt, judge ye who shall answer it at the dreadful day of judgement, such as seeks another man's life to enjoy what is his right; or that man who stands in his defence to save what is his; we have bestowed our times to good purpose to be proclaimed traitors and rebels for demanding our own and no more. But what yourself and those mercenaries desires, that you have brought to murther us, and take the bread out of the mouths of our wives and children. I have no more but this as David spoke to Saul when he hunted after his life. The Lord be judge between us whose heavenly protection I am assured of, knowing his cause to be just. I have not else to trouble you but rest
> Your humble servant
> John Poyer[8]

Fleming must have felt a sense of frustration, even anger, as he read yet another rehearsal of Poyer's demands. It was a further exercise in time-wasting and brought them no nearer a solution. Some historians have suggested that the long delays in answering Fleming's correspondence occurred because Poyer was awaiting replies, either from Royalist contacts who were encouraging him in his defiance, or from Fairfax himself. Poyer later admitted that he had written to the General, offering to surrender Pembroke to him in person rather than to Fleming. No contemporary documents, however, have survived to indicate what Poyer was planning, but what is noticeable in his letter to Fleming is that, for the first time, he puts in writing his intention to fight. Perhaps by this point he had sought and been given assurances of Royalist support, for Fairfax appears to have taken no notice of his offer to surrender. Whatever the truth, the feud that had been born out of Poyer's dislike and distrust of Royalist turncoats had now gone beyond a local disagreement. A second civil war was looming and amongst its several causes was John Poyer's intransigence.

In a last desperate attempt to avoid a breach, Colonel Fleming, in consultation with the County Committee, replied to Poyer's demands by offering new terms. Poyer was to receive £200 in cash. He and his followers were to be paid upon disbanding on the same terms that had been offered to all supernumeraries; Poyer's arrears were to be audited and security given for payment. As a further concession, the local gentlemen with whom he was in dispute would cease all suits and actions-at-law against him. This last condition was the most important to Poyer personally. It released him from the fear of prosecution by his enemies and might conceivably have reduced the likelihood of an investigation by Parliament. Unfortunately, he was now too deeply committed to the Royalist cause to draw back. He returned no reply to Fleming's offer, but within days of it 'he put out his flag of defiance', and without warning opened fire on the Parliamentary head-quarters in Pembroke. Casualties were heavy; Fleming reported to the Commons that 14 men were wounded, whilst the Royalist newspapers boasted of 16 dead and the rest of the enemy sent away 'with a flea in their large ears'.

Fleming seems to have been caught unawares. He assured Westminster that he had been about to land two guns from the warship *Expedition*, then anchored in the Haven, which he thought would overawe his opponents. He added, however, that he feared that the Tenby garrison would join Poyer's revolt. This particular worry appears to have been shared by others, for on 10 March a group of eight officers, including Captain Hugh Laugharne, had issued a statement that they would obey the Ordinance for Disbandment, promising that they had no inten-tion of holding Tenby against the state, neither did they intend to seize any of the Commissioners for Disbandment who were then in the town. They promised to disband whenever and wherever they were instructed. Moreover, they pointed out that they were innocent of any complicity in Poyer's actions and desired the power from Parliament to be able to reduce him to obedience.[9]

On 16 March, Colonel Rice Powell, the governor of Tenby, and all his officers except one ensign were absent from the town. Given the uncertainty of the times and the doubts current about the loyalty of the garrison it seems to have been an unwise move on his part, unless he suspected what was about to happen and wished to distance himself from it. Whatever the truth, the soldiers took full advantage of his absence. A letter written by Sampson Lort and other members of the Pembroke Commission, and received at Westminster on 27 March, describes events:

> Sergeant Henry Stephens with twelve or fourteen soldiers went to the castle on that night.
>
> On Friday night one of the soldiers was sent from the castle to draw in the rest of the company, and bring the Commissioners (who were then upon the work of disbanding) with them: to which purpose they gath-ered themselves in a tumultuous way and seized the persons of Mr Wm. Phillips, Mr Thos. Barlow, Mr Sedgewick ... and Mr Lort, the Parliamentary Commissioners. The rest got out of town.

*Tenby Harbour, the scene of an attempt in March 1648 by the men of Tenby garrison
to force Parliamentary officials aboard boats bound for Pembroke Castle*

Sampson Lort went on to describe how the Commissioners had been
dragged through the streets to the castle with the soldiers taunting them as they
went. The terrified men were locked up for a period in the castle cells before
being brought down to the quayside in the darkness, where they were loaded into
a boat manned by some of the troops, who had drawn their swords, whilst others
leapt into nearby craft. This little convoy prepared to set off, 'with most hideous
oaths and execrations', for Pembroke, but for some reason were prevented from
doing so. Nevertheless, for the following three nights small parties of men slipped
away from Tenby Castle and made their way to Pembroke.

As Fleming's men still occupied the town, the Tenby rebels must have entered
Pembroke Castle through one of its postern gates. No attempt to stop them seems
to have been made by the Parliamentary forces and as they conveniently arrived in
the night hours, it is possible that Poyer knew in advance of their plans.

Poyer was also heartened by news from Lampeter. Five troops of Laugharne's
men had been disbanded there early in March and, though they had received their
arrears of pay, a number of them were hurrying to Pembroke. From Glamorgan,
the companies of Captain Addis and Captain Agborow, despite promising to
disband as ordered, were also offering support.

At Westminster, news of the revolt in Pembrokeshire was received with
dismay. On 21 March, the Commons ordered the Derby House Committee

to confer with Fairfax over measures to crush the rebellion and within days the General had issued a number of dispatches. Two companies of Colonel Overton's regiment were ordered to march from Bristol to Pembroke; Fleming was instructed to bring the rebels to submission by any means, but he was not to grant them any conditions without the agreement of Parliament; and Colonel Horton, an experienced officer of the New Model Army, was to assist these efforts by any means necessary. A warning note was also sent by Fleming to Laugharne, Powell and Poyer, making it clear that their men would be disbanded troop by troop and any hesitation in obeying would be taken severely amiss.

By the time Fleming wrote this note, Poyer was already planning his next step. On learning that Agborow and Addis were marching to Pembroke, he sent a message to them, indicating that he intended to launch a sortie against the enemy and requesting them to attack from the rear. According to Sampson Lort, who described the action in his letter of 27 March, Fleming's men were already exhausted with day and night guard duties, and when the attack occurred on 23 March, they were taken by surprise. Many were killed or injured, whilst others fled the town and were pursued far into the surrounding countryside. Fleming's two heavy guns were captured, along with the gun-crews and all the ammunition. Fleming and his officers defended themselves as best they could, beating off their attackers for at least half an hour before eventually retreating. In the confusion Fleming went missing, feared dead, and it was some time before it was discovered that he had taken refuge in Griffith White's house at Henllan, where he lay sick for several days.

Sampson Lort added to his letter a warning of the serious disorders that were sure to follow Poyer's seizure of Pembroke town: '... if great care be not taken to crush this cockatrice in the egg, he will be able to raise a new war ... all men in these parts generally fearing him ... if he have time to victual the town and castle it will cost about one thousand lives to regain it.'

On receiving news of the Pembroke affray, the Commons set about raising extra troops to send into west Wales. Their efforts received added impetus when the members learned that Poyer had sent a ship to France, where Prince Charles was in exile, presumably carrying news of the rebellion and a plea for help.

Five days after Poyer's attack, a force of about 350 men of Colonel Overton's regiment arrived in Milford Haven from Bristol. They came ashore from their ships near Pwllcrochan, about four miles west of Pembroke, and immediately occupied the church of St Mary until more suitable accommodation could be found for them. It was not long before Poyer learned of their presence and on the following day he surrounded the church with about 100 foot and two companies of horse. Overton's men put up a fierce resistance, but were eventually forced to surrender on terms. They were allowed to leave with their weapons, providing that they promised not to return again to Pembrokeshire. They set off for Cardiff, possibly

Pwllcrochan Church, where Colonel Overton's regiment surrendered on terms to John Poyer

in the boats that had brought them from Bristol.

Amongst them was Colonel Fleming, who had narrowly escaped capture at Henllan. A bare half mile of countryside separated the church and the house and the sound of firing as Overton's men defended themselves interrupted a conference being held to discuss the quartering of the recently arrived troops. Amongst those present besides Griffith White and Fleming were Roger Lort, John Lort, and others sympathetic to the Parliamentary cause. They galloped away from the house in such confusion that Griffith White, who had stuffed his pockets with money before escaping, left a trail of gold coins in the road to mark his passage. It was only just in time; within minutes John Poyer and his men arrived with sledgehammers and iron bars to smash in the doors of the house. For a short time at least, Poyer had the upper hand.

15   Skirmish at Llandeilo

In the aftermath of the attack on Fleming, the Parliamentary press, not surprisingly, published a spate of vituperative denunciations of John Poyer. On 21 March, *The Perfect Diurnall* gave an account of his character based on letters sent to the Speaker of the Commons:

> The man is certainly in two dispositions every day, in the morning Sober and Penitent, but in the afternoon drunk and full of plots. Some days since he sent four of his Bullies (clad only in the best apparel he could get for them) out of the sally-port before the sun rising, and received them again at the Gate in great ceremony, as if they had been Princes and then shot off some guns for their entertainment, giving out among the peoples of the Town that they were Collonels and Commanders sent out of France to him by the Prince of Wales and that more of them would follow speedily ...
>
> He takes it very ill the King is in the Isle of Wight, and calls the Generall King Thomas Fairfax ... we lie close and have not made one shot at him but we keep him up so that not one man of his dares keep out of the Gate ...
>
> He got a gentleman the other day and prest him to tell him whether he was an Independent or Presbiter. The gentleman answered 'Neither, for he was a Protestant'. 'Why, so am I' quoth Poyer, 'therefore let us be merry.' So in they went and drunk so hard that neither was able to stir in four and twenty hours after. A thousand of these stories might be told of him.[1]

Articles such as this did much to shape the public perception of Poyer at the time and ever since. He must have known what was being written about him, but as much of it flowed from the pens of the men who had a personal grudge against him, he might not have been surprised by it. It is a striking fact that other contemporaries make no mention of his alleged drunkenness. There was, in any case, too much for Poyer to worry about for him to give any attention to the London news-sheets. At some unknown point, he and Rice Powell, back in command of the garrison at Tenby, had decided to act in concert. A declaration was drawn up by a confederate, Colonel Culpepper, based in Carmarthen, which attempted to prove that they still fought for the rights and privileges for which the country had originally gone to war:

> The errors of the former government ... were now exceeded in Church and State: the King had been in the Reformers hands for two years, yet no reforms had been made: the King had not been allowed to treat personally with his Parliament: to satisfy the avarice and ambition of a few men 'who now labour to disband us, not to ease the country but ... to bring in other forces ... make the gentry subject to sequestration, inslave the people ... establish Excise, taxes and other intolerable charges ... and put down the Book of Common Prayer'. Religion, Laws and Liberties have been trampled upon. We do now declare -
>
> That wee do still continue to our first principles, to bring the King to a personall treaty with his Parliament with Honour, Freedome, and Safety so that the just Privileges of Parliament, Lawes of the Land and Liberties of the People may be established in their proper bounds.
>
> That wee will as much as in us lyes protect the people from injury and maintaine the Protestant religion, and the Common Prayer as it is established by Law in this Land, and therefore crave the assistance of the whole Kingdom therein.[2]

The existence of this declaration was rumoured in Pembrokeshire by late March and a copy had been sent by Poyer to Prince Charles in France. It was accompanied by a number of propositions which basically asked the Prince to appoint a general to lead the revolt in Pembroke, to grant Poyer and Powell a pardon for their conduct during the previous war, including all suits-at-law resulting from it, and to guarantee the payment of their arrears and confirm them in the offices they already held.[3]

The Prince replied to this on 3 April, appointing Poyer as Governor of Pembroke and, though no commission has survived, he probably also confirmed Powell's governorship of Tenby. In a further letter on 13 April, the Prince encouraged them in their struggle, promising assistance.

By this time, the Declaration had been published (10 April), to be followed ten days later by the correspondence sent to Prince Charles. At about the same time, there appeared a pamphlet entitled *Declaration of Divers Gentlemen of Wales concerning Col. Poyer*. This recounted the main points of the Poyer-Powell declaration but went on to express the views of various gentlemen concerning the two rebels. Like the article in *A Perfect Diurnall*, it became the source of many inaccurate stories about Poyer and was probably written by John Eliot.

Pembroke had now become the centre of Royalist hopes and expectations and their broad-sheets were reporting that 'Great England's honour lies in the dust and Little England [Pembrokeshire] lends a hand to raise it up'. Poyer's stance had encouraged people in other areas of Britain to give voice and action to their own dissatisfaction. In London, early in April, the apprentice boys marched through the streets with ringing cries of 'Now for King Charles'. The unrest was quickly crushed, but it was discovered that many of the rioters came from Kent and Surrey, where the cost of maintaining the army was much resented. There were similar riots in East Anglia and there was discontent in Brecon, Radnor and Monmouth.[4] A popular verse summed up the prevailing attitude: 'Hey diddle diddle, I heard a bird sing; The Parliament soldiers are up for the King'.

Just as many discontented soldiers and Royalists had made their way westwards in support of Poyer, so columns of Parliamentary troops were marching along the roads that converged on Pembroke. Colonel Horton, acting on orders received from Fairfax, left Brecon on 8 April for Neath where he would shortly rendezvous with Colonel

John Poyer, said to be a memorial portrait painted after his death (National Library of Wales, Aberystwyth)

Okey's dragoons, who had marched from Cardiff. The Derby House Committee had instructed Captain Crowther, Vice-Admiral of the Irish Sea, to make for Tenby on 'the first opportunity of wind and weather'.

In Pembroke itself, feverish preparations were made to challenge Horton's advance. Poyer and Powell demanded contributions from many Pembrokeshire parishes, which caused great resentment within the county. Warrants were issued for the county militias to assemble at Colby Moor, Carmarthen and Lampeter. The disbanded supernumeraries were ordered to gather at Carmarthen with three days' provisions and rumour suggested that the warrants had raised a force of about 4,000 men. The real total was probably just over a quarter of that, but Poyer had high hopes of receiving help from Ireland, where Lord Inchiquin had recently declared for the King.[5]

On 15 April a skirmish took place at Llanelli, when Colonel Fleming led a raid on the quarters of a detachment of Powell's men, capturing ten troopers and fourteen horse. A day or two later some of Powell's officers deserted and made their way to Horton's camp at Neath, bringing news that they had left behind them others who were unhappy about Powell's change of loyalties.

Horton now issued a statement justifying the advance into west Wales, which he claimed was taking place only because Powell had refused to disband his soldiers. Powell had engaged others in a plot aimed against Parliament on the pretence that the Army was threatening the people's peace. Horton gave an assurance that he and his men would withdraw as soon as obedience to the orders of Parliament had been obtained.

By 17 April Horton had joined forces with Colonel Okey and had advanced into Carmarthenshire. His road was blocked at Carmarthen by a large force of 'English, Scotch, Irish but mostly Welsh', who were backed by 'diverse porters, butchers and rascally fellows come from London'. With a numerically inferior force and with the bridge over the Towy held against him, Horton was forced to swing eastwards, marching towards Pont-ar-gothi, which he reached by 24 April. Here, a large force of Powell's men awaited him on the far bank of the river, having broken down the bridge that spanned it.

For the next two days there was a stand-off until Horton received information from local sympathisers of a ford across the river some five miles further upstream. Wading through the shallows, his men were soon in a position to advance again on Carmarthen from the east and north. Realising that Horton now had the advantage, Powell retreated with his men to the top of a nearby hill.

Anxious to bring the insurgents to battle, Horton staged a mock retreat, but Powell remained immovable at the summit of his hill. Horton then sent Colonel Fleming with a troop of horse and two of dragoons to seize a pass about seven miles distant, on the far side of Powell's army. As he approached his objective, Fleming found himself facing an advance party of the enemy under Major Roach and a fierce fight erupted. The men of Powell's force fell back under a withering fire, suffering many killed and wounded, whilst others were taken prisoner. Eager to press home his advantage, Fleming embarked on a pursuit of the fugitives, but to his horror he blundered on a reserve force under Colonel Butler which was waiting in ambush. Within minutes, the pursuers became the pursued, many of them abandoning their horses and seeking refuge on foot.

Fleming and 119 of his men managed to find shelter in Llandeilo church where, according to contemporary reports, 'the Pembrokians broke in upon them and made, as they say, a slaughter of them'.[6] In fact, about 100 of Fleming's men were taken prisoner on quarter of their lives, but Fleming himself was found dead in the church with a pistol in his hand. The cause of his death was never established, some reports saying that he had been shot by Major Roach, others that he had committed suicide to avoid falling into Poyer's hands. In the words of one newspaper 'Fleming became his own Executioner, a remarkable heavy judgement of God'.

The defeat of Fleming and the capture of so many of his men resulted in a major change in Horton's plans.[7] Unable now to force his way through to

Llandeilo church, where Fleming was killed and most of his troops surrendered

Carmarthen, he fell back on Brecon, where he could replenish his supply of ammunition.

News of Fleming's death reached London by 29 April, just as many of the leading figures in the New Model Army were gathering at Windsor for a prayer meeting during which they also laid plans for the future. Aware that many Presbyterians had joined the Royalist movement, they decided to continue the fight against all enemies of the state, including the King: 'if ever the Lord brought us back again in peace, to call Charles Stuart, that man of blood, to account for the blood he had shed and mischief he had done to his utmost'.[8]

It was also on this day that a letter was read out to the Commons from a correspondent in Wales. It described the firing of guns by the Welsh as a salute to welcome home Major-General Laugharne. On 30 April, newspapers reported that 'Major-General Laugharne is with the Welsh Army and hath or shall have the Prince's commission'. These are the first indications of Laugharne's return to south Wales. At some point in mid-April he must have been released from, or broke, his parole and left London to travel back to Pembrokeshire. His reasons for doing so, and for joining Poyer's revolt, have never been fully understood. A.L. Leach suggests that he was hoping to restrain Poyer and Powell and to prevent a premature rising before adequate preparations had been made. As events had already overtaken him, Laugharne had no choice but to take part, ready or not. He must have known how great a gamble this was, but like many another former supporter of Parliament, he probably felt he had no choice. The first civil war had been fought for principles which seemed clear and just – to bring the King to an agreement with his Parliament and to safeguard the royal prerogatives, the privileges of Parliament and the ancient laws and liberties of the land. Somehow the rush of war had swept the nation beyond those boundaries, into an unfamiliar landscape. Laugharne now found himself in a conservative minority, whilst more radical thinkers than he occupied the seats of power. With no real contacts or support amongst the leading figures of government and resentful of the ex-Royalists who now occupied places in the county committees in south Wales, it would not be surprising if he decided to change allegiances.

We do not know when or how quickly he came to this decision, but he was certainly in communication with the Prince of Wales by mid-April. In a letter dated 19 April, Prince Charles assured Laugharne that his loyalty to the King was recognised and promised to give him a suitable reward for his services. He granted Laugharne the power to issue General Pardons in the King's name and gave a further assurance that arms and money would be sent to him. It is possible that a commission accompanied this letter from the Prince, appointing Laugharne to be the King's General in south Wales – one certainly seems to have been issued, though it has not survived.

On 29 April, Laugharne was at Haverfordwest and on the following day he rode eastwards to join up with Rice Powell, whose men were moving into Glamorgan.[9] It is doubtful that he did so with any great confidence, for he must have known that all the resources of Parliament were ranged against him.

On 3 May, having received orders from General Fairfax, Lieutenant-General Cromwell marched out of Windsor at the head of a large body of men and took the road to Wales. Poyer, upon hearing of his approach, was said to be unimpressed. He boasted that he would be the first man to charge old 'Ironsides' and would not be deterred 'even if he had a back of steel and a breast-plate of iron'.[10]

Horton had left Brecon a few days before this, his troops rested and re-armed, and was leading them southwards over the mountains. He had received news that Rice Powell had seized Swansea and Neath and was threatening Cardiff. In drenching rain, Horton's men staged a series of exhausting forced marches that enabled them to reach St Fagans, a few miles west of Cardiff, by 4 May. Hoping to block Powell's approach from Swansea, Horton immediately set up guard posts at the key crossings of the Taff and Ely rivers, though in fact the rebels were already within two miles of St Fagans. For the next day or so, minor skirmishes took place as scouting and foraging parties from the two armies patrolled the surrounding countryside.

Meanwhile, the two commanders indulged in a brief exchange of letters. On 4 May, writing from his camp at St Nicholas, a few miles from St Fagans and close to Cottrell, the home of his brother-in-law, Miles Button, Laugharne demanded to know by what authority Horton had entered the districts which Parliament had entrusted to him:

> … otherwise your perseverance in these affronts to myself and the soldiery and the country will not be without some difficulty. Sir, if you please to withdraw your forces out of this county it may be the special means to prevent several inconveniences besides the necessary resolutions which may otherwise be forced upon, Sir,
> Your servant
> Rowland Laugharne'.[11]

If this rather pointless show of bravado was intended to overawe Horton, or to prevent bloodshed, it failed in its effect. On the following day, Laugharne received a reply.

> Sir,
> I thought it had not been unknown to you that his Excellency the Lord Fairfax is General (by Ordinance of Parliament) of all forces both in England and Wales and is empowered to dispose of them into such places

and in such manner as he shall see cause for the preservation of the peace of this Kingdom.

Horton reminded Laugharne of the steps by which Poyer and Powell had alienated themselves from Parliament and encouraged rebellion. He ended his letter on a note of regret:

> … considering the former trust the Parliament reposed in you and your late obligations to them, I would rather have believed that you came with an intention to join with us for the suppressing of that tumultuous assembly with you, than to appear amongst and own those who have manifestly violated the authority of Parliament, which you seem to maintain and insist upon in your letter to me.[12]

Also on 4 May, Poyer and Powell published yet another declaration, which again promised

> that we will use our best endeavours to bring the King to a personall treaty with his Parliament in freedom, honour and safety: to the End that the Just prerogative of the King, Privileges of Parliament, Lawes of the Land, Liberties of the People may be maintained and preserved in their proper bounds and the Protestant religion, as it now stands established by the Law of the land, restored throughout the kingdom with such regard to tender consciences as shall be allowed by the Act of Parliament.[13]

Once this war of words was over it was down to the real business. Blood would have to be shed. Laugharne may well have felt that his army, by virtue of numbers, had a definite advantage, but he must also have known that a battle with Horton would only be the first of many if his cause was to triumph. He surely hoped that the confrontation at St Fagans would be the initial move in a series of risings across the country, otherwise he, Poyer, and everything they fought for were doomed.

16 The Battle of St Fagans and Siege of Tenby

In the days immediately prior to the battle, Rowland Laugharne drew his army back from the vicinity of St Fagans to the Llancarfan-Penmark area to regroup and consider his options. He may have wished to avoid a fight, hence his letter to Horton, but he also knew that to retreat would ruin Royalist morale. It would also give Cromwell time to reinforce Horton and gain an advantage in numbers.

Laugharne had at his command some 8,000 men, of whom about 2,500 were musketeers. A further 4,000 were said to be clubmen armed with a variety of weapons, the remainder consisting of a thousand or more pikemen. Few of these had much experience in battle and there were a limited number of horsemen to support them.[1]

The officers and gentlemen are said to have adorned their hats with blue ribbons bearing the embroidered motto 'We long to see His Majestie' and the royal crowned rose with the letters CR.[2] They included not only Rice Powell, but Phillip Sammage, who possibly came from Newcastle Emlyn, and Major-General Stradling of the St Donats family, who had commanded the defeated Royalist army at Colby Moor. It is unlikely that there was any real liking or trust between Stradling and Laugharne.

Several Glamorganshire gentlemen had offered their support. Miles Button was probably amongst them, as was Edward Kemeys, a relative of Miles' wife Florence. It is almost certain that Poyer was not present at St Fagans, though some reports and later histories have him leading a troop of soldiers. Horton, writing to Fairfax after the battle, mentioned that 'Col. Poyer keeps Pembroke Castle with 100 men' and the *Moderate Intelligencer* of 11-18 May stated that 'Poyer yet doth not appear was in the fight but in his castle'.[3]

The Royalist army was more than twice the size of Horton's, but the Parliamentarians were well-equipped, experienced fighters. Horton had been wounded at Naseby, and his officers included other old campaigners such as Colonel John Okey, Major Walter Bethell and Major Nathaniel Barton. Between them they mustered about 1,200 horse, 1,400 foot and 700 dragoons, although some of these troops were away guarding the river crossings leading into Cardiff.[4]

Having arrived in the area in advance of Laugharne, Horton had been able to choose his ground, with the River Ely on his left flank and a line of high ground to his right, or northern, flank. On the evening of Sunday 7 May, he drew his forces close around the village of St Fagans. At about the same time, Laugharne moved his army towards St Nicholas and beyond, fording the Ely near Peterston and deploying his men on a north-south axis along the vale of the Nant Dowlais, a stream that runs out of the hills to join the Ely.

Early the next morning, probably between 7 and 8 o'clock, about 500 of the Royalist infantry, the 'Forlorn Hope', advanced on the Parliamentary position, occupying the hedgerows on the way. Horton hurried forward his own 'Forlorn Hope', consisting of 'Lieutenant Godfrey with ... 30 horse and 20 dragoons (who) charged and routed them, doing great execution, which gave us the advantage of new ground, so we advanced with horse and foot upon them ...'.[5]

Horton's general advance covered, according to his statement, almost a mile of ground. The fighting was hard, groups of men pushing forward through the waterlogged fields and enclosures that barred the way, disputing every hedgerow with volleys of musket fire and bludgeoning at the faces of their opponents with their gun butts. At last, Horton's troops 'came to a bridge where the enemy's

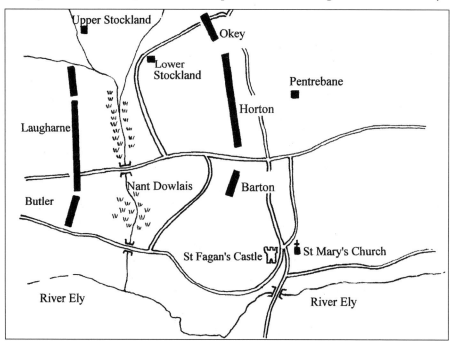

The Battle of St Fagans, 8 May 1648

greatest body were placed. The horse all this while and dragoons following this first success with much vigour were constrained to stand the enemy's shot for sometime before the foot (though they made great haste) could come up to them'.[6]

It is probable that a fierce fire-fight now took place across the muddy waters of the Nant Dowlais, during which the Royalists found themselves outflanked by a division of Horton's army, which splashed across the stream to attack from the south. A troop of about 60 of Laugharne's men charged down upon them, hoping to drive back Horton's foot soldiers, but was beaten off. As Horton was later to report, 'By this time the horse and dragoons on the right wing were gotten over also, the enemy's foot standing very stoutly to it, until our horse began to surround them, and then they presently all ran, and we cleared the field, our horse and dragoons persueing them for eight or ten miles'.

In less than two hours, Laugharne's army had been thoroughly routed, about 200 of them killed, including his brother Thomas, and over 3,000 taken prisoner. Others were rounded up as they fled and, after surrendering their weapons, were allowed to go home. The majority of prisoners were probably held in Llandaff Cathedral, a few miles away. Many of the Royalist officers had been killed and most of the others were captured, amongst them Major-General Stradling and Miles Button. These two men, along with nine others, were held aboard Vice-Admiral Crowther's flagship, the *Bonaventure*. Regarded as amongst the principal rebels and therefore the most culpable, all were court-martialled and condemned to death. Three were hung and a fourth was shot. Stradling was imprisoned at Windsor Castle, where he later died in captivity. The other officers, including Button, were exiled for two years. Of the common soldiers who had been taken prisoner, most were released after swearing an oath not to fight again, but some 240 unmarried men were shipped off to Barbados to help colonise the island, first occupied by English settlers in 1627.[7]

In the chaos of the retreat from the battlefield, Laugharne managed to slip away, riding hard for the west and Pembroke. He had been wounded at some point in the battle, but not so seriously that he could not endure a long ride of over 100 miles to the temporary safety of Pembroke Castle. Also galloping westwards was Rice Powell, though the two men may not have kept company. According to rumour they had quarrelled, but the cause is unknown. As the fugitives hurried through Carmarthen, they withdrew some guns from Carmarthen Castle, Powell pressing on to Tenby and Laugharne to Pembroke.

On 11 May, Parliament received news of the victory at St Fagans and appointed Wednesday 17 May to be a Day of Public Thanksgiving. It was observed 'but very slightly in the city'.

Three days earlier, on 14 May, an advance guard of Horton's troops arrived before Tenby and attempted to take the town by storm. Powell had clearly wasted no time in preparing some kind of defence, for the attack was driven off and the Parliamentarians sat down before the medieval walls to wait for the arrival of their main force.

Horton reached Tenby a few days later. Including the advance guard, he now had a force of some 1,230 officers and men of Colonel Overton's regiment with which to besiege the town. In addition, there were two companies of Colonel Sir William Constable's regiment from Gloucester. Vice-Admiral Crowther anchored off-shore with two warships, the *Bonaventure* and *Expedition*, and began a naval blockade of the town, cutting off all hope of assistance by sea. Within the walls of Tenby were crammed between 300 and 600 men, plus the population of about 1,000 men, women and children.[8] Most of the soldiers were probably quartered in the castle, or perhaps in St Mary's Church.

During the first week, Horton made no obvious effort to storm the town. He may have been testing the strength of the defences or perhaps he was awaiting reinforcements. These arrived on 23 May, when Cromwell marched into the leaguer.

Cromwell had been delayed for several days at Chepstow, which he reached on 11 May after a forced march from Windsor. The strongly fortified castle, towering above the River Wye, had been held for the King during the first Civil War, but had surrendered to Parliamentary forces in October 1645. In the spring of 1648 it had been seized in the King's name by Sir Nicholas Kemeys, a relative of Miles Button's wife, Florence, and quickly became a focus for Royalist hopes in south-east Wales.

Cromwell's forces retook the town of Chepstow with relative ease, forcing the town gate and scattering the defenders. The castle, however, resisted all efforts to capture it and without artillery Cromwell was unable to mount a prolonged siege. In any case, he was anxious to deal with Tenby and Pembroke lest the rebellion should spread further afield. He decided to continue his march westwards, leaving a Colonel Ewer to deal with the castle. The end came for Sir Nicholas Kemeys and his garrison less than a fortnight later, on 25 May. Colonel Ewer was able to obtain heavy guns from Gloucester and Bristol, which were used to batter down the outer walls on the landward side of the castle. In the subsequent storming of the stronghold, Kemeys and an unknown number of his men were killed.

Upon arrival at Tenby, Cromwell found Horton to be a man in whom he could place his confidence, for on the following day he moved on to invest Pembroke. Horton now ordered an attack on 'a certain work' in the suburbs, in which up to 30 of the defenders were killed or captured. The ease with which this was achieved seems to have sapped the determination of Powell's men, for they sent out an appeal for surrender on conditions. Horton, however, 'would give no ear to them knowing the serpentine malevolency of their natures, especially of that proud and insolent Col. Powell that shameful apostate who indeed deserves no mercy at all'.[9] This refusal seems to have been given extra point by a bombardment of the walls, for by 31 May a breach had been opened up in the ancient stonework. At this point Cromwell urged that terms should be offered to the garrison and it was made clear to Powell that if these were not accepted, the defenders could expect no mercy.

The threat of wholesale slaughter, which might well have been visited upon the townsfolk as well as the soldiers, had an immediate effect. Powell, whose men were already divided by 'great discontents', found himself facing a rebellion of angry, frightened citizens, who 'seeing nothing but ruine, brought the desperate officers and country gentlemen to a compliance'. An answer was returned to Horton the same day, in which Powell desired him 'to take them into protection and mercy upon which they did freely and willingly surrender all, both arms and ammunition'.[10]

The terms of surrender were better than might have been expected. Rice Powell, Colonel Edward Kemeys, who had fled from St Fagans, four captains and 30 other officers were taken into custody. Of the common soldiers, those who desired it were allowed to go to their homes, providing that they took an oath never again to make war against Parliament, whilst others were sent on service to Italy. A list made out immediately after the surrender shows that amongst the booty taken were 20 guns, 300 arms, four broken barrels of gunpowder, 40 horses, five colours (regimental flags), the standard of the castle and a large amount of baggage and provisions.[11]

News of the capitulation of Tenby was received in the Commons on 5 June and was jubilantly reported in the newspapers.

> Colonel Powell ... who indeed deserved no mercy at all, but that he should be cast into that Current of the Fludgate of Justice and made exemplaire to posteritie and to all perfidious villains.
> This nest of vermin did not desist from creeping and crawling until they were not able to subsist no longer and then they were forced to strike sayle and submit to mercy and our pleasures.[12]

The messenger who brought the joyful news was awarded £20. On the same day that it was announced to Parliament, the members ordered that the estates of Rowland Laugharne, Powell and Poyer should be sequestered and their owners tried by court-martial because 'they had failed in their trust and deserted the service of the Parliament'. Powell was removed from Tenby under heavy guard and taken to Carmarthen, where he was kept in prison to await events. Some at least of the townspeople were sorry to see him go, for the bailiff's accounts show that he was sent 'on[e] pottle of sack and on[e] pottle of white wine at his going away a prisoner ... 4s.'

It was to be Pembroke's turn next. An anonymous writer, possibly Colonel Horton, had written to the Commons from Tenby on 3 June to give details of the surrender of the town and had added in his concluding paragraph, 'And I doubt not in short time (after our mortar pieces are come and ready) that a good account will suddenly be given of Pembrook Castle, where are the rest of the fry, that have occasioned the disturbance of these parts'.

17 The Siege of Pembroke

On 13 March 1648, the *Kingdomes Weekly Account* published a brief outline of events in Pembroke, together with an explanation of why the town might prove difficult to capture: 'Neither are our forces able for the present to approach very near the castle by reason of the high tides which flow about the town'. The correspondent who provided the account clearly knew Pembroke well and it is likely that Cromwell, as he drew near, was already aware that a formidable task awaited him.

The town of Pembroke is perched upon a narrow limestone ridge, which at its western end rises into a rocky bluff. Upon the steep cliffs of this crag a massive castle had been built by William Marshall during the thirteenth century, the walls of which in places towered up from the rocks to present a continuous precipice. Around the foot of the limestone ridge flowed the tidal waters of the Pembroke River, which formed a natural barrier along the northern perimeter of the town. To the south, a narrow stream flowed through a shallow valley, which flooded on an incoming tide, and which at the ebb consisted of mud flats that could be crossed only by a narrow bridge at the eastern extremity and by an arched causeway at the western end.

The town walls, which Poyer had repaired, were originally built in the thirteenth century and extended from the north-east corner of the castle towards the nearby North Gate, where a bridge carried the road from the town northwards over the river. Two mills stood upon the bridge, which formed a dam through which the tidal water was channelled to turn the mill wheels. Beyond the bridge, stretching eastwards, the river was overlooked by a continuation of the walls, which ran from the North Gate to Barnard's Tower, a strong fortification at the east end of the town. From Barnard's Tower the walls turned south to the great East Gate of the town, where roads radiated outwards to Carew, Tenby and Manorbier. From the East Gate the walls continued south and then west, running along the rim of the limestone ridge until they culminated in the West Gate, immediately below the castle, where a road crossed the causeway to the outlying suburb of Monkton. The wall was further strengthened in a number of places by small towers, most

The stout medieval town walls of Pembroke provided a formidable obstacle to the besieging Parliamentarians; the ground level was even lower in 1648

of which stood along the eastern and south-eastern stretches, the sections most approachable by land.[1]

Within the circuit of the walls the town consisted, as it does today, of one long street running from the West Gate to the East Gate. This thoroughfare, Main Street, was lined with houses, behind which gardens and orchards reached down to the walls. Some of these houses still exist, particularly opposite the castle on Westgate Hill. The town's two churches, St Michael's and St Mary's, to which Poyer had donated the chalices in 1645, stood at opposite ends of Main Street. A narrow lane known as Northgate Street, or Dark Lane because the leaning houses that lined it blocked out the light, ran past St Mary's from Main Street to the North Gate.

Several small suburbs existed outside the town. A scattering of houses stood around the Green to the north of the town beyond the river, and outside the East Gate the roads were lined with dwellings. Across the causeway to the south-west of Pembroke was the village of Monkton, centred on the remains of the medieval priory.

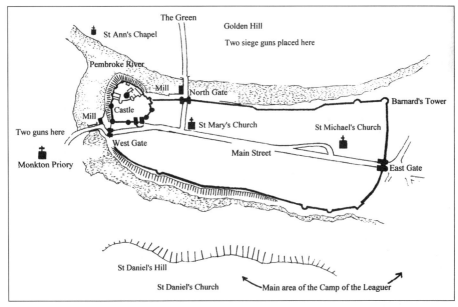

The Siege of Pembroke, 24 May – 11 July 1648

Even before he arrived at Pembroke on 24 May, Oliver Cromwell was already at a disadvantage. The heavy siege guns intended to reduce the town's defences were seriously delayed – the ship carrying them was wrecked in the River Severn near Berkeley and it took several weeks to recover the guns and, even then, storms

These houses on Westgate hill, opposite the castle, survived the siege

137

held up their eventual arrival. Moreover, as he marched towards Pembrokeshire, Cromwell found it difficult to supply his troops. At his approach, the inhabitants of the districts through which he passed fled into the hills and forests, taking all their cattle with them. 'Many of their smiths are also gone, they themselves having cut down their bellows before they went'. Anything that might have been useful to the Parliamentary army was hidden or destroyed.[2]

Cromwell, however, wasted no time in forming his siege camp, which became known as the 'Leaguer before Pembroke'. It stretched across the lower slopes of St Daniel's Hill to the south of the town, in the area known as Underdown.[3] Encamped within the Leaguer were the men of Cromwell's own regiment, together with Colonel Pride's regiment of foot, Colonel Okey's dragoons and, from 6 June when they arrived from Tenby, Colonel Horton's horse and Overton's foot

Barnard's Tower, at the east end of Pembroke's defences, probably housed a small garrison during the siege

soldiers under Lt.-Colonel Reade.[4] They originally numbered about 8,000 men in all, though some were garrisoned at Tenby, Haverfordwest, Carmarthen and Cardiff to prevent further risings and to keep open Cromwell's lines of communication with London. This left about 6,000 troops at Underdown and in its satellite camps at Monkton and The Green, north of the town. Cromwell himself stayed at Welston, the home of the Cuny family, about three miles north-east of Pembroke, within sight of Carew Castle. Some of his officers also appear to have been quartered there, for one of the fields close to the present house, an early 19th century building that replaced the one Cromwell knew, is called the Bowling Green because of the tradition that they played bowls there.

As soon as the Leaguer had been established, the siege began in earnest. The main sources of information about events at Pembroke are four letters which

Cromwell wrote to the Speaker of the House of Commons, four other pieces of correspondence by an anonymous author – or authors – and some extracts from other letters that were published in contemporary newspapers. All were written by members of the besieging force. No letters or diaries appear to have been produced by those trapped within the town and what we know of conditions within the walls comes from the Parliamentary reports, which sometimes contain nuggets of information obtained from deserters.

From the beginning of the siege there were dissensions amongst the defenders, the most serious of which was between Poyer and Laugharne. When the latter reached Pembroke after the flight from St Fagans, he was 'very sicke of body and minde'. Poyer allowed him to enter the town but, according to a letter written on 5 June by someone known only as 'W.S.', admittance was then refused to other fugitives from the battle. The same source also states that Poyer distanced himself from Laugharne, claiming to stand for his original principles and emphasising that he was 'not confederate with Laugharne and Powell in that rebellion'. Exactly why he did so is unclear; perhaps there had been a disagreement between the three men over the timing of Powell's march into Glamorgan; or Poyer may have been excluded from the plans for the revolt. It is even possible that he wanted to obtain more favourable terms for himself should Pembroke be taken.

Main Street, Pembroke,
the scene of bitter fighting in June 1648

Tensions were only to be expected amongst those occupying Pembroke. There were some 2,000 Royalists defending the town, in addition to the inhabitants. Many of the soldiers would have been sheltered within the castle, and the two churches may well have become dormitories, stables or storage depots. A small garrison seems to have been placed within Barnard's Tower, but a large number of men must have been billeted in the houses along Main Street. Some of these homes might have been abandoned by their owners but, as at Tenby, it is likely that the majority of townsfolk had no other choice than to stay put. As well as sharing their accommodation, they would also have been forced to share their supplies of food under the time-honoured rule of free quarter.

The loss of the heavy guns meant that the siege went on for longer than it might otherwise have done, but Cromwell and his men quickly improvised. Hugh Peters, Cromwell's army chaplain, obtained 'two drakes, two culverins and two demi-culverins with all their accoutrements' from the guardship *Lyon*, then stationed in the Haven. Tradition has it that two of these were placed in Monkton churchyard, from where they were able to shoot directly into the town and castle. Their fire was so accurate that 'a man dare not stand upon the castle walls to shoote without a blinde'.[5] Poyer was said to have lowered the red flag which flew over the castle to prevent it from being shot down; this was probably a flag of defiance rather than a personal standard.

The siege was not a static affair in which the besiegers were content to starve out their enemy. From the beginning, both sides launched a series of attacks and counter attacks, sometimes on horseback, sometimes on foot. One of the first of these took place about 4 June, less than two weeks into the siege. A storming party of Parliamentary soldiers carrying scaling ladders approached the walls, probably during the night hours. When the ladders were thrust against the stonework, the troops were horrified to find that they were too short. During the resulting confusion, a heavy fire was opened up from the battlements, killing 23 men and wounding many more. Cromwell, writing to the Speaker, tried to make light of the incident: 'We lost a few men; but I am confident the Enemy lost more. Captain Flower, of Colonel Dean's Regiment, was wounded; and Major Grigg's Lieutenant and Ensign slain; Captain Burgess lies wounded and very sick'.[6]

A day or two later, it was Laugharne's turn to attempt an attack upon the camp of the Leaguer. He was by now healed of the wound he had received at St Fagans, a return to good health facilitated by Cromwell himself who, at the beginning of the siege, allowed Ann Laugharne and a doctor to enter the town to tend to her husband's injuries. He also ordered the return of some of Laugharne's cattle that had been seized by foraging troops.[7] At the head of a troop of horse, Laugharne now galloped out through one of the town gates, only to be driven back at a cost of nine dead and 20 taken prisoner.

By 6 June Horton had arrived from Tenby and the encirclement of Pembroke was complete. Extra guns were brought in from the *Lyon*, to supplement those already in use. The following day news was received that a Royalist rebellion in Kent had been successfully crushed. A thanksgiving salute was fired from the cannon of the Leaguer and from ships lying in the Haven, the noise of it causing some consternation in Pembroke.[8] Poyer seized the opportunity to assure his men that 'it was ... Prince Charles and his revolted ships, coming with relief', but whether this boosted morale as intended is doubtful.

The guns brought from the *Lyon* had been keeping up a steady bombardment of the castle and town, so much so that on 9 June Cromwell wrote to Carmarthen requesting the Committee there to procure extra ammunition from the iron works. As well as shot for the demi-cannon and culverins, shells of 14-inch diameter were needed for the mortars. If these extra supplies were provided, they soon ran low, for by the end of the month the Parliamentary gunners 'shot stones into the town with [their] mortar pieces which killed divers'.[9]

In addition to ammunition, Cromwell was also anxious to obtain food supplies. On 28 June, in a letter to Fairfax, he explained his difficulties:

> The county, since we have sat down before this place, have made two or three insurrections; and are ready to do it every day; so that – what with looking to them and disposing our horse to that end, and to get us in provisions, without which we would starve, this country being so miserably exhausted and so poor, and we no money to buy victuals – indeed, whatever may be thought, it's a mercy we have been able to keep our men together in the midst of such necessity, the sustenance of the foot being but bread and water.[10]

Some supplies were received from Haverfordwest. The municipal records show that on 3 June, 43 barrels – their contents were not recorded – and 11 hogsheads and 50 barrels of beer were sent to the Leaguer. The provisions were taken from the storehouses down to the riverside in carts, where they were loaded aboard boats that took them to Carew for onward transport by road to Pembroke. Other supplies stored in 100 butts, hogsheads and barrels followed them, but it was noted in the accounts that the containers were not returned when empty. Nine days later, 18 gallons and 3 pints of cider were dispatched, and later a cask of cider and a piece of loaf sugar weighing 4¾ pounds went the same way. Bread was also sent, as well as salt at 3s 4d a bushel.[11] The cost of carts at Haverfordwest was recorded as 2s and payments were also made to the boatmen.

Most communities in Pembrokeshire were expected to contribute to the upkeep of the Leaguer. The cost of foodstuffs was taken from the Monthly Assessments, but the care of the sick and wounded was paid for out of the funds of Haverfordwest Corporation and the charges were carefully recorded in the accounts: 'Two muttons for the sick at 9s 6d, each wrapped in canvas; Mutton...4s; Barrel of Beer...10s; Five dozen loaves...5s; Four quarts of oatmeal...1s; A couple of pullets...8d; Paid for shrouds for 24 souldiers which were wounded against Pembroke and for burying them £4 8s 6d'.

It is also clear from the accounts that some prisoners taken at Pembroke were transferred to Haverfordwest to be incarcerated in the Guildhall. Three women were paid for cleaning the building and five loads of straw were brought in for the men to sleep on.

However difficult conditions were for the troops in the Leaguer, within Pembroke they were much worse. By 10 June, rations had been cut to ½ pound of beef and an equal amount of bread per day for each man of the garrison, but whether the civilians were included in this reduction is unclear. Even the horses suffered privation; early in June they were being fed on thatch pulled down from the roofs of the houses.

In his first letter, dated 14 June, to the Speaker, Cromwell had predicted an early end to the siege. 'Confident I am, we shall have it in Fourteen days by starving'. He was also certain that the town mills could be destroyed by gunfire and that 'we can take away his [Poyer's] water in two days, by beating down a staircase, which gives into a cellar where he hath a well'. The mills referred to were probably the ones on the bridge outside the North Gate. It is unlikely that they were still operating during the siege and as Cromwell never again mentions them in his letters, he presumably did not carry out his threat.

The entry concerning the well raises a thorny question: where exactly was it? Cromwell does not disclose its location, but by tradition there was a well in the Wogan Cavern below the castle; if one existed there, no trace of it has been found. There was another well in the basement of Barnard's Tower. No attempt seems to have been made to destroy either of these wells, as the stonework around them bears no scars from gunfire and Cromwell makes no further reference to the water supply in his later correspondence.

It is worth noting that water was also obtained from one of several springs near Norgan's Hill, south-west of Pembroke. From this point it flowed through earthenware pipes that ran underground until they came to the creek surrounding the castle, where they were supposedly laid across the riverbed before entering the building through an arch in the vicinity of the Monkton Tower.[12] A long-established legend insists that this was the only water supply for the castle – and perhaps the town – and that the severing of the pipes led to an eventual surrender. This is untrue; the pipes may have been broken on Cromwell's orders, but he was probably pinning his hopes of success on starvation and the eventual arrival of the heavy siege guns (see Appendix II).[13]

By 13 June the guns had still not arrived, so two smaller cannon were placed on Golden Hill overlooking the Mill Pond. Towards evening, a steady bombardment of the town commenced and as the timber-framed walls and roofs of the houses crumpled under the hammer blows, the thatch burst into flame. That night Main Street blazed, and as the fires spread from house to house, men with long bill hooks tried to pull smouldering thatch from the roofs amidst showers of sparks and the inhabitants struggled to rescue their possessions from the flames. By the morning of the next day the bombardment was over but the flames still burned, as Cromwell informed the Speaker in the letter of 14 June: 'Last night we fired divers houses; which "fire" runs up the town still: it much frights them'.[14]

A day or two later an even greater terror was added to the miseries endured by the inhabitants of Pembroke. The Parliamentary guns had opened up a breach in the town walls, possibly somewhere at the east end of the town. A storming party led by Colonels Horton and Okey forced their way through the opening and a running battle took place along Main Street. Despite fierce resistance and hand-to-hand fighting, the defenders were driven back almost to the gates of the castle, losing a hundred men. Pembroke might have fallen at that moment but one of the Parliamentary majors, who should have brought in a reserve of pike and musket to reinforce Horton, failed to do so. The reason for his non-appearance is unknown, but it gave Laugharne a chance to counter attack. There is evidence that Laugharne was in command of troops at the East Gate and Barnard's Tower. A pamphlet entitled *A Great and Bloody Fight at Pembroke Castle*, printed in London in July 1648, contains extracts from a letter written at the time:

> Major-General Laugharne came in the rear of them [Horton's men] with a party of horse and forced them to quit the town, out of which they were driven, and about 30 of our men killed and some few wounded – the rest made good their retreat.
>
> Of the enemy it is supposed their loss was many more as appears by the confession of divers who have since deserted that service and come into the Lieutenant General [Cromwell].[15]

Once again Main Street was a nightmare scene, littered with dead and wounded men, abandoned weapons and bloodied garments. The ordinary men and women of the town, crouching in their cellars, attics and outhouses, must have prayed for it all to be over.

Though many of the garrison were determined to fight on, the morale of others was ebbing away. Desertions continued at a steady rate, men dropping over the walls and surrendering at the Parliamentary outposts. They brought with them tales of the conditions within the town. An anonymous correspondent, writing on 19 June, gave some details:

> This town is almost at the last gasp, being much discontented and divided, occasioned by want of victuals, but Colonel Poyer studies how to delude the soldiers, declaring to them that before Monday he will warrant relief from Major General Langdale.[16]

Sir Marmaduke Langdale had seized Berwick for the King on 28 April and was rumoured to be marching south, backed by a Scottish army. He may never have intended to send help to Pembroke, but Poyer was willing to tell any lie if it kept his men at their posts.

Cromwell had his own worries to deal with. The threat from Scotland was only too real. The Marquess of Hamilton was said to be gathering men and munitions to aid Langdale in the north of England. Parliament was anxious to see an end to the siege of Pembroke, but on 25 June Cromwell was forced to send a detachment of his troops northwards to counter the threat of invasion.

> The number I sent are six troops: four of horse and two of dragoons; whereof three are Colonel Scroop's – and Captain Pennyfeather's troop and the other two dragoons. I could not, by the judgement of the Colonels here, spare more, nor send them sooner, without manifest hazard to these parts. Here is, as I have formerly acquainted your Excellency, a very desperate Enemy, who being put out of all hope of mercy, are resolved to endure up to the uttermost extremity; being very many of them gentlemen of quality, and men thoroughly resolved. They have made some notable sallies upon Lieutenant Colonel Reade's quarter, to his loss. We are forced to keep divers posts, or else they would have relief, or their horse break away. Our foot about them are four-and-twenty hundred; we always necessitated to have some in garrisons'.[17]

Towards the end of June the heavy siege guns and mortars finally arrived at Pembroke. With these in place, it did not take long to open up several breaches in the town walls. As a result, Cromwell's Council of War decided to make yet another assault upon the battered town. One of the besiegers wrote:

> Tuesday last we gave the town another strong alarm. One hundred and twenty of Poyer's men laid down their arms, vowing never to take them up again; but by the importunity of Poyer and Laugharne telling them, if relief came not within four days they would yield, and they should hang them, they have engaged again. We are informed that they have not provisions for 14 days. We expect every day that most of them will come to us through want – they only have a little rainwater and biscuit left. But it is still feared that Poyer and Laugharne, when they can hold out the town no longer, will betake themselves to the castle, and leave the rest to mercy. If we get the town, we doubt not to carry the castle suddenly.
>
> Our mortar pieces have played hard against the town and done great execution; have battered down many houses and killed at the least thirty of the enemy, as appears by the confession of two of Poyer's men who came over the walls to us.[18]

Many of those killed by the mortar fire were townspeople and their deaths underlined the possibility that if Pembroke were taken by storm, innocent civilians might die. This likelihood surely weighed upon the consciences of Laugharne and his officers. It was clear that no help was coming; Sir Marmaduke

Langdale was too far away and was intent on joining forces with Hamilton; Lord Inchiquin's troops were still in Ireland; and Prince Charles, despite the promises of his advisors, could give no aid. Nor was this all. After a six-week siege during which at least 2,500 people had to be fed daily, food stocks must have dwindled to worrying levels. Despite claims in the Royalist newspaper *Mercurius Elenticus* that the castle was well provided with beef, salt, butter, herrings and cheese, the reports of shortages given by the deserters may have reflected the truth of the situation.

The fact of their isolation spurred Poyer and Laugharne to consider surrender. Poyer sent out a message to the Leaguer asking for terms and claiming that he had always been faithful to the Parliament and, rather pathetically, wondering why a 'David should be persecuted by a Saul'. Cromwell's first inclination was to offer no terms at all and to insist on an absolute surrender, but there were good reasons for considering a more moderate approach. Firstly, if the Pembroke garrison refused to surrender, the siege might drag on for weeks. Secondly, and more importantly, his troops were urgently needed elsewhere to counter the threat from the Scots. To delay sending reinforcements to the north might have catastrophic results. After consultation with his army colleagues, Cromwell drew up terms and sent them into Pembroke by the hand of Hugh Peters.

The conditions upon which Cromwell prepared to accept surrender were much harsher than Poyer had anticipated. All the principal officers within Pembroke were expected to offer unconditional submission to the mercy of Parliament. Realising that this could result in a death sentence, if not immediate execution, Laugharne, Poyer and the others seem to have spent hours debating the terms. Hugh Peters remained a hostage in the town whilst the discussions went on and was removed from the castle to Poyer's house, where he was locked in the cellar. His confinement lasted some time, but provided him with a treasure trove of evidence against the rebels. In a letter dated 23 July and written from Swansea, he described what he had found:

> I being commanded in a hostage and to wait upon Major-General Laugharne and Poyer and lay in Poyer's house and in a vault there, found his commission under the Prince's own hand and seale which shews that they fought not for arrears; besides all the transactions betwixt the prince and them: together with many other letters of theirs manifesting the whole design of this year's trouble.[19]

Eventually Peters was brought out of his confinement and dispatched back to the Leaguer with a plea for easier terms. Cromwell made a few unimportant alterations and the document was sent back to Poyer with an accompanying letter:

Sir,

I have (together with my Council of War) renewed my propositions I thought fit to send them to you with these alterations, which if submitted unto I shall make good. I have considered your condition and my own duty: and (without threatening) must tell you that if (for the sake of some) this offer be refused and thereby misery and ruin befall the poor soldiers and people with you, I know where to charge the blood you spill. I expect your answer within these two hours. In case this offer be refused, send no more to me about this subject.

    I rest your servant

    Ol. Cromwell

    July 10, at 4 a'clock this afternoon 1648

Anyone reading this letter could be in no doubt as to what would happen if Pembroke did not submit. The town would be taken by storm and those within, soldiers and civilians alike, would face the same fate as had befallen the luckless people of Leicester, Birmingham, Bolton and Liverpool, where hundreds had been slaughtered in the streets.[20]

The majority of the Royalist officers agreed to accept the terms, though both Poyer and Laugharne had to be 'overswayed' into submission and neither of them signed the articles of surrender. The main signatory for the garrison was David Poyer, John's brother, who had been by his side throughout the siege.

    Articles for the Surrender of Pembroke Town and Castle

That Major-General Laugharne, Col. Poyer, Col. Humphrey Matthews, Capt. William Bowen, and David Poyer do surrender themselves to the mercy of Parliament.

    That Sir Charles Kemeys, Sir Henry Stradling, Mr Miles Button, Major Pritchard, Lieut-Col. Stradling, Liet-Col. Laugharne and eleven other officers do within six weeks next following depart the kingdom and not to return within two years from the time of their departure.

    That all officers and gentlemen not before named, shall have free liberty to go to their several habitations, and then live quietly, submitting to the authority of Parliament.

    That all private soldiers shall have passes to go to the several houses without being stripped, or having any violence done to them – all sick and wounded men to be carefully provided for, till able to go home, etc.

    That the townsmen shall be free from plunder and violence and enjoy their liberties as heretofore they have done, having freedom to remove themselves and their families wither they shall think fit, etc.

    That the Town and Castle of Pembroke, with all the arms, ammunition and ordnance, together with all the victuals and provisions for the garrison, be forthwith delivered into my hands or such as I shall appoint for the use of the Parliament

    Oliver Cromwell

    David Poyer

On 11 July, Commissioners were sent into the town to receive the formal surrender of the castle with all its weapons and ammunition. Poyer, Laugharne and the other named officers were taken into custody and presumably locked up within the castle. In order to facilitate matters Cromwell moved out of Welston Court and took up residence in the York Tavern in Main Street, where he lodged for five days.[21] On the day of the surrender, Cromwell wrote to the Speaker, enclosing a copy of the terms.

> Sir
> The Town and Castle of Pembroke were surrendered to me this day, being the eleventh of July, upon the propositions which I send you here enclosed. What arms, ammunition, victuals, ordnance, or other necessaries of war are in [the town] I have not to certify you – the Commissioners I sent in to receive the same not yet being returned, nor like suddenly to be; and I was unwilling to defer the giving you an account of this mercy for a day.
> The persons excepted are such as have formerly served you in a very good cause; but being now apostatised I did rather make election of them than of these who had always been for the King; judging their iniquity double, because they have sinned against so much light and against so many evidences of Divine Providence going along with and prospering a just Cause, in the management of which they themselves had a share.
> I rest, your humble servant
> Oliver Cromwell[22]

The letter reached London on 15 July and was read to the Commons two days later. The messenger was awarded £20 and the members of the House sent instructions to Cromwell to begin marching north with all possible speed. Cromwell had in fact already left Pembroke on the first leg of his journey, having attended a thanksgiving service conducted by the Reverend Peregrine Phillips, vicar of Monkton.[23] He also gave instructions for the demolition of sections of the town walls and of parts of the castle.

The man entrusted with the task of overseeing the destruction was Poyer's old enemy Roger Lort and he did his job well.[24] Which sections of the town defences were actually removed in 1648 is unclear, but the castle is known to have fared badly. The outer walls of the Bygate, Henry VII, Westgate and Northgate towers were all brought down by gunpowder.[25] An attempt was made to blow up the Barbican Tower, though it was so stoutly made that the explosion only cracked open the walls, lifted the roof and blasted a hole on the western wall.[26] The townspeople subsequently took stones from the ruins to repair their shattered houses, causing even more damage to the fabric of the building.

When Cromwell left Pembroke about 16 July he took with him as prisoners Rowland Laugharne and John Poyer, together with a number of others. Rice Powell joined them as they passed through Carmarthen on 18 July.[27]. Each of these men must have wondered if they would ever see their families and Pembrokeshire again. We do not know if Ann Laugharne had remained with her husband after Cromwell had allowed her entry into Pembroke, nor if she returned to the family home at St Brides following the surrender, but Elizabeth Poyer is said to have been with John throughout the siege. After the capitulation, she apparently took refuge at Templeton, about 12 miles away, where her children had been sent for safety.[28]

By 23 July, Cromwell had reached Gloucester en route to Nottingham, where a brief stop was made in order to place the prisoners in safe custody. They were incarcerated there until the autumn, when they were sent to the Army Headquarters at Windsor for trial.

18   The Trial

The decision to bring Laugharne, Poyer and Powell to trial on charges of treason was taken by Parliament. The three men were brought by slow stages to Windsor, which became their prison for the next few months. Efforts were already being made to secure their freedom, or at least to reduce the charges they faced. At the end of July or early in August Prince Charles wrote to Fairfax appealing for a less rigorous course to be taken against them and pointing out that they had acted under his commission. Fairfax replied that all three had betrayed the trust placed in them by Parliament and that the House itself had decided that they should be tried under martial law. He promised to lay the Prince's letter before both Houses for consideration, which he did on 19 August 1648.

This seems to have had some effect. Parliament agreed in November to the banishment of Laugharne, though no similar decision was taken regarding his companions. If Laugharne's family breathed a sigh of relief at the news, it was too soon. On 6 December, Colonel Pride carried out his famous 'Purge' of Parliament, denying entry to about 240 members and arresting 39 of them. Most of those excluded had refused in the previous August to declare the Scottish invaders to be traitors and had voted in favour of a treaty with King Charles, but as Hugh Peters pointed out, the remaining members were now responsible not to the people but to the army.[1]

It did not bode well for the prisoners at Windsor. Their executions were confidently forecast by many of the newspapers and at some point they were brought to the capital in anticipation of their trial. Some histories state that they were imprisoned in the Tower of London, but for the period of their court martial they were held at Whitehall.

On 15 March the Council of State appointed a committee which included Colonel Okey, Hugh Peters and Colonel Pride to prepare charges against the prisoners. The members were also to make a case against three other prisoners, David Poyer, Major Phillips and Captain Phillip Bowen.

The military court was in session from 4 April until 12 April. A full record of the proceedings appears not to have survived, but at the end of it Laugharne,

Poyer and Powell were all condemned to death. Their families immediately mounted a campaign to have the sentences commuted. Ann Laugharne begged that Rowland's actions at St Fagans and Pembroke 'might not cause all his former eminent services to be forgotten'. Rice Powell's sisters Maud, Mary and Elizabeth joined forces to try and obtain a pardon for him. Elizabeth Poyer also made pleas on her husband's behalf, but it was John himself who on 21 April addressed an appeal for mercy to Colonel Fleetwood, citing in mitigation his previous services to Parliament:

> Be pleased to cast your eye over these few lines, and present the truth to his Excellency. It is known how faithfully I have served the Parliament in their lowest ebb of affairs and at such time that the King had taken Bristol, all Wales – Pembroke excepted – declared for the King, our forces routed at Emling Castle by Gerett [Gerrard] myself then on shipboard bound for London: but on receipt of so sad news I repaired to Pembroke, prepared for a siege, and withstood Gerett and his forces for 11 weeks and at last forced him to raise the siege.
>
> I refused his offer of preferment with £5,000 to boot, and although not commissioned by Parliament, nor receiving a penney from them, I stood firm to my principles. I am proclaimed traitor without proof of disaffection, the small sum I prayed to relieve my poor wife and four children is denied me and despairing of right done me against my bloody enemies drove me desperate to defend myself and to secure some of them, but in obedience to the General's letter I released them, whose liberty hath produced much misfortune, brought myself to this deplorable condition.
>
> Had I intended to desert Parliament I should not have set at liberty Col. Fleming's soldiers and the seamen taken at Pembroke nor have sent privately to the Lord general [Fairfax] to surrender the town.
>
> Pardon my boldness for life is sweet and all lawful means are to be sought to preserve the same.[2]

This was not the only attempt that Poyer made to clear his reputation of some of the slurs cast upon it and to obtain mercy. At some point during his imprisonment he wrote an answer to *A Declaration of Divers Gentlemen of Wales concerning Collonel Poyer*, which had been published during April 1648. Entitled *Poyer's Vindication in answer to a lying Pamphlet*, it was printed in March 1649 and set out to answer many of the personal insults which the writers of the earlier piece had levelled against the Governor of Pembroke. Poyer recounts his version of the events of his life and is in no doubt as to who is the author of the Declaration; '... one John Eliot; who to satisfie his insatiable desire, hath thus mask'd himself in a dark Scene (without name) being ashamed to own such falshood as is there set forth'.

The combined pleas of the families clearly had some effect, for the Council of State announced that only one of the condemned men should actually die. The Council granted them the right to draw lots for their lives, but they were unwilling to choose for themselves. Three pieces of paper were prepared and placed in a bag; two bore the words 'Life given of God' and the third was blank. A child, possibly the daughter of the gaoler, was instructed to draw lots for the prisoners. A persistent legend was that, not understanding its significance, she gave the blank paper to the most handsome of the three men and thus Poyer received his death sentence.[3] 'Did I do well, sir?' she is said to have asked, frightened by the expression on his face. 'Yes, child', he replied, 'you did very well'.

Poyer's execution was fixed for 24 April. To those who came to inform him of the date, 'that he might the better fit himself for that great work', he seemed to accept the news calmly. He declared to them

> that he had but one life to lose, and in sacrificing of it in this World, hee hoped to have a blessed and joyful restauration thereof in the World to come, desiring God to forgive them, who were the causers of it, and that for his part he freely forgave them, being at peace with all men … desiring that his death might close up the breach of the people, and that his bloud might bee the last that should issue forth in streames within the Bowels of this Commonwealth.

He would presumably have been allowed to settle his affairs, such as they were, and no doubt was allowed visits from his friends. If, as is likely, Elizabeth was in London, there would have been one last, difficult farewell.

For some unknown reason, the execution was delayed for 24 hours. Early on the morning of Wednesday 25 April, John Poyer stepped into a coach at Whitehall and was conveyed through the streets of London to Covent Garden, where he was to die. Two troops of horse and three companies of foot of Colonel Hewson's regiment guarded him in his journey and he was accompanied by two ministers, Mr Knight and Mr Walter Cradock, the latter of whom he was supposed to have injured in a quarrel at Pembroke.

Upon arrival at Covent Garden, Poyer and his companions alighted from the coach and he was escorted to the spot chosen for his execution. At that time, Covent Garden was a large open space, bordered on its northern perimeter by a row of houses and to the west by St Paul's Church. The garden wall of Bedford House formed the southern boundary and Poyer was placed between two 'bulges' in the wall. He was allowed to make a short speech, during which he told his listeners that

> he desired the prayers of all good people for his present wading through the vaile of misery; that he was willing to sacrifice his life; that he freely

forgave all men; that he had ever acted for the liberty and freedom of the subject; that he was an unfeigned and cordial lover of the peace of England; that he died a true protestant according to the Discipline of the Church of England and that he desired a speedy period might be put to the present distractions between prince and people.

With this formal address over, he knelt in prayer and then, with remarkable courage, summoned the six musketeers who were to shoot him. The signal to fire, he told them, would be the holding up of both his hands. He spoke again to the friends gathered near.

> I confess that I have lived very loosely ... though I was once low yet I became very high ... but now I must leave all ... although my fortune changed my affections to the Parliament did not alter ... I was always honest with them until an unhappy disaster which hath brought this misery to me.

There was one more brief prayer. Turning to face the firing squad, Poyer called aloud 'Come Lord Jesus. Lord receive my soul' and having now 'prepared an embracement for death', he lifted up his hands and 'the Executioners (with their fire locks) did their Office, who at once bereaved him of his life'.[4]

The corpse was quickly taken up and placed in the coach which bore it away. Colonel Hewson's regiment was marched back to Whitehall. Poyer's friends sorrowfully made their way to their homes and lodgings, whilst behind them the acrid smell of gunpowder hung briefly in the air and curious crowds gathered at the spot where the infamous Colonel Poyer had died.

19 Aftermath

The execution of John Poyer was preceded, almost three months earlier, on 30 January, by that of King Charles, who perished on a scaffold outside the Banqueting Hall of Whitehall Palace. If Poyer was at that time a prisoner at Whitehall, he may have heard the groan of horror that went up from the watching crowd as the axe fell. It was a horror certainly felt by many Welshmen, who still saw the monarch as an essential pillar of the social order. James Howell, an ardent Royalist who had been thrust into the Fleet Prison in London on suspicion of being 'a dangerous malignant', could not believe what had happened: 'the more I ruminate upon it, the more it astonisheth my imagination, and shaketh all the cells of my brain'.[1]

There were those who regarded Charles Stuart's death as a necessary evil. Colonel John Jones of Maesygarnedd and Thomas Wogan of Wiston, MP for the Cardigan boroughs, had both signed the King's death warrant.[2] Morgan Llwyd, a determined Puritan, believed that the sentence of death was a just one: 'Unhappy Charles provoked the lamb, to dust he must withdraw'.[3]

Whatever their views about the King, no one could have been happy at the state of Wales at the end of the Second Civil War. The country had been ravaged: every shire had seen military action of some sort, with castles and houses plundered and stores of cattle and food appropriated by passing armies. Churches had suffered particularly badly, serving as dormitories, stables and ammunition stores. St Davids Cathedral lost much of the lead from its roof to make musket balls and at Wrexham the organ pipes of the parish church had been put to the same use.[4]

Towns that had been known for their prosperity were in a ruinous state. Wrexham and Oswestry had been deliberately fired during the war. John Taylor, known as the Water Poet because he worked as a waterman on the Thames, travelled through Wales in 1652 and found Harlech 'had neither hay, grass, oats or any relief for a horse; there stands a strong house, but the town is all spoild and almost (un)inhabitable by the late lamentable troubles'.[5] Riding his beloved nag Dun, Taylor made his way to Pembroke, which had clearly not recovered from the siege of 1648: 'The shire town, Pembrook, hath been in a better estate, for as is now, some houses down, some standing and many without inhabitants ...'.[6]

Many Welsh communities were still complaining bitterly about the assessments they were having to pay and about the continued quartering of soldiers and their behaviour. As early as December 1648, Colonel Horton was forced to issue a warning order to his men:

> Whereas I have been informed that divers soldiers both dragoons and foot under my command within this county of Pembrock have by disorderly carriage and misbehaviour in their quarters forced their landlords to quarter them in inns and alehouses, the dragoons at 3s 6d per diem and the foot a 1s per diem, as well for the punishment of the said offence as the prevention of the same and others for the future I do declare that if any soldier or soldiers have or shall commit the said offence or any other contrary to the articles of war ... the party offended shall have due reparation and the offender undergo the judgement of a court martial ...[7]

Tenby was in such dire straits that Cromwell, passing through on his way to Ireland in 1649, gave the mayor £10 for the relief of the poor. During the previous October, Colonel Dawkins had issued a written order to Captain Beale, one of his officers: 'In regard to the poverty of Tinby, you are to march to Haverfordwest and to quarter your soldiers there until further notice.'[8]

This instruction raised a howl of protest from the councillors of Haverfordwest, who pointed out how much they had already spent on the care of wounded Parliamentary soldiers and that the town was already suffering under a heavy rate of assessment and a tax for the relief of Ireland. In 1649, the situation worsened; a new rate for the support of troops was introduced. A monthly payment of £45 was now expected, three times what had been paid before, even though, as the councillors made clear in a new petition:

> the army in August and September last in their march to Milford Haven to take shipping for Ireland were maintained ... for the most part upon free quarter and continued a long time on them there and do daily quarter there as they go. And by reason hereof your petitioners are brought very poor, and most of the inhabitants of this town not able to maintain themselves and families, and many of them forced to leave this town by reason of the said heavy assessment, will be to your petitioners utter undoing.[9]

By November of that year the council was seeking compensation for the £500 it had cost to give the troops free quarter. Four years later the unpaid arrears owed by the town amounted to the enormous sum of £1,260 and Haverfordwest had no alternative but to keep a representative in London constantly to petition

Parliament for relief. Eventually, success was achieved; the monthly rate was reduced to £25 and the arrears were remitted on immediate payment of £120.[10]

By this time much of Pembrokeshire was in the grip of an outbreak of plague. In Haverfordwest, 207 people perished within nine months, with many more dying later. Although Pembroke seems to have escaped the worst of it, Tenby was hard hit. It has been estimated that out of a population of about 1,000, between 300 and 400 died. The town was cut off from the rest of the county, with traders leaving food supplies for the inhabitants outside the town walls.

The problems were further exacerbated by a series of poor harvests that, after 1646, had led to a huge increase in food prices. In some areas restrictions were imposed on the consumption of corn, whilst other parts of the countryside had been so denuded of food supplies by the war effort that there was very little left. The people in the rural areas around Haverfordwest were still complaining in 1650 that Gerard's forces had 'so eaten, spoiled and made desolate' the surrounding parishes that no crops could flourish.

For the majority of merchants and tradespeople, the resumption of peace brought no immediate easing of hardship. The drovers and cloth merchants of north and mid-Wales had found their supplies and trade routes disrupted during the war and their stocks had been appropriated by the warring armies. Towns that had been important market centres had been abandoned by the merchants who had contributed to their commercial success and who had moved elsewhere to set up business. It was not until the Restoration that some towns recovered their fortunes.[11]

Marine trade had also suffered. Many ships were absorbed into the navy of one side or the other, often serving as auxiliary warships. Even when peace was restored, the owners found themselves involved in a long struggle for compensation, as a petition presented to the Lord Protector on 16 August 1655 makes clear:

> John Whicker and other owners of the *Gillyflower* .... In 1644 when Pembrokeshire was almost lost to Parliament for want of money, arms and ammunition from their good affection and at request of the County Commissioners, they furnished the public with money and goods from their ships, value £557 12s 6d and have a receipt therefore. The said Commissioners then took up the ship at £150 a month for four months to guard the port and town and land men and ordnance, make the entire claim £1,157 12s 8d.

For the principal figures of the Civil Wars in south Wales, the coming of peace did not guarantee success or contentment. In truth, their fortunes were often in inverse proportion to the commitment and determination with which they had supported their cause.

The Lort brothers and John Eliot, who had changed sides as the wind blew, were all accused of delinquency by Parliament because of their support for the King during 1643. Roger Lort was fined £1,000, but there is no record of its being paid. In March 1649 the accusations were dropped in view of their later loyalty to Parliament and because of their opposition to John Poyer. On the day before their discharge they were granted a lucrative contract from the Admiralty Committee to supply ships arriving at Tenby and Milford.

Roger Lort had already been chosen by Cromwell to oversee the destruction of some of Pembrokeshire's castles. Both he and Sampson were appointed as Justices of the Peace, having already joined the Committee administering the collection of a fine levied on south Wales for delinquency during the Second Civil War. Sampson in particular was prepared to aim high; not only did he serve as High Sheriff of Pembrokeshire in 1649 (he was followed by his brothers Roger in 1651 and John in 1652), but when the Propagation Act was passed in 1649 to promote the 'Better Propagation and Preaching of the Gospel in Wales', his Puritan views ensured that he was one of the nominated commissioners. There must have been some family tension in 1654, when Roger was one of those appointed to investigate the finances of the Propagation and Sampson's part in its conduct.[12] Small wonder that one of Sampson's contemporaries described him as one who could 'pray as long as there is profit'.

During the 1650s, Sampson made several attempts to get himself elected as a Member of Parliament for Haverfordwest. His most determined effort came in 1660 when the Long Parliament was to be recalled. 'All the fanatic party' of Pembrokeshire gave him their support and went about armed to the teeth. These men seem to have included some members of the county militia and as the likelihood of a restoration of the monarchy increased, they gathered together a rag-tag crew of cobblers, hatters, weavers and tailors and paraded with their troop colours to which had been added the motto 'Noe kinge, Noe Lorde, We are ingaged'. Lort, as captain of the troop, ordered the words to be removed, but this did not improve his chances of election. As he was not a burgess of Haverfordwest the sheriff would not acknowledge him as a candidate and the opposition candidate, William Phillips, was elected. Sampson then petitioned the Houses of Parliament to disqualify Phillips. On 27 June the result was declared void, but two months later Phillips was again returned and thereafter Sampson seems to have given up his Parliamentary ambitions.

To Rice Powell, who might once have expected no mercy for his part in the events of 1648, fate was kind. He was pardoned after petitioning Parliament and, on 7 May 1649, was given his freedom. What happened to him afterwards is unclear. He may have returned to Pembrokeshire, but his life was far from comfortable. In 1665 he was forced to appeal to King Charles II for assistance to meet debts he had incurred in the Civil War, but there is no indication as to whether or not he was successful.[13]

Rowland Laugharne had also petitioned Parliament for a pardon and was released on the same day as Powell. Many of his estates had been sequestered and sold by Parliament because of his involvement in the 1648 rebellion, but he managed to retain some properties. However in 1650 there were suspicions that he was involved in 'designs against Parliament' and he was re-arrested. Once this particular squall was over, he was released and spent much of his time in Pembrokeshire, where he involved himself in the life of the county. When Tenby was struck by plague in 1650-1, he sent the Mayor, David Palmer, a gift of 45s 6d for distribution to the poor, accompanying it with a box of powder recommended as a cure for the disease. He visited the town later in the year and was entertained at the Mayor's expense. An entry in the account books reads 'Paid for beare [beer] bestowed on maior generall Laugharne at John Devereux with Mr Rice Barrow and Mr Will Bowen 5s 6d'.[14]

In November 1649 Laugharne had been fined £712 for his delinquency in making war against Parliament. This was not immediately collected, but by 1655 there were calls for it to be paid. The only way for this to be done was through the sale of more land, which had been mortgaged to offset debts, and the sale would have to take place quickly, before the claims on the estate amounted to more than it was worth. Laugharne now faced abject poverty, but he was fortunate that several factors were working in his favour. It was remembered by the Council of State that he had performed many good services to Parliament; that as a result he had lost £1,000 a year and estates to the value of £30,000; that he was £4,000 in debt; and that he had been living in peace and seclusion ever since 1649.[15] The fine was remitted.

In 1659, however, there came another whiff of political troubles. The details are murky but Laugharne was required to give security to behave peaceably.

The Restoration appeared to mark an improvement in his prospects. He was elected as MP for the Pembroke Boroughs in 1661, a position he held until his death in 1676. He had also been granted by Parliament £3,000 out of the Excise. This generous sum was presumably intended to help him at a time of financial difficulty, but he never received even half of the amount.

For the rest of his life Laugharne struggled against debt and both he and his wife addressed several petitions to Parliament. On 19 March 1662 he requested some sort of recompense, as he had lost £37,630 and had been forced to sell most of his estates. Upon receipt of this address Parliament voted him a grant of £500 but dawdled for two years before paying it.[16] At the same time he was assured of a pension of £500 but within a year he was petitioning 'for continuance and arrears of his pension of £500 lately stopped'. Two years later his debts had grown so great that he appealed for £3,000 'that he may return to his own county'.

In 1665 Ann took up the cudgels, writing to Lord Arlington 'to obtain for her husband the request in his petition that he may return to his own county and not stay to his utter ruin. He lost £37,000 of which £12,000 was cash left at Derby House: though absent from his own county he is so well beloved that he had been chosen as Member of Parliament and can do good service'.

As they struggled with their poverty, Rowland and Ann cannot have been pleased to learn that Roger Lort, the man described as being 'of any principle or religion to acquire wealth' had been granted a warrant making him a baronet. There was heartache too in their private life. In 1667 they lost two of their sons; Arthur was killed during a naval action against the French in the West Indies and Thomas, also serving in the navy, fell in battle against the Dutch.[17]

There was some hope in 1669 that his financial situation would improve, when Laugharne, together with several others, was granted a licence to hold plate lotteries in Ireland, but he remained burdened with debt. He had to forward yet another petition 'for present relief to pay his lodgings and clothe his family, having waited 8 years in expectation also for a weekly pension till the £3,500 due to him from the late King [Charles I] is paid ... his real estate is extended for £8,000 and is almost past redemption'. The following year there was a further appeal, this time from Ann to Lord Arlington, 'for relief for her poor husband who had been ill 8 weeks and in want of all things. Has been obliged to pawn his cloak and sword and has only 3s in the world'.[18]

By now Laugharne was an elderly man. He had managed to retain the core of his estates, the land at St Brides, but the extensive acres his family had once owned were all gone. He still commanded respect in Pembrokeshire and in 1674 he became Deputy-Lieutenant for the county. The pension he had been granted was now £4,000 in arrears and it must have been with great relief that he heard that the Lord Treasurer had recommended that this sum should be paid to him.

He died in 1676, probably in London, where he had spent much of his time since his election as an MP. His place of burial has been suggested as St Margaret's, Westminster. The £4,000 of arrears remained unpaid at the time of his death and Ann was to receive not a penny of it.[19]

There is one last, sad glimpse of Ann in 1680, shortly before her own death.

> Ann Laugharne, relict of Major-General Laugharne, asks his Majesty to remember that she has lost two sons in his service. She, being in danger of arrest and forced to keep several lodgings to secure her from prison, is living under the protection of Sir Edmund Windham.
>
> She prays for £400 to pay her debts and 40s a week during her life and one year after to bury her, she being near seventy-two years old. If shee be not blessed with a settlement before your Majesties removal shee must perish. If your Majesty thinks not this convenient your petitioner humbly prays your Majesty to give her what you please.[20]

The thought of this aged lady having to hurry from place to place to avoid arrest for debt is a pathetic one. Her petition went unanswered.

Life for Elizabeth Poyer was equally harsh. After John's execution she was left virtually destitute with four children to bring up. She chose to settle in Pembroke, where she spent the rest of her life. On 20 September 1649, an 'Elizabeth Poyer, widow' presumably John Poyer's wife, took out a 21 year lease on a house and two closes of land in St Michael's parish within Pembroke, at a rent of £5 per annum.[21] In an attempt to recover some of the fortune her husband had spent on the defence of Pembroke, Elizabeth begged Charles II for help on numerous occasions. In addition to the joint petition of 1660 in which she and Miles and Florence Button were signatories, she presented at least four others, in each of which she reminded the King that her husband had died in the Royalist cause. In the first of these she claimed that John had lost £8,000 during the war, whilst she had lost 'her whole estate'.

Elizabeth seems to have achieved a measure of success through her various applications, for in 1663 she was granted £100. This was followed by a further grant of £3,000 to be paid at a rate of £300 a year for 10 years, 'which would save her perishing family and give them bread to eat and time to glorify God for His Majesty's Christian relief'.[22]

The money appears to have been paid via Sir John Prettyman, 'formerly receiver General of First Fruits and Tenths'. It is probable that some of the people to whom the Poyer family was in debt to the tune of £1,500 intercepted the money before Elizabeth received it, for in 1665 she sought from Lord Arlington 'a warrant for a caveat that none interfere with her grant'.[23] Even when she received this assurance all did not go smoothly, for on 21 February 1669 a declaration appeared in the Calendar of State Papers Domestic to the effect that 'Sir John Prettyman's arrears, granted to Francis Rogers on 16 January last are on trust for payment of moneys due to widow Poyer, the residue to be disposed of as Barbara, Countess of Castlemaine, in her own writing (shall) appoint for her benefit.'

Elizabeth was still living in Pembroke in 1670, when her name appears in the Hearth Tax Survey. Two years later she wrote yet another letter in support of her petitions for relief, but thereafter she disappears from history, the date of her death unknown.[24]

As the last decades of the seventeenth century slipped by, they bore away with them the men and women who had experienced the terrifying, exhilarating events of the Great Rebellion. With their passing, memories became legends and legends were distorted as they were repeated down through the generations. The severing of the pipes supplying Pembroke with water became the sole reason for the surrender of the town in 1648; Cromwell became the victor of Colby Moor and visited St Davids Cathedral in person to strip the lead from the roof; and what most people chose to remember about John Poyer was his drunkenness and dishonesty.

Of the three principal characters in this book, it is probably the reputation of Rowland Laugharne that has fared best. It rests on his successful campaigns in Pembrokeshire in 1644 and 1645 and on his subsequent success in Glamorgan, all of which earned him the trust and gratitude of Parliament. An unknown contemporary summed up the prevailing attitude to him by describing him as a 'forward sword-man and a slow pen-man'.

It seems that Laugharne did not often commit himself to paper, though it is always possible that much of his correspondence has been lost. He never commented either in writing or verbally on religious or political matters and prior to 1648 he made no effort to use his growing reputation for personal advancement. There are no stories of corrupt dealings and as far as we know he did not hold grudges. He seems to have been regarded as a man of integrity who enjoyed the respect of his peers and even after his change of allegiance he never became the victim of a smear campaign. This is all the more remarkable when one considers that Parliament obviously had doubts about his loyalties and ordered his detention on several occasions. Perhaps he was seen as a man who sincerely championed a particular cause and adhered to a code of conduct that others recognised but with which they no longer agreed.

Some modern historians have questioned Laugharne's military ability. Although he eventually succeeded in clearing the Royalist forces out of South Wales, he fared less well when faced with determined and experienced commanders such as Gerard or Horton. In 1645 he allowed himself to be surprised at Newcastle Emlyn and had to withdraw into the strongholds of Tenby and Pembroke. It was only the King's defeat at Naseby that allowed him to emerge and re-establish control of the area.

He may have had concerns about the ability of his own men to stand up to Gerard's troops. Some of his soldiers were said to be ex-members of Ormonde's Irish army, men who had taken service with Laugharne to avoid being thrown into the sea when Captain Swanley captured their transports. They were hardly likely to be the most committed of Parliamentarians and on each of his campaigns in Pembrokeshire, Laugharne had to strengthen their resolve with a healthy injection of men from the navy ships anchored in Milford Haven. At Colby Moor this may well have swung the balance of the battle in his favour, for though the Royalists were numerically superior, Gerard had already taken the cream of his troops back to England.

The situation in Glamorgan in 1645-7 was on the whole favourable to Laugharne. The opposition was fragmented and divided within itself and strong Parliamentary support was forthcoming from the navy and from Gloucester and Bristol. Laugharne had also put in place agreements with the gentry of

Glamorgan, Brecon and Powys, which made at harder for the Royalists to gather long-lasting and cohesive support.

The real tragedy of Laugharne's story is that ultimately he identified himself with a cause that could not succeed. Either through inclination, or lack of opportunity, or because of geographical distance, he failed to develop meaningful links with the men who were responsible for a new political climate and so he found himself isolated. Even the close religious and familial links he had shared with others of the west Wales gentry failed him. The Owens, Wogans and Meyricks, to whom he was related, all managed to reach an accommodation with the political elite and in doing so preserved their estates and fortunes.

In the same way and for the same reasons Rice Powell found himself distanced from his former companions. The Cunys made clear their loyalties by allowing Cromwell to stay at Welston and during 1648 other members of Powell's large family apparently kept very quiet. It is difficult to appreciate Rice's reasons for acting as he did because few of his personal papers have survived. Most of what we know of him comes from the writings of other people and he remains a shadowy figure, the least substantial of the leaders in Pembrokeshire.

Not so with John Poyer. He is arguably the most famous of them all, a larger than life, rumbustious, buccaneering figure, and the one whose presence we are aware of in the background even when focussing on the activities of others.

It has already been pointed out that our view of Poyer is influenced by the writings of John Eliot and others. Besides drunkenness and embezzlement, they also accused him of never having married Elizabeth and of fathering several illegitimate children upon her. He is also supposed to have severely beaten the Reverend Cradock and another minister, Mr Evan Roberts, in Pembroke and to have held Presbyterian, if not downright irreligious views.

These charges are complete nonsense. No other contemporary refers to Elizabeth as John's mistress and in a small community like Pembroke, where he was a major figure, everyone would have known their business. Besides, Elizabeth would never have petitioned King Charles II in the way that she did – as John's legal wife – had she been anything less, nor would Miles and Florence Button have agreed to present a joint appeal with her in 1660. She may well have been pregnant when John married her in about 1643, but we can be sure that they were legally wed.

As to Poyer's religious views, he stated on several occasions – most notably in his speech immediately before he was shot – that he was 'a true protestant according to the Discipline of the Church of England', which should settle the matter for good. The story of his treatment of the two ministers should also be treated with caution. He may well have quarrelled with them at some point, but he was on respectful enough terms with Cradock for that gentleman to accompany him to his death.

Some of the other charges laid against Poyer may well contain an element of truth. How much of a drunkard, if at all, Poyer actually was we shall never know, but there is no doubt that he never hesitated to take advantage of circumstances and that he was prepared to use force when it suited him. In doing so he differed very little from others amongst his contemporaries, to whom war presented many opportunities for self-advancement. By his actions, he gave his enemies the chance to bring him down and furthermore, by resisting in the way he did a suggested inquiry into his conduct, he placed himself beyond any hope of redemption.

It is that vivid mixture of wrong-headedness, determination, opportunism and courage that has ensured his name has lasted. Most people in Pembroke today are aware of who he was and what he did. A street in the town is named after him and places associated with him can still be pointed out. No visitor to the castle can leave without discovering something of his part in its history. It is a kind of immortality and it would probably have delighted him.

Appendices

Appendix I

Peregrine Phillips was a staunch supporter of Parliament, though not of its soldiers. It is said that a number of men were billeted in his house during the siege of Pembroke. Determined to preserve at least some of his supplies from forage, Phillips had all the pillows in the house stuffed with flour, which the soldiers slept on each night without ever realising what they contained. Another tale tells how his maid milked the cows sitting between two the of cannon which were sited in the vicarage garden. The daily bombardment of the castle could not begin until she had finished; a nice story, if apocryphal. A strict Puritan and Dissenter, Phillips was later ejected from the livings of Freystrop and Llangwm in Pembrokeshire, to which he had moved from Pembroke. His beliefs resulted in a spell in prison and his treatment by the sentencing magistrates so enraged one of his parishioners that the man declared that 'he cared not a turd for any justices of the peace'. Phillips' life seems to have been filled with incident. Once, whilst riding home late one night near Freystrop, he and his horse fell down an abandoned mineshaft. Both became securely wedged in the narrow opening until rescued in the morning.

Appendix II

According to legend, Cromwell was anxious to find the location of the underground pipes which supplied Pembroke Castle with its water. None of the local people would divulge the secret until a carpenter named Edmonds pointed out where the pipes lay. As a result, the water supply was cut off, forcing the surrender of the castle. Not long after, Edmonds was hung on Cromwell's orders, either because he had betrayed Cromwell's trust over another matter, or because Cromwell himself despised what Edmonds had done. The general is supposed to have said that if Edmonds would betray his own townsmen, he would betray anyone. The Edmonds family were later banned from living within the town and took up residence in a cottage below the walls. Edmonds himself was supposed to have been buried in the hole which had been dug to break the pipes. A stone carved with the representation of a cat was placed near the scene of his burial; the significance of the cat is unknown, unless it is that in the seventeenth century a cat was regarded as an untrustworthy animal. The stone can now be seen in the castle museum.

Appendix III

In 1883 the American writer Mark Twain was reading a copy of Carlyle's *Letters and Speeches of Oliver Cromwell* when he came across an account of the execution of John Poyer. He was fascinated by the tale of the child who had chosen the lots which decided Poyer's fate and eventually wrote a short story entitled *The Death Disc*, also called *The Death Wafer*.

The central figure is the 7-year-old Abby, the daughter of Colonel Mayfair, an officer in Cromwell's army. Mayfair had disobeyed Cromwell's orders during an attack on a Royalist position. As a result, he and two others were tried by military court and sentenced to death. Only one of them is to be executed and the victim is chosen by lot. Abby draws the lots and without knowing its significance she gives the red disc representing death to her father. When Cromwell realises what has happened, he pardons Mayfair.

The Death Disc was first published in the 1901 Christmas issue of *Harper's Magazine*. In February 1902 it was staged as a one act play at the Children's Theatre at Carnegie Hall. Seven years later it was made into a silent film by D.W. Griffith, arguably the greatest director of the early cinema.

Bibliography

Abbreviations

CSPD   Calendar of State Papers Domestic
CCRO   Carmarthenshire County Record Office
DCC   Dyfed County Council
HL   Haverfordwest Library
HMSO   Her Majesty's Stationery Office
NLW   National Library of Wales
OUP   Oxford University Press
UWP   University of Wales
PCRO   Pembrokeshire County Records Office
PTC   Pembroke Town Council

Magazines and periodicals

Archaeologia Cambrensis 1846, 1851, 1853, 1859, 1869, 1872, 1880, 1882, 1883, 1896, 1898, 1915, 1922, 1933, 1938, 1988

Archaeology in Wales Vol. 39 1994, PCRO

'Biographies' news cuttings HL.

Cambrian Quarterly Magazine, Vol. 1, No. 1, January 1829

Francis Green news cuttings, Vols 1, 10, 15 and 16, HL

Local Newscuttings, Vols 5, 17, 26, HL

Rees, W. 'A remarkable co-incidence' in *Journal of the Welsh Philatelic Society Newsletter* No. 91, Sept. 2002

Bennet, M. 'Dampnified Villagers: Taxation in Wales during the first Civil War' in *The Welsh History Review ,*Vol. 19, June 1998

Phillips, J. Pavin *Notes and Queries* Series 2, Vol. 3, Bell and Daldry 1857

Richards, Dr B.W. 'Colonel Poyer and Relatives; Some mistaken assumptions' in *Dyfed Family History Journal*, April 1989, Vol. 3, No. 3, PCRO

Roberts, S.K. 'How the west was won: Parliamentary Politics, Religion and the Military in South Wales1642-49' in *The Welsh History Review* Vol. 21, Dec. 2003, No. 4

Vaughan, H. 'Oliver Cromwell in South Wales 1648-9: a retrospect' in *Transactions of the Honourable Society of Cymmrodorion*, 1936

West Wales Historical Review Vol. XII, p.169

Manuscripts

Calendar of Records of the Borough of Haverfordwest, PCRO

Green, F. Transcripts, Vol. 5, PCRO

Haverfordwest Records, PCRO

Norton, B.L. 'Civil War General: Major General Rowland Laugharne; a study', Privately printed manuscript, PCRO

Thomason Tracts, NLW

Books

Adair, J. *Roundhead General* Sutton, 1997

Atkins, M. & Laughlin, W. *Gloucester in the Civil War* Sutton, 1992

Beardsworth, T. *The Sieges of Pembroke and Tenby 1648* Stuart Press, 1998

Bennet, M. *Travellers Guide to the Battlefields of the English Civil War* Webb & Bower, 1990

Cadw *Buildings of Special Architectural or Historic Interest: Templeton*
Carlyle, T. *Oliver Cromwell's Letters and Speeches* Chapman & Hall, 1871
Carradice, P. *Pembroke, for King and Parliament* PTC, 1992
Charles, B.G. *The Place-names of Pembrokeshire* NLW, 1992
Clark, G.T. *The Genealogies of Morgan and Glamorgan* London, 1886
Edwards, O.M. *The Story of the Nations: Wales* T. Fisher Unwin, 1933
Emberton, W. *The English Civil War Day by Day* Sutton, 1995
Fenton, R. *A Historical Tour through Pembrokeshire* Cultural Services Department, DCC, 1994
Fletcher, A. *The Outbreak of the English Civil War* Edward Arnold, 1981
Gardiner, S.R. *History of the Great Civil War* The Windrush Press, 1987 reprint
Gaskill, M. *Witchfinders* John Murray, 2005
Gaunt, P. *A Nation under Siege*, Cadw, London HMSO, 1991
Gregg, P. *King Charles I* Phoenix Press, 2000
Guest, B. & K. *British Battles* Harper Collins, 1996
Hunt, T. *The English Civil War at First Hand* Weidenfeld and Nicolson, 2002
James, D.J. *The Town and County of Haverfordwest and its Story* J.W. Hammond, 1957
Jenkins, G.H. *The Foundations of Modern Wales 1642-1780* OUP, 1993
Jones, F. *Historic Houses of Pembrokeshire* Brawdy Books, 1996
Jones, F. *Treasury of Historic Pembrokeshire* Brawdy Books, 1998
Jones, I. *Modern Welsh History from 1485 to the present day* G. Bell and Sons, 1934
Kishlansky, M. *A Monarchy Transformed; Britain 1603-1714* Penguin, 1997
Lacey, R. *An Elizabethan Icarus* Weidenfeld & Nicolson, 1971
Laws, E. *The History of Little England beyond Wales* Cultural Services Department, DCC, 1995
Leach, A.L. *History of the Civil War 1642-1649 in Pembrokeshire* 1936
Lloyd, H.A. *The Gentry of South-West Wales* UWP, 1968
McGarvie, M. *Meyrick of Bush; the story of a Pembrokeshire Family* Privately printed, 1988
Miles, D. (ed.) *A History of Haverfordwest* Gomer, 1999
Pembrokeshire County History, Vol. 3, Editor Brian Howells, Pembrokeshire Historical Society, 1987
Phillips, Reverend J. *The History of Pembrokeshire* Elliot Stock, 1909
Phillips, J.R. *Memoirs of the Civil War in Wales and the Marches 1642-49* Longmans, Green and Co., 1874
Plowden, A. *In a Free Republic* Sutton, 2006
Purkiss, D. *The English Civil War; a People's History* Harper, 2006
Rees, J.F. *The Story of Milford* UWP, 1957
Rees, J.F. *Studies in Welsh History* UWP, 1965
Royle, T. *Civil War; The Wars of the Three Kingdoms 1638-1660* Little, Brown, 2004
Snow, V.F. *Essex the Rebel* University of Nebraska, 1970
Stickings, T.G. *Castles and Strongholds of Pembrokeshire* H.G. Walters Ltd, 1972
Stoyle, M. *Soldiers and Strangers; an ethnic History of the English Civil War* Yale University Press, 2005
Webb, D. *The Battle of St Fagan's, 1648* Stuart Press, 1998
West Wales Historical Records, Vol. II 1911-12. F. Green editor, Spurrell and Sons. 1911
Williams, D. *A History of Modern Wales* John Murray, 1977
Williams, G. *Renewal and Reformation; Wales 1415-1642* OUP, 1993
Woolrych, A. *Britain in Revolution 1625-1660* OUP, 2002

References

Chapter 1
1. NLW MSS 1370B.
2. Leach, p.212.
3. Local tradition in Pembroke. The maces went missing after the siege of Pembroke. Whether they were taken away by Cromwell as a sign of the subjection of the town or by sympathisers of the condemned men is uncertain. They were not recovered until the late 19th century and are now kept at the Town Hall in Pembroke.

Chapter 2
1. 'Poyer's vindication in answer to a lying pamphlet' British Museum MS E548, quoted in Leach, p.27.
2. 'A declaration of Divers Gentlemen of Wales concerning Collonel Poyer ...', British Museum MS E36 (7). John Eliot may have had a hand in its composition.
3. British Museum MS E436 (7), quoted in Laws' unpublished manuscript.
4. NLW MS 1377 (b).
5. *PCH*, Vol III, p.167.
6. Cadw: Templeton. The farm bore an inscription dated 1672.
7. NLW MS 1377 (b) p.90.
8. Clark Papers, Glamorgan Genealogies MS 517F, NLW.
9. Dr B.W. Richards, *Dyfed Family History Journal* Volume 3, No 3, April 1989.
10. One clue to Rowland's date of birth is that, at the outbreak of the Civil War in 1642, he was said to be about 30 years of age.
11. A Reeve held local office under the king and served as chief magistrate of a town or district; he might also supervise an estate or a manor for its lord. A burgage was a strip of land, usually within a town, held from the lord for an annual rent or service.
12. Schedule of Picton Castle Collection, pp.6, 12, 13, 14, 15.
13. Charles, Vol II, p.632.
14. Fenton, p.97.
15. H.A. Lloyd, p.113.
16. *Ibid*, p.115.
17. Laws, p.314.
18. H.A. Lloyd, p.114.
19. Lacey, p.274.
20. Adair, pp.8-9.
21. Snow, p.184.
22. This marriage also failed. Devereux believed that Elizabeth had been unfaithful and threatened to separate from her. On learning that she was pregnant, he agreed to recognise the child as his if it was born by 5 November. The child arrived on that date, but when it subsequently died, Essex carried out his threat.
23. Snow, p.185.
24. Lort Papers, Carmarthen Record Office.
25. *Ibid*.
26. Sir Thomas Button (d.1634) was a noted sailor and explorer. Born in the Vale of Glamorgan, he first went to sea in about 1589 and probably served under Drake, Hawkins and Raleigh. In 1612, he commanded an expedition to locate the missing explorer Henry Hudson, which was also to find a North-West Passage around northern Canada to the Pacific. Although the expedition failed in its purpose, Button did discover and name Mansel Island and also explored the west coast of Hudson Bay. He was later involved in expeditions against the pirates of Algiers. Knighted by James I, he was appointed as Admiral of the Irish Sea. He fitted out at his own expense a squadron of privateers, which he used to clear coastal waters of pirates. He managed to recoup some of his money

by capturing ships and selling their cargoes.

27. Leach, p.85.
28. PRO, MF 202; WWHR, Vol XII, p.169.
29. *Ibid.*
30. *PCH*, Vol III, p.162.
31. *Ibid*, p.150.
32. Cadw, Lamphey Palace guide book, p.10.
33. *WWHR* ,Vol XII p.169.
34. *PCH*, III, p.164; McGarvie, p.33.
35. J.F. Rees, p.96.
36. *Ibid.*
37. Leach, p.38, quoting a letter from Rowland Laugharne.

Chapter 3
1. G. Williams, p.381.
2. P. Gaunt., p.7.
3. *PCH*, Vol 3, p.19.
4. J. Gwynfor Jones, p.36.
5. Lloyd, p.53. G. Williams, pp.406-09.
6. G. Williams pp.386-87.
7. *Ibid*, p.396.
8. *Ibid.*
9. H.A. Lloyd, p.82.
10. *Ibid*, quoted on p.17.
11. *PCH*, Vol III, quoted on p.38.
12. G. Williams, p.413.
13 *PCH*, Vol III, quoted on p.64.
14. Dickers, dikers or dykers, a quantity of ten, usually of hides; fardels were bundles, loads or packs of goods.
15. *PCH*, Vol III, p.54.

Chapter 4
1. *PCH*, Vol III, p.153.
2. Woolrych, p.54.
3. Glanmor Williams, p.373.
4. *PCH*, Vol III, p.153.
5. CSPD 28 August 1627.
6. CSPD 25 September 1627.
7. CSPD 18 August 1628.
8. CSPD 23 October 1628.
9. CSPD 15 April 1629.
10. CSPD undated, 1627.
11. *PCH*, Vol III, p.153.

12. CSPD February 1628.
13. This might not have been the retrograde step that it sounds; the rate of fire of a bowman is faster than that of a musketeer, who takes longer to reload.
14. *PCH*, Vol III, p.153.
15. J.R. Phillips, Vol I, p.42.
16. *Ibid.*
17. Glanmor Williams, p.485.
18. Woolrych, p.67.
19. Lloyd, p.215.
20. Laws, p.319.
21. Lloyd, p.122.
22. *Ibid*, p.122.
23. *Ibid*, p.215.
24. Leach, p.23.
25. Glanmor Williams, p.485.
26. *Ibid.*
27. *Ibid.*
28. Woolrych, p.146.
29. Kishlansky, p.141.
30. Glanmor Williams, p.485.
31. Plowden, p.12.

Chapter 5
1. Leach, p.26.
2. *PCH*, III, p.156.
3. Emberton, p.12.
4. Hunt, p.65.
5. James Butler, Earl later Marquess of Ormonde, an Irish Protestant landowner and staunch royalist; Lieutenant General of the Irish army, Lord President of Munster. He had serious doubts about using the Irish army against Scottish Covenanters, as the king planned. It has been suggested that he knew in advance of the Irish rebellion but did nothing to stop it.
6. Leach, p.28.
7. *Ibid*, quoted pp.29-30.
8. Hunt, quoted p.78.
9. Their duties were to prevent the levying of fines under the King's Commission of Array; to declare Parliament's intentions in regard to the king's safety; to ensure the publication of Parliamentary declarations; to take charge of the

county magazine of arms; to put in force laws against Popish recusants; to ensure transmission of dispatches to Parliament; to repel by force if necessary any attempt to prevent disobedience to Parliament's ordinances.

10. *PCH*, III, p.157.
11. Leach, p.32.
12. Gaskill, p.22.
13. Fletcher, quoted pp.264-265.
14. G.H. Jenkins, quoted p.3.
15. *Ibid*, p.5.
16. Lloyd, quoted p.128.
17. PCH, III, pp.157-58; Snow, pp.253-54.
18. G.H. Jenkins, pp.6-7.

Chapter 6

1. Gaunt, p.31.
2. *Ibid*, p.25.
3. Stoyle, p.11.
4. Emberton, p.38.
5. Leach, p.41.
6. *AC*, 1853.
7. Michaelmas was otherwise known as the Feast of St Michael, 29 September.
8. 'Declaration of Divers Gentlemen of Wales', British Museum MSS E436 (7).
9. Rees pp.84-85; *PCH*, III, pp.175-176.
10. Scott, Turton, von Arnim, p.65. John Gunter is known to have fought in several battles of the Civil War. Thomas was killed on active service during the war.
11. G.H. Jenkins, quoted on p.9.
12. Woolrych, p.241.
13. CSPD, 28 April 1654. The sum of £208 10s would be worth £25,152.62 by today's (2004) values. Source: http://eh.net/hmit/powerbp/
14. Leach, p.41.
15. *Ibid*, quoted p.49.
16. Archdeacon Rudd was taken prisoner at the capture of Tenby in March 1643.
17. The amount they agreed to raise for the royal coffers was £2,000 each.

Chapter 7

1. Gaunt, p.33; Durant, pp.65-66.
2. Stoyle, p.28.
3. Atkin and Laughlin, p.31.
4. Gaunt, p.34.
5. Guest, p.125.
6. Bennet, pp.76-77.
7. Lynch, p.115.
8. J.F. Rees, p.10.
9. Simon Thelwall's letter to the Speaker of the House of Commons, quoted in Laws, p.324.
10. Traces of these foundations were still visible in the early 20th century, as were the remains of the banks until the late 1980s/early 1990s, when they were bulldozed to allow building on the site. Castle or Prix Pill is a long tidal inlet situated on the eastern extremity of the modern town of Milford.
11. The warships were the *Leopard* 38 guns, under the command of Richard Swanley, Admiral; *Swallow* 36 guns, William Smith, Vice Admiral; *Expedition* 18 guns, Joseph Jordan, Rear-Admiral; *Lyon* 42 guns, William Swanley; *Bonaventure* 36 guns, captain unknown; *Signet (Cygnet)* 18 guns, J. Weild; *Cressent (Crescent)* 14 guns, T. Plunkett; *Lilly* 10 guns, L. Lambert; *Starre (Star),* 12 guns, T. Clarke. The merchant vessels were the *Ruth, Peter, Employment, Leopard, Friendship, Mary, John, Pennington, Exchange, Prosperous* and two other unnamed vessels. See Leach p.53 and Laws p.322.
12. Letter of William Smith quoted in J.R. Phillips p.77.
13. Rev J. Phillips, p.492.
14. *AC*, 1915. It's worth noting that all the sources say that Carbery visited the town, not that he attacked or captured it, which must reflect the possibility that Haverfordwest had no hard and fast loyalties to one side or the other. When, later in the year, there was a threat to bring Royalist troops into the

town, the mayor informed Rowland Laugharne, who visited the town on 6 June and was entertained by the council.

15. Leach, quoted p.55.
16. Richards, *DFHJ*, Vol III no 3.
17. Norton, p.4. As we have already seen, the name Laugharne was spelt in a variety of ways in the 17th century; Langhorn, Laharne, Lachan are all variations that appear in letters and documents of the time.
18. A cannon dredged up from the seabed off the Sker Rock and now in Tenby Museum may have come from this ship.
19. *PCH*, III, p.178.
20. Leach, p.58; *PCH*, III, p.178.

Chapter 8

1. Laws, quoted p.325.
2. NLW MSS 1377b.
3. Captain Smith's letter, quoted in Laws, p.325.
4. Quoted in Leach, p.62.
5. Rev. J. Phillips, p.493.
6. Lieutenant Jones seems to have been half-hearted in his allegiance to the King. He took up service with Parliament and a few months later fought with Laugharne at the storming of Tenby.
7. These numbers are given in Leach, p.65. In Poyer's *Vindication*, he mentions that, upon his first joining forces with Laugharne, he had present at Pembroke one troop of horse, two troops of dragoons and three foot companies, 250 men in all. It is not clear why they were not included in Laugharne's total. Were they being held in reserve to defend Pembroke Castle, or had they been sent elsewhere before Swanley's arrival?
8. NLW Thomason Tracts E 42.
9. NLW MSS 1377b.
10. Laws, p.325.
11. NLW MSS 1377b.

12. In a petition to Parliament dated 19 February 1647, signed by Roger and Sampson Lort and Sir Richard Phillips, a plea was made for financial relief for Thomas Bowen for all he had lost at Trefloyne. The blame for the storming of the house was laid at Lord Carbery's door for, according to the Lorts, he had seized and garrisoned the place. Bowen had moved to Pembroke, where he was living quietly under the protection of John Poyer.
13. Quoted in Laws, p.331.
14. Captain Smith's letter, quoted in Leach, p.70.
15. A gabbard or gabbart was a barge-type sailing vessel or lighter used for inland navigation.
16. Thelwall's letter, quoted in J.R. Phillips, p.143.
17. NLW Thomason Tracts E42.
18. NLW MSS E3(12).
19. NLW Thomason Tracts E42.
20. *Ibid*. The chapel still exists. During the 1930s it was restored and re-roofed. It is today screened from the road by modern housing, which blocks the view that the soldiers would have had of the fort. Local legend also relates that pieces of armour and horse gear were discovered beneath the fields near Pill Priory, to the south-west of Steynton church (see map). These finds were said to mark the location of a fight between 'Cromwell's men' and the Royalists. Nearby is an ancient earthwork said to have been raised by Cromwell, but actually much older. Is this the site of the 'ambuscado', where the Royalists lay behind a line of hedges?
21. NLW Thomason Tracts E42.
22. Captain Smith's letter, quoted in Leach, p.72.
23. NLW Thomason Tracts E24. Sir Hugh Owen must have been preparing for bed. He had obviously taken off his doublet or shirt. Pantables or pantoufles were slippers.

Chapter 9

1. The letters are quoted in Leach, pp.76-77.
2. AC 1896, p.182. At the time this description was published in *Archaeologia Cambrensis*, it was still possible to see what was thought to be the remains of this breastwork in the stable yard of the Gate House Hotel. It consisted of a wall 35 paces long and must have originally been 5 or 6 feet high. It was pierced by 4 arches, each one about three feet high, interspersed with 5 or 6 apertures which might have been musket loops about 2 foot off the ground.
3. Leach, pp.80-81. Some accounts kept by David Hammond for materials and equipment bought for the defence of Tenby mention 'Frank the Gunner'. Is this the master gunner who was killed on 9 March? (Leach Papers, Tenby Museum).
4. Rudd was taken to Milford Haven and was imprisoned aboard the guardship *Lyon*. He died in October 1648, but may have been released before that date. A memorial to him may be seen in the parish church of St Florence.
5. Leach, quoted p.85.
6. *PCH*, III p.187.

Chapter 10

1. Gaunt p.51.
2. Stoyle, p.59.
3. Gaunt, p.44.
4. NLW Thomason Tracts E284 (20).
5. Stoyle, p.60; Gaunt, p.44.
6. Gaunt, p.45.
7. G.H. Jenkins, p.15.
8. For a further and more detailed examination of this vexed question, see Mark Stoyle's excellent *Soldiers and Strangers*.
9. Stoyle, pp.158-9.
10. G.H. Jenkins, p.25.
11. Leach, pp.89-90.

Chapter 11

1. J.R. Phillips II, p.190.
2. *Ibid.*
3. I. Jones, quoted p.92.
4. CSPD, 1 July 1644.
5. CSPD, 27 July, 1 August 1644.
6. Cadw, Laugharne Castle guide book, pp.20-21.
7. *Cambrian Quarterly Magazine*, No 1 Vol 1 p.63.
8. J.R. Phillips, Vol II, quoted p.228. Doctor Jeremy Taylor was one of the most eminent clergymen of the time.
9. From a pamphlet entitled 'God appearing for the Parliament in sundry late Victories bestowed upon their forces.' Quoted in J.R. Phillips, II pp.229-230.

Chapter 12

1. Quoted in Leach, p.102.
2. *Ibid*, p.103.
3. *Ibid*, p.115.
4. Quoted in Leach, p.105.
5. Quoted in J.R. Phillips, II, p.250.
6. Thomason Tracts, E285.
7. Quoted in J.R. Phillips, II, p.250.
8. *Ibid*, p.251.
9. The facts do not fit the legend. Erasmus Philipps was not a small boy in 1645. His marriage agreement, drawn up in 1651, has his age as *'about 37'*, which would make him 30 or 31 in 1645. He married the 19-year-old Katherine Darcy, daughter of Edward Darcy of Drury Lane, London, and later served as High Sheriff for Pembrokeshire and as an MP. He died in 1696.
10. Quoted in Phillips, II, p.249; Miles, p.182.
11. Quoted in Leach, p.109.
12. CSPD 28 April 1654. The amount specified in the Bill would today be worth over £89,430. Source: Economic History Services: http//eh.net/hmit/powerbp/. Mary Gunter never recovered the full amount owed to her. On 28 April 1654, she and her second

husband, William Denny, presented a petition to Parliament begging for payment of her monies. The couple had been imprisoned for debt. One of Thomas Gunter's surviving brothers had obtained '£700 of the property and £20 worth of apparel' and had given nothing to Mary. She took out Letters of Administration, by which she became liable to debts on a bond of £2,000, and was thrown into prison. Mary produced the receipts given to her by Poyer and Laugharne and was eventually awarded a portion of what she was owed.

13. AC 1988. Bridget Powell, Thomas' widow, later presented a petition to Parliament for recompense for her husband's losses.

14. Quoted in AC 1882.

15. AC 1882, p.67.

16. AC 1988, Vol 137, p.14.

17. CSPD 26 May 1645.

18. CSPD 30 June 1645.

19. CSPD 2 July 1645.

20. Amongst the defeated Royalist troops at Naseby were contingents of Welshmen, many of whom were taken prisoner. In the weeks after the battle, Parliament provided a Welsh speaking chaplain who preached to the men in their native tongue and tried to convince them of the error of their ways. Less fortunate were the female camp followers of the King's army who, during the flight from the battlefield were overtaken by vengeful Parliamentary mounted troops. On hearing the women screaming out in a strange tongue, the soldiers assumed them to be Irish and slaughtered over 100 of them, slitting the noses and slashing the cheeks of others to brand them as harlots. It is more probable that the women were Welsh.

21. CSPD 1 August 1645.

22. The number of troops is given in a letter written by Laugharne shortly after the battle and published in a pamphlet entitled 'A true Relation of the late success of Parliament's forces in Pembrokeshire'. Captain Batten, however, states that there were 800 men in Laugharne's army.

23. Local information.

24. The exact site of the battle has been disputed, but the discovery over the years of musket and cannon balls during ploughing in the fields of Colby Moor, Claridale and Roger's Hook farms would seem to fix the location beyond doubt.

25. Although there is no information about the weather on that day, there are clues. If there had been rain, which would have hampered the movement of troops and guns, Batten and Laugharne would surely have mentioned it in their letters; and if the Royalists really did intend to burn the cornfields, they wouldn't have tried it in wet weather.

26. Quoted in Laws, p.330 and Phillips, II, p.266.

27. Quoted in Laws, p.330.

28. Phillips, Vol I, p.355.

29. *Ibid.*

30. *Ibid*, Vol II, p.305.

31. *Cambrian Quarterly Magazine*, No 1, Volume 1, January 1829.

32. J.R. Phillips, Vol II, p.305.

33. Leach, p.113.

34. Phillips, pp.274-77.

35. *Ibid.*

36. *Ibid.*

37. Roberts, WHR, p.66.

38. Phillips, II, p.273.

Chapter 13

1. Quoted in Leach, pp.117-8.

2. *Ibid*, pp.118-9.

3. *Ibid*, p.119.

4. *Ibid.*

5. Quoted in Royle, p.332.

6. J.R. Rees, p.74.

7. *Ibid.*

8. *Ibid*, pp.74-5; G.H. Jenkins, p.18.

9. J.R. Rees, p.74.
10. Quoted in Stoyle, p.168.
11. Quoted in J.F. Rees, p.75.
12. Gregg, p.400.
13. *Ibid*, p.403.
14. Phillips, II, pp.298-300.
15. Quoted in J.F. Rees, p.78.
16. Phillips, II, pp.298-300.
17. Roberts, WHR, p.662.
18. Leach, p.120; Gregg, p.409.
19. Leach, p.191.
20. Quoted in Leach, p.122.
21. Hudson had been imprisoned in the Tower of London but escaped, perhaps with the collusion of the authorities, in order to inform the King of a planned rising in his favour.
22. *PCH*, III, p.198.
23. J.R. Phillips, Vol II, p.335.
24. Quoted in Leach, p.126. The sum of £6,000 would be worth about £744,400 in today's (2005) values.
25. *Ibid*, p.127.
26. *PCH*, III, p.199.
27. It was not unusual for the armies of the Civil War to forage for provisions in their immediate locality, taking what they needed wherever it could be found. The same charges were laid against Gerard's troops and against Laugharne's.

Chapter 14
1. Royle, p.416; Woolrych, p.399.
2. Hunt, p.163.
3. Woolrych, pp.418-9; Hunt, p.165.
4. Hunt, p.166.
5. Calendar of State Papers Domestic, 25 January 1648. One explanation for Laugharne's possible involvement in a plot was given in a letter published in London in February 1648. According to this story, several castles in South Wales had been surrendered to Laugharne on condition that the officers in them should not be tried as delinquents. This promise was broken through no fault of Rowland's, who as a result felt himself to have been dishonoured. It seemed logical to some within Parliament that he would therefore give his support to the Royalists and so he was arrested.
6. Quoted in Leach, p.138.
7. *Ibid*, p.145.
8. *Ibid*, p.146.
9. *Ibid*, p.150.

Chapter 15
1. Quoted in Leach, p.157.
2. *Ibid*, p.161.
3. *PCH*, Vol III, p.203.
4. Royle, pp.433-4.
5. Leach, p.167.
6. *Cambrian Quarterly Magazine* No 1 1829, Vol I, p.70.
7. Many of the prisoners were sent to Pembroke, later being transferred to Haverfordwest.
8. Leach, p.173; Fraser, p.237.
9. *PCH*, Vol III, p.204.
10. J.F.Rees, p.80; Leach, p.174.
11. Phillips, Vol II, p.362.
12. *Ibid*, p.363.
13. Quoted in Leach, p.175.

Chapter 16
1. Webb, p.12; Gaunt, p.68.
2. Webb, p.12.
3. Thomason Tracts, E443.15 and E. 443.21.
4. Webb, p.11.
5. Phillips, Vol II, pp.3, 65.
6. Quoted in Webb, p.19.
7. *Ibid*, pp.21-24.
8. These figures are based on those given in documents written shortly after Tenby surrendered. Three hundred 'common soldiers' are mentioned as being within the town in a letter of 1 June and if to this are added officers and other sympathisers, the true figure may well be near 500 or more.
9. Quoted in Phillips, Vol II, p.377.
10. *Ibid*.

11. Leach Papers, TM. Some estimates mention that the provisions could have lasted for ten weeks.

12. Thomason Tracts, E446 (27).

Chapter 17

1. Pembroke is still encircled by the remnants of its walls. Long sections exist along the northern perimeter and along the south-eastern edge of the town, where two of the towers look out over the stream which now runs through a culvert. The area of the mudflats once covered by incoming tides is known today as the Commons and consists of car parks, a children's playground and wide lawns. All the town gates have gone, though faint vestiges of the West Gate are visible below the castle. Barnard's Tower still frowns down upon the Mill Pond, grey and formidable-seeming even on a bright summer day.

2. Phillips, II, pp.353-4.

3. Buttons, belt buckles and musket balls have been discovered in the fields of Underdown.

4. Leach, p.194.

5. A blinde was a strongly made screen behind which a musketeer could shelter.

6. Carlyle, Vol II, p.4.

7. Beardsworth, p.14.

8. Carlyle, p.4.

9. Leach, p.199. Round stone shot has been found in several locations around Pembroke.

10. Carlyle, Vol II, p.10.

11. Beardsworth, p.13.

12. Leach Papers, TM. In a letter to A.L. Leach written in June 1930, a Mr A.G. Matthias of Pembroke described the discovery of these pipes in the fields adjacent to Norgan's Hill. They were laid in masonry and covered by flat stones, though it is not clear if they reached the castle over the Monkton causeway or were laid along the

riverbed. They seem to have entered the castle through a postern.

13. One of the famous legends of the siege is that of the breaking of the water pipes. See Appendix II.

14. Carlyle, p.4.

15. Phillips, II, p.395.

16. *Ibid*, p.392.

17. Carlyle, pp.9-10.

18. Phillips, II, pp.395-6.

19. Quoted in Leach, pp.163-4. Local tradition gives two possible locations for Poyer's house, one close to the East Gate, the other near the present Post Office. It is possible that, as a wealthy merchant, he owned two properties in the town, though after his death his widow is known to have rented a house at the east end of the town. An ancient cellar still exits beneath the building close to the Post Office, which may be the vault in which Peters was kept. He later made public Poyer's commission from the Prince as well as one of the letters, but this haul of correspondence has since vanished.

20. These towns had all been taken by the Royalists, but rumour assigned the same ferocity to the Parliamentarians, as their slaughter of the camp followers at Naseby testifies.

21. Whilst staying at Welston, Cromwell apparently suffered a severe attack of gout and was forced to keep to his bed. He wrote all his correspondence sitting up amongst the pillows and on one occasion upset his inkwell over the coverlet. This counterpane, of white quilted material lined with crimson, became a family heirloom and remained in the Cuny family's posses- sion for generations, though it has since been lost. The damage to the counter- pane was not the only inconvenience suffered by the Cuny family during Cromwell's stay. All Walter's stock and crops were appropriated for the use of the troops, a loss of some £200 in 17th

century values, for which he subsequently received £150 compensation.

22. Phillips, II, p.397.

23. Peregrine Phillips, Vicar of Monkton seems to have been a remarkable character. See Appendix I.

24. Roger Lort was one of several local gentlemen entrusted with the task of deciding which of Pembrokeshire's castles were to be slighted. His brothers Sampson and John were amongst the others, as was Thomas Barlow. They summoned the inhabitants of Haverfordwest and the surrounding area to demolish the castle there, but the Town Council wrote to them informing them that the job had proved too difficult without gunpowder. In any case, it would 'exhaust an Immense some (*sic*) of money and will not in a longe time be effected.' The Council asked for gunpowder to be made available, but in the event seem to have made little effort to destroy the building; large parts of it remain standing today.

25, Carradice, p.68.

26. There is a tradition that Cromwell actually witnessed the attempt to blow up the Barbican Tower.

27. Another old tradition states that on 16 July Cromwell was in Haverfordwest, where he stayed with the Prust family. He was said to like to drink fresh spring water each morning and was taken by the young son of the household to a spring in City Road known as Gwen's Ditch or Queensditch. The house in which he stayed no longer exists, but the site, near St Martin's Church, was known as Cromwell's Corner.

28. PRO, MSS Q12/228.

Chapter 18

1. Woolrych, p.428; Royle, pp.484-5; Emberton, p.196.

2. Leach Papers 3/177, TM.

3. Francis Green News cuttings, Vol 16, p.6, HL.

4. Most of the information concerning Poyer's execution comes from *The Declaration and Speech of Colonell John Poyer*, published in London on 26 April 1649; I have also made use of other accounts current at the time. After Poyer's death, his family took the motto 'Destiny is against me' in his memory.

Chapter 19

1. G.H. Jenkins, p.31.

2. Jones was later executed as a regicide. Wogan apparently evaded the same fate. For many years after the Restoration a melancholy old man, believed by many to be Thomas Wogan, lived in the church porch at Walwyn's Castle in Pembrokeshire. He had the white hands and manners of a gentleman, but refused all offers of help except food and drink, which were brought to him by the villagers. He claimed that his name was Drinkwater and was eventually found dead in the porch.

3. G.H. Jenkins, p.32.

4. *Ibid*, p.29.

5. Chandler, p.271.

6. *Ibid*, 273. John Taylor (1578-1653) celebrated his 74th birthday during this journey. Born in Gloucester and self-educated, he had worked as a Thames wherryman and had turned to writing to earn his living. The author of some 200 published poems, religious tracts, travel books and a joke book, he travelled widely through England and Wales. He served in the Elizabethan navy, took part in the theatre of Shakespeare's time and ran a pub in Covent Garden.

7. Haverfordwest Corporation MS 265.

8. Haverfordwest Corporation MS 262.

9. Haverfordwest Corporation MS 532.

10. *PCH*, III, p.210.

11. G.H. Jenkins, p.117.

12. *PCH*, III, p.214.
13. CSPD 29 March 1665.
14. Quoted in Leach, p.215.
15. The £30,000 he lost would today be worth in the region of £3,722,000.
16. The money was given 'on secret service' which probably does not mean that Rowland was acting as a secret agent, but that cash was being transferred to him out of a confidential fund so that his debtors could not seize it.
17. The toll on the Laugharne family during the mid-17th century was high. Rowland's two brothers died during the Civil Wars, Thomas at St Fagans and Hugh at Cahill in Ireland. As well as his brothers, Rowland also lost his two sons and three nephews in the military campaigns of the time.
18. CSPD 1670.
19. The National Library of Wales possesses an inventory of the goods of one Rowland Laugharne and a deed of administration granted to his wife, dated 1677. These have been suggested as documents relating to Major General Rowland Laugharne, but this is most unlikely. The woman named in the deed is Judith Laugharne, and as we know, Rowland's wife was Ann. Also, the man in the inventory and deed is stated to be Rowland Laugharne 'of the town of Haverford'. The Rowland Laugharne described in this book was always known as 'of St Brides', the place of his main residence. Gentlemen of his rank always added the name of their estate to their own names – as for example John Barlow of Slebech, Colonel John Jones of Maesygarnedd, Roger Lort of Stackpole.
20. Quoted in Leach, p.217.
21. NLW MS 1371 B. The house was described in the lease as being 'between the lands of Erasmus Phillipps [*sic*], Barronett in the occupation of Thomas Clin (or Glin) on the west part, the lands of Thomas Powell, gentleman in the possession and occupation of An Morgan widow on the East side. The street of the said town on the south side and the Town Walls in the north part.' There were also two closes of land, one called St John's Close and covering an area of about 8 acres.
22. CSPD 13 August 1664.
23. CSPD 1665.
24. Journal of the Welsh Philatelic Society Newsletter No 91, September 2002.

Index